NOT
PROVEN

By the same author:

THE TRIAL OF JEANNIE DONALD
THE TRIAL OF PETER MANUEL

NOT
PROVEN

JOHN GRAY WILSON

LONDON
SECKER & WARBURG
1960

TO
E.W.W.

Printed in England by
Western Printing Services Ltd, Bristol
and first published 1960
by
Martin Secker & Warburg Ltd
7 John Street, London
WC1

CONTENTS

ACKNOWLEDGEMENTS

My thanks are due, first, to William Hodge & Co. Ltd for permission to quote from the *Scottish Law Review* for February 1959, and from three volumes in their invaluable Notable British Trials series: *Trial of Madeleine Smith*, edited by A. Duncan Smith; *Trial of A. J. Monson*, edited by John W. More; and *Trial of John Donald Merrett*, edited by William Roughead.

I have also to thank the Scottish Council of Law Reporting for permission to quote from the reports of the McMillan and Withers cases in 1940 and 1947 Justiciary Cases; Judge Gerald Sparrow and Robert Hale Ltd for permission to quote from *Murder Parade*; and Miss Sybille Bedford and William Collins Sons & Co. Ltd for permission to quote from *The Best We Can Do*.

Dr C. A. Malcolm of the Signet Library, Edinburgh, and Mr D. J. Stevenson, Depute Clerk of Justiciary, generously allowed me free access to the late William Roughead's collection of books on crime and Madeleine Smith's letters respectively. And the Commissioner of Police for the Metropolis was helpful in relation to A. J. Monson.

J.G.W.

INTRODUCTION:
BASTARD VERDICT?

A SCOTTISH jury is not restricted to the two verdicts of Guilty and Not Guilty. There is a third possibility, a verdict of Not Proven. After such a verdict the accused is acquitted and cannot be tried again on the same charge. In this respect it has the same effect as a verdict of Not Guilty.

Scottish jurists are as a rule patriotically proud of their native legal system and probably the great majority of the legal profession in Scotland approve of the Not Proven verdict. But they do so in silence. Those who speak or write of it tend to be critical, even strongly so: publicly expressed admiration comes from outside.

On 20th February 1827, after the trial of Mrs Mary Smith for poisoning a servant girl, Sir Walter Scott wrote in his diary: "Waited to see the poisoning woman. She is clearly guilty, but as one or two witnesses said the poor wench hinted an intention to poison herself, the jury gave that bastard verdict, *Not proven*. I hate that Caledonian *medium quid*. One who is not *proven guilty* is innocent in the eye of law." Note, however, that although Mrs Smith was not proven guilty to the satisfaction of the jury she was not innocent in the eye of Sir Walter Scott.

In *Blackwood's Magazine* for June 1906 Lord Moncreiff, who had recently retired from the bench on which his father and grandfather sat before him, forcefully criticised the verdict, which he called both theoretically and historically indefensible. The usual criticism, as he pointed out, is that it leaves a stigma on an acquitted person. But he thought that a more serious objection was that it was "favourable to a criminal and there are many cases in which, if the jury were driven to choose between the verdicts of 'Guilty' and 'Not Guilty', they would probably find the prisoner 'Guilty'."

7

More recently Lord Wheatley made the same criticism in an address to the Glasgow Juridical Society.

This, incidentally, involves an oblique attack on the integrity of the Scottish jury, either actual or potential. It means one of two things: either juries today return verdicts of Not Proven when they are satisfied of the guilt of the accused or juries faced with a choice between two verdicts would say Guilty even in cases where doubt remained and they were not fully satisfied of guilt.

In his introduction to the *Trial of John Donald Merrett*,[1] William Roughead described the verdict as "that indefensible and invidious finding" and in 1948 Lord Justice-General Cooper said that he would not like to offer a logical justification for its retention. And neither Roughead nor Lord Cooper could be criticised for falling short of the respect due to the Scottish system.

Finally, an article in the *Scottish Law Review* for February 1959 arrived at the same conclusion: "There is no logical half-way house and no place for the verdict of Not Proven. Where the facts and circumstances libelled are proved beyond reasonable doubt, the panel (accused) is guilty, and where they are not so proved he is innocent."

In view of these attacks on the logic of the third verdict it is interesting to find an Englishman, Judge Gerald Sparrow, writing: "I have often thought that the distinction typifies the different spirit of Scottish and English law: the Scottish being the more logical, the English more sporting."[2]

This is the onlooker seeing more of the game (if the phrase is not too sporting for a Scotsman to use). Not Proven is in fact a logical—even coldly logical—verdict. Consider what a jury has to do. If after hearing the evidence they are satisfied beyond reasonable doubt that the accused committed the crime with which he is charged they return a verdict of Guilty. That verdict, put into the form of a proposition, means "We are satisfied that the accused committed the crime". There are two ways in which they can deny that proposition: they can say "We are not satisfied that he committed the crime" or they can say "We

---

[1] Hodge, Notable British Trials Series, 1929.
[2] *Murder Parade* (Robert Hale, 1957).

are satisfied that he did not commit the crime". These two negative statements, of course, do not mean the same thing. The first
includes the second but the second does not by any means in-
clude the first. They correspond more or less accurately to the
verdicts of Not Proven and Not Guilty respectively.

From this it would appear that, if the three verdicts are to be
reduced to two, the one to be discarded is Not Guilty. Its only
justification would be if it were reduced in status from its
present almost positive meaning to the purely negative sense
of Not Proved Guilty—in which case we might as well say Not
Proven.

In many cases two verdicts are probably enough, either Guilty
and Not Proven or, more logically and tidily, Proven and Not
Proven. This is because usually the only issue raised is that
raised by the prosecution, namely the guilt of the accused. The
accused does not as a rule put his innocence positively into
issue. But he sometimes does so. For example, if he pleads alibi,
he undertakes to prove that he was at a different place when
the crime was being committed. If he succeeds there is no question of his being guilty, unless perhaps some form of conspiracy
is involved. Normally, however, a man in Edinburgh does not
commit a crime in Glasgow. If such a defence succeeds the jury
is entitled to say "We are satisfied that he did not commit the
crime". And similarly with the other special defences, as where
the accused successfully charges some other person with the
crime charged against himself.

This is not to say, however, that the only cases where a Not
Guilty verdict is possible are those in which an accused person
pleads a special, or positive, defence. It can easily happen that
the whole evidence in an ordinary case points quite clearly to
the innocence of the accused. When this is so there is no reason
why he should not get a verdict to that effect, so long as there
are three verdicts. But on the whole the most appropriate cases
for Not Guilty verdicts are those where an accused person successfully puts his innocence in issue.

When we consider the matter historically, in spite of the
criticisms quoted earlier, we find support for this view. In the
earliest Scottish criminal records, the verdicts were not standard-
ised. Convictions were usually expressed by the words "fylit"

(fouled), "culpable" or "convict"; acquittals by the words "cleanse" or "acquit". Commentators tend to equate these with Guilty and Not Guilty, but there is no reason to suppose that "acquit" at least meant more than Not Proven. There were a few occasions when a verdict of "innocent" was returned, and this is obviously the equivalent of Not Guilty. But speculation about the meaning of the old verdicts is not very profitable.

The verdicts of Guilty and Not Guilty seem to have entered Scots legal language during the period known as the Usurpation, when Cromwell imposed English Judges on Scotland, a period which apart from these two verdicts has left little mark on our jurisprudence. For some time they continued to be used after the Restoration along with the older ones, which revived.

In the later years of Charles II's reign a further change took place. That monarch's religious policy was unpopular in Scotland and it was often difficult for the Crown to obtain from reluctant juries convictions for such crimes as attending conventicles or field preachings. The Lord Advocate, Sir George Mackenzie, is said to have evaded this reluctance by introducing the doctrine that juries had no concern with anything except the evidence; their only function was to decide the facts and leave it to the Judges to determine the legal quality of these facts. They had to say, in other words, whether the Crown had proved the facts alleged or not and so the verdicts of Proven and Not Proven became standard forms in their turn.

Eighteenth-century writers could find nothing good to say of Mackenzie, who is still popularly if unfairly known as the Bluidy Mackenzie. It was axiomatic to them that whatever was done under the Stuarts and before the Hanoverians was oppressive and tyrannical. But the distinction which Mackenzie drew between the functions of the jury and those of the Judges is sound enough, however suspect his motives may have been. It can only be exceptionally that a jury is not told in so many words that it has to decide questions of fact upon the evidence, while the Judge has to decide all questions of law. Today that direction, like all other directions from the presiding Judge to the jury, is given after counsel's speeches and just before the jury retires to consider the verdict. In this procedure the presiding Judge can tell the jury what facts it must find proved before the accused can be found guilty; he can also tell them in advance the legal result of finding certain facts or combinations of facts proved. In such a procedure a jury is not deciding any question of law by holding that a particular combination of facts has the legal quality of guilt; it is merely applying the law as that has been laid down for it by the presiding Judge to the facts which it has decided upon the evidence.

But in the seventeenth century there was no practice of the Judges charging the jury before the verdict. The Judges had to hold, before the trial began, that the facts set forth in the indictment were relevant, that is that if they were proved the accused was guilty. But they did not deal with the legal effect of finding only some of the facts proved and this question was therefore left until after the verdict was given.

It was not until the trial of Katharine Nairn and Patrick Ogilvie[1] for murder in 1765 that a Judge charged a Scottish jury and he did so then only in spite of vigorous, even violent, protests from defence counsel that he was in breach of an Act of the Scottish Parliament which provided for the defence having the last word. This, it may be observed, was a legacy from the "tyrannical" reign of the same Charles II. It is still the foundation of the right which the defence always has in Scotland to address the jury after the prosecution—a right which is lost in England if a law officer prosecutes.

In 1728 a verdict of Not Guilty was returned in the trial of Carnegie of Findhaven for the murder of the Earl of Strathmore. This trial may be taken as the effective reintroduction of the Not Guilty verdict although a similar verdict was given in the trial of Samuel Hale two years earlier.

On the evidence in Carnegie's case there was no doubt that he did kill the Earl. The defence was that he was so drunk that he did not know what he was doing, that he bore no ill will against the Earl and that he had no intention of killing or even injuring him. The evidence was that Carnegie, who was certainly very drunk, was grossly insulted and abused by one Lyon of Bridgetown, who ended by pushing him into a "kennel" or gutter two feet deep in mud and probably, though we are not told about this, even less salubrious matter. He was nearly

[1] Hodge, Notable British Trials Series, 1926.

smothered and had to be rescued by one of the Earl's servants,
who took it upon himself to rebuke Lyon for his conduct. This
shows clearly that Lyon's behaviour was outrageous: servants
were not in the habit of criticising gentlemen. Carnegie drew his
sword and rushed at Lyon. Lyon apparently had no sword and
tried to draw the Earl's. The Earl either stepped forward to
intervene or was drawn in front of Lyon and received Carnegie's
thrust. He died two days later. On several occasions he told the
doctors who attended him that he was sure Carnegie had not
meant to injure him. Carnegie himself had been on good terms
with the Earl and was overwhelmed with remorse when he
learned what had happened.

On these facts Carnegie's counsel demanded a verdict of Not
Guilty. If the jury did not make that positive declaration, he
told them, the Judges would construe their verdict as one of
guilty of murder. He also urged them to stand up for the rights
of jurymen; they had to assert these rights now against the
claims of the Judges or lose them for ever. By the practice of
the day the Judges had no right to reply. And so the jury, with
these words ringing in their ears, paid perhaps more attention
to their constitutional rights than to the facts of the case and
found Carnegie Not Guilty. Yet he was surely guilty of that
lesser degree of killing known in Scotland as culpable homicide
and in England as manslaughter, if not of actual murder.

There have no doubt been many bad verdicts of Not Proven.
This verdict of Not Guilty seems at least as open to criticism
as any of them. But it supports the view for which I have
already argued that Not Guilty is appropriate when a special
defence has been established. Logic and history are less hostile
to Not Proven than the critics have made out.

Even if the verdict is "logically indefensible", there are other
more serious illogicalities in the criminal law which reformers
tend to ignore. Take the way in which a jury arrives at its verdict, whatever that verdict may be. In criminal cases, in Scotland and in England alike, the prosecution must prove the
guilt of the accused beyond all reasonable doubt. Now the Scottish jury of fifteen does not have to be unanimous; a simple
majority is enough for any verdict. But where only eight out
of fifteen are convinced of guilt, it is not easy to say that reason-

able doubt has been excluded. Yet in such a case the verdict is Guilty just as much as if all fifteen had been unanimous.

In England a jury must be unanimous. This seems more logical where conviction is concerned. But if an English jury is not unanimous the result is not acquittal but a new trial. This process can go on in theory though not in practice until a unanimous jury is found. Even if eleven members of a jury are positively convinced of innocence and only one of guilt a new trial results, though surely in such a case the prosecution has failed to prove guilt beyond reasonable doubt.

A compromise (in Scotland, for I dare not speak for England) might be to require at least a minimum majority, say 10–5, for a conviction. During the recent war, when the jury was cut down to seven, no verdict of Guilty could be pronounced unless the majority was at least 5–2. Where the majority was for Guilty but was too small to return such a verdict, Not Proven would seem admirably apt to express that result. This, however, is a digression.

It is often said that a Not Proven verdict leaves a stigma on the reputation of an acquitted person, namely the suggestion that he has been lucky to get off only because the Crown did not have enough evidence to prove his guilt. This is no doubt true. But in England a Not Guilty verdict may mean exactly the same thing. In the trial of Adelaide Bartlett in 1886 the jury returned their verdict in these words: "We have well considered the evidence, and, although we think grave suspicion is attached to the prisoner, we do not think there is sufficient evidence to show how or by whom the chloroform was administered." That verdict was recorded as one of Not Guilty but it was far more stigmatic than many Not Proven verdicts.

Where, as in England, some verdicts of Not Guilty mean no more than Not Proven, there is a risk that any or every verdict of Not Guilty may be so interpreted. The result is that in England there is no positive verdict of innocence. As Sybille Bedford says in her account of the trial of Dr John Bodkin Adams,[1] "A man accused of murder, with whatever aloofness the law may have held him innocent before the verdict, is nearly always presumed not to have been quite that after his acquittal."

[1] *The Best We Can Do* (Collins, 1958).

That is, of course, a lay view, not a legal view, but it is all the more important for that: it is among laymen that, as a rule, an acquitted person has to live. It is the great merit of the Not Proven verdict that it makes Not Guilty of real worth.

The trials which follow have not been chosen to prove or disprove any thesis but for their intrinsic qualities as human documents and mysteries. They come from different periods: two (Madeleine Smith and Monson) from what has been called the "classic period" of British crime (Madeleine in 1857 to Crippen in 1910), one (Christina Gilmour) from an earlier period and one (Merrett) from a later. The two women were tried for poisoning, the two men for murder by shooting. Poisoning has always an aura of mystery about it because of the insidious operation of the means of death and poisoning cases may therefore seem made for Not Proven verdicts; but the opinion has been expressed that, if the Not Proven verdict were open to English juries, they would most often use it in shooting cases.

Some apology may seem needed for trying once again to tell the story of the trial of Madeleine Smith when it has been told so often. But could she have been omitted from any book called "Not Proven"?

(I)

CHRISTINA GILMOUR

The dog it was that died.
Goldsmith

FOR many years the Ayrshire parish of Dunlop has been noted for its cheeses, whose excellence is due to their being made from sweet instead of skimmed milk. According to one tradition this method was introduced into the parish by Barbara Gilmour, who had been driven into exile in Ireland during the reign of Charles II. The Ayrshire historian Paterson, writing in 1852, rather sourly observes that this tradition "seems extremely doubtful, seeing that the Irish do not understand cheese-making at the present day".

Whether Irish by origin or not, the fame of the Dunlop cheeses had so grown by the beginning of the nineteenth century that a Mr Cochran was able to build up a considerable fortune by trading in them. He died about the year of Waterloo, leaving the bulk of his fortune to his eldest son Alexander, who had been in partnership with him. Alexander settled down, took a wife and worked the farms he inherited. In due course at least four daughters and a son were born.

Christina, the eldest daughter, was born, according to the parish register, on 16th November 1818. She was educated at the local parish school, then at boarding schools in Paisley and Glasgow. For a short time she was trained at a dress-making establishment kept by the Misses Parker in Paisley. While she was at home she took her full part in the domestic work at the farm. Ayrshire farmers of those days, even when they were as comfortably situated as the Cochrans, did not indulge in the luxury of domestic help.

As Christina grew up she attracted a number of suitors. She was a good-looking and pleasant girl, fair of hair and of complexion, with a natural good humour and gaiety. If

17

her right arm was slightly disabled so that she could not raise it to her head, this was no doubt compensated by her rich father and her sound training in household management. Many of her suitors came from higher ranks than herself but neither she nor her parents were ambitious for a marriage out of her class. Her own affections were fixed on John Anderson, son of the farmer at Broadley, about a mile from the Cochran farm of Grange. He had known her when she was a child at school, for the parish school was conducted in a house belonging to his father. Although he was ten years older than she was the two planned marriage. There was, however, no formal engagement; John Anderson's financial position did not allow him to take a wife.

In 1842 John Gilmour, son of another farmer in the parish, came on the scene. It is pleasant to speculate that he was related to the Barbara Gilmour who may or may not have introduced into the parish the secret of cheese-making on which the Cochran fortune was founded; but there is no proof of that. He had, however, some qualities which made him more immediately preferable to Anderson. He was more independent. Though younger he had his own farm at Town of Inchinnan, near Renfrew. He was also a more determined suitor. Once when Christina refused him he threatened suicide.

Christina was flattered by this determination and appeared to relent. Some time later she gave him to understand that she accepted him. Whether there was paternal compulsion, as Christina later claimed, we cannot now say. But there is no doubt that Alexander Cochran, a strong-minded father, approved of a match with young Gilmour. Christina sometimes suffered from a weakness of will and the approval of such a father may well have seemed to her indistinguishable from compulsion.

In the meantime John Anderson continued his visits, though his affection for Christina and hers for him were unknown to Gilmour. Christina told Anderson of her promise or half-promise to Gilmour, perhaps hoping to rouse him out of his stolidity to a more passionate declaration than he had yet made. If this was her object she failed. Anderson at first refused to believe her but when he was at last convinced he behaved, disappointingly, like a perfect gentleman and, urging her to be true to her word, retired from the field.

According to a more romantic contemporary account Gilmour owed his success to Christina's parents. She herself showed the most determined opposition and pleaded to be allowed to remain single for the rest of her life. Eventually Christina and Anderson met, declared their love for one another and then parted "both deeply bathed in tears at the cruel fate which awaited her, and which neither of them seemed to have the power to avert".

Her engagement with Gilmour and Anderson's philosophic acceptance of it had a disastrous effect on Christina. She had once been lively and cheerful, afraid only of being alone in the dark. Now she was abstracted and given to roaming alone about the house and the fields at night. She was not, however, the complete lovesick heroine. Her appetite did not dwindle but grew so insatiable that her mother had to restrain her to a diet. From time to time her new habitual gloom was broken by signs of the old good humour and merriment. Oddly enough these occurred when John Gilmour, the reluctantly accepted suitor, was present. And she seemed so far to accept her fate that she made at least two expeditions with him to Paisley and Glasgow to choose "the braws" or wedding dresses.

The wedding after two postponements took place on 27th November 1842 at Grange, the bride's father's home. The parish minister, Matthew Dickie, who performed the ceremony, observed nothing remarkable about the conduct or appearance of the two young people. On 29th November they went to take up their new life at Town of Inchinnan, accompanied by the bride's eldest sister Elizabeth, who stayed with them for a week.

Gilmour leased his farm at Whitsunday 1842 from Mr Campbell of Blythswood—a first, tenuous link with Madeleine Smith of Blythswood Square. From the evidence at Christina's trial in January 1844, we know the names of some of the farm servants. There was first Mary Paterson, who had been employed by John's father Mathew Gilmour in Dunlop before John set up on his own. Her duties were not domestic but had to do with the cows in the byres. Then there were Alexander Muir, whose brother John helped occasionally, and William Arthur, the ploughman. In addition to this staff there was in residence for practically the whole duration of the marriage one or other of Christina's three sisters, for the tradition that started when Elizabeth went with the newly married pair on their honeymoon was maintained. Andrew Gilmour, a fourteen-year-old cousin of the bridegroom, had been living on the farm before the marriage and continued to do so after it.

The house was a commodious one. Mr and Mrs Gilmour occupied a bedroom on the ground floor and took their meals in another room on the same floor, off the kitchen where the servants ate. Christina cooked the meals for herself and her husband—porridge and tea for breakfast; dinner; and tea in the evening. On some occasions at least the resident sister ate her meals alone in the kitchen.

The only witness at the trial who described the domestic life of the young Gilmours was Mary Paterson. Once Mrs Gilmour told her that she had been unwilling to take John Gilmour and would have preferred Anderson. Mary did not, however, suspect any unhappiness from their conduct towards one another. Until the end of December 1842—that is one month after the marriage—things were normal, with John Gilmour, a healthy sober man of thirty, going quietly about his business at the farm.

From two contemporary reports of the trial a blacker picture emerges. Both agree that the marriage was never consummated. The more romantic of the two assures us, "on good authority" (whose?), that Christina never undressed during the whole six weeks for which the marriage lasted: it had the single virtue of brevity. She promised her husband to be a faithful and loyal servant though she could be no more. To the outside world they behaved with propriety though one visit to hospitable neighbours was rather spoiled by Christina falling into a stupor from which she recovered only by "a sort of epileptic start".

Our information so far depends very much on the two reports of the trial already referred to. From 26th December 1842 the evidence gives a very full picture of what happened at the farm. The dispute was far less about facts than about the inferences to be drawn from them. One editor says tantalisingly that "the witnesses adduced, *with perhaps one exception*, told the facts with remarkable accuracy".

On Monday 26th December 1842 (characteristically described not as Boxing Day or St Stephen's Day but as the Monday before New Year's Day) Mary Paterson went to visit her sister in Dunlop. On her way there she had to pass through Paisley. Before she left Mrs Gilmour gave her twopence and told her to call at a house there. The people in the house were to send a boy with the twopence to buy arsenic. Mary forgot the name of the house but not the errand. On her way back next day she went to Dr Vessey's druggist's shop in Paisley where she said that she wanted arsenic for Mrs Gilmour, Town of Inchinnan, who proposed to use it to poison rats. The shop assistant gave her a paper parcel with the words "Arsenic, Poison" written on it, which she handed to Mrs Gilmour.

The killing of rats is of course one of the classic, not to say hackneyed, excuses for the purchase of arsenic. Before the marriage John Gilmour had in fact used it for that purpose. He got it from Paton, a smith near Inchinnan, and he kept it in a kist or wooden chest which sat in the kitchen before the marriage and was then moved into the bedroom. But that was not Mrs Gilmour's intention, as she admitted in the judicial declaration which was read at her trial. According to that solemn statement she meant to use the poison to put an end to her unhappy marriage—by suicide.

On Wednesday 28th December Mary Paterson was in the boiling-house next to the farmhouse when Mrs Gilmour entered with a paper packet in her hand, like the one Mary had given her. She threw it into the fire before Mary's eyes saying she was frightened in case she did not use it properly. In her declaration she said "I was frightened with what she told me about its sudden effects in producing death at once and I therefore destroyed it." If suicide had in fact been her object there would have been great virtue in that very suddenness. If she had been told the truth, that arsenic produces its fatal issue as a rule some hours after ingestion, she would have had more reason to fear its suicidal use. Of course it may be that her suicidal intention, if it existed, was not serious and that she confidently expected and wanted to be saved after a spectacular and convincing demonstration of unhappiness. A quick-acting poison would have been in every sense fatal to such a project.

John Gilmour's illness began next night, Thursday 29th December. Till then he had been healthy but now until his death on 11th January 1843 he was almost constantly vomiting "a kind of brownish stuff" and complaining of pain in his stomach and chest and swelling in the face.

On Monday 2nd January 1843, however, he and Christina were able to visit the Cochrans at Dunlop, where they spent the night. Neither Christina's brother nor her father, both of whom were Crown witnesses at her trial, described Gilmour's condition while he was with them. On the way home on Tuesday morning the young couple called on the senior Gilmours and spent two hours with them. John was then complaining of having been ill and had a fit of vomiting in his parents' house.

On their way to Dunlop on Monday the Gilmours met in Paisley John Muir, the occasional hand, who was then on his way to the farm. He noticed nothing peculiar about John Gilmour's appearance then. On Wednesday after the return from Dunlop he saw Gilmour in the stable: "his face was kind of swollen ways and his eyes were swelled and a kind of watering about them from throwing".

Friday 6th January is an important date in the history of the case. Christina left the house early that morning telling Mary Paterson that she was going to Renfrew to get something for her husband. She told Mary not to let the other servants know that she had gone from home. This instruction was painted in sinister colours by the Lord Advocate for the prosecution at the trial. But her reason for wanting Mary to keep silence may have been to conceal the fact that there was no person in authority at the farm for the time being, for John was confined to bed that morning.

Soon after Christina's return John Muir found in a corner of the boiling-house a black bag, which he opened. In it were a small phial, unlabelled, containing a dark brownish liquid with a sweet smell. It was like oil and he thought it was scent. It was not turpentine, which he knew. (The defence theory was that this phial contained turpentine to rub John with.) There was also a small paper parcel with the one word "Poison" written on it. He gave the bag to Mary Paterson and showed her what was in it, telling her that the word "Poison" was on the parcel: she could not read. In her turn Mary gave the bag with its contents to Mrs Gilmour, whose property it was. Mrs Gilmour said nothing.

That evening Christina visited her uncle Robert Robertson, who lived in Paisley and held the responsible position of treasurer of the Poors' Funds of the Abbey Parish. About 9 o'clock when she was ushered into the parlour her uncle was writing and she had to introduce herself as he did not recognise her. Robertson remarked "You are not far from us now" to which Christina somewhat ungraciously replied that it was against her will that this was so. She explained that she would have preferred to marry another person named Anderson. She did not complain of any unkindness on her husband's part though she seemed in great grief—not enough, however, to impair her faculties.

Robertson, like a good uncle, took the opportunity to deliver a short homily. He reminded her that at her marriage she had vowed to be an obedient and affectionate wife and that she was bound by the laws of God and man to act accordingly. In a more mundane key he went on to say that many persons had not got the husband they liked best but that if they studied one another's tempers they would come in time to like one another.

Christina seemed to receive this advice quite pleasantly and then turned to the real purpose of her visit—or if one cares to be suspicious the ostensible purpose. Her husband was unwell and had been so for just over a week. Robertson asked if a doctor had seen him and she said no, that the Gilmour family as a whole was averse to seeing doctors. [This was long before the National Health Service. There was therefore nothing surprising in a normally healthy and thrifty family refraining from incurring a possibly needless expense by calling a doctor. Many ailments cure themselves in the course of time with or without medical intervention.]

Robertson was not convinced and suggested calling on Dr Robert McKechnie, a well-known Paisley practitioner. Christina was still reluctant and asked her uncle to call and consult her husband first. She then returned to the farm, between 11 o'clock and midnight, to find an unexpected visitor.

While she was away John Muir the temporary farmhand visited his master in his room. Gilmour was then complaining of pain in his side and Muir asked if he would like to see a doctor. This was because of what he had found in Mrs Gilmour's black bag that morning but he did not mention this to Gilmour or to anyone else. Gilmour's reply confirms his reluctance to consult the medical faculty, as he said he would wait and see how he felt in the morning. Muir insisted and asked for the name of a doctor. Gilmour suggested Dr McLaws of Renfrew, which is about two miles east of the farm. Before he left Gilmour said "Jock, this is an unco thing", which Muir did not understand.

Muir did not know the way to Renfrew and took the ploughman with him. They did not have to complete the two miles' journey as they found the doctor at Inchinnan Tollhouse on the way. All three arrived at the farm between 10 and 11 o'clock. Mrs Gilmour was still away. According to Muir the doctor was not quite sober and John Gilmour told Robertson next day that he had been tipsy. In spite of this he bled the patient and said he would return next day. He did not do so.

The doctor's own evidence at the trial was fairly short and did not agree altogether with that of the other witnesses. This may have been due to his condition, about which he was, tactfully, not questioned. He thought he had been called after midnight and was not sure of the date. He said nothing about bleeding his patient; all he remembered was that he gave instructions to the servant (whom he took for Mrs Gilmour) that Gilmour should be rubbed with turpentine. He thought the trouble was inflammation due to a cold as he knew nothing of the vomiting that had taken place.

Next morning about 8 a.m. a "respectably dressed female" called at the shop of Alexander Wylie, druggist in Renfrew, and asked if he sold arsenic, which she wanted to kill rats in the field. Wylie asked who it was for and she said "John Ferguson". Wylie did not know any farmer of that name and asked for the name of the farm. The customer had forgotten. Wylie named all the farms in the district that he could remember but she recognised none of the names, explaining that she had come so recently to that part of the world that she could not remember.

The druggist was not satisfied and called in James Smith, an elderly grocer in Renfrew, who was passing the shop at the time. He had not heard of a Ferguson with a farm in the district and in his turn named all the farms nearby, no doubt with all the detail that an old inhabitant would give. Still the mysterious customer failed to recognise the name of the one she had come from. She explained at last that it was "up by Paisley", which is only some three miles from Renfrew. This explanation was satisfactory and the customer, who gave the name of Miss Robertson, received her twopennyworth of arsenic in a paper marked "Poison, Arsenic". Before she left the shop Wylie made an entry in the book he kept for sales of arsenic: "January 7th 1843. For John Ferguson, per Miss Robertson, for killing rats in the field. James Smith, witness."

As he handed her the packet Wylie remarked with grim humour "Don't take it yourself or give it to anyone else, for here is James Smith who will be a witness against you."

At the trial when both he and James Smith were in fact witnesses against the accused, Wylie identified "Miss Robertson" as being Mrs Gilmour. Indeed she never denied this purchase under a false name. But her account of this parcel confuses it with the one found by John Muir in the boiling-house corner the day before. Apart from the all-important point of the administration of the arsenic the only question of fact that was at all strenuously contested was whether Christina bought two or three packets of arsenic. The Crown said three: the first was that bought by Mary Paterson and marked "Arsenic, Poison", the second was that found by John Muir and marked "Poison" and the third was that bought from Wylie and marked "Poison, Arsenic".

The defence case, that the second and third packets were one and the same and that the witnesses were mistaken in the dates, will hardly do. Muir was positive that it was the finding of the second packet that induced him to go for Dr McLaws. That was on Friday 6th January as Dr McLaws' visit coincided with Christina's visit to her uncle. Her uncle was quite clear about the date of that visit; he visited the sick man next day and sent Dr McKechnie in place of Dr Laws on Sunday. John Gilmour's father had visited his son on Saturday, after Dr McLaws had been. The entry in Wylie's arsenic book gives the date of the sale of arsenic to "Miss Robertson" as 7th January, which was Saturday. Wylie also remembered a servant coming for soda and tartaric acid for John Gilmour the next day, Sunday. This was prescribed for Gilmour by Dr McKechnie who did not see him until Sunday morning. The sequence of events therefore makes it clear that the packet found by John Muir was found by him the day before "Miss Robertson" bought arsenic from Wylie. Further, each of the three packets was differently inscribed.

To some extent this anticipates counsel's arguments at the trial. But it is as well to have the facts clear at this stage. To return to the chronological scheme of things, Mathew Gilmour, John's father, heard on Thursday that he was worse than he had been and went to Inchinnan on Saturday morning to see for himself. He found John ill in bed, still complaining of "throwing up", swelling and pain in the breast and stomach and constant thirst. He stayed for some time and then went home, although his son asked him to remain: he feared his further absence would cause alarm at home.

Between 3 and 4 o'clock just as Mathew was going away Robert Robertson arrived in accordance with the arrangement made the evening before. The patient was obviously ill and Robertson offered, as he had done to Christina, to send for Dr McKechnie. Gilmour again said he would rather not see a doctor that day but would wait and see how he felt next day. He may have been even more than usually reluctant for medical attention after being bled by the tipsy Dr McLaws.

Robertson thought that this was quite reasonable and arranged with Christina that she would send him a message if her husband got worse. Before he left she again spoke of her unhappy marriage. There was nothing bitter in her voice but she seemed grieved and depressed.

Next morning about 9 o'clock a servant came to Robertson's house asking him to send for Dr McKechnie. Robertson passed the message to the doctor and went himself to Town of Inchinnan, where he arrived about noon. Dr McKechnie arrived about an hour later.

The patient was feverish, complaining of pain in his side and of vomiting, the vomit being like bile. The doctor prescribed calomel powders and effervescing powders—soda and tartaric acid. He also ordered a blister to be applied. John Muir was sent for the medicines: he went to Wylie's. On learning that the powders were for "throwing" Wylie strongly approved the remedy, remarking that he was sometimes "sair fashed" with the trouble himself.

Before he left the doctor prudently asked for specimens of Gilmour's vomit and evacuations to be kept for examination. He does not seem to have had at the time any suspicion of poisoning and this may have been part of his normal routine. One wonders how many lives would have been saved, how many murders prevented and how many unknown murders detected if other doctors had adopted the same routine. Unfortunately his instructions were not carried out. When he came back next day and asked to see the specimens Christina told him she had not retained them: there was so little she did not think it worth while.

When the doctor left, Robertson stayed at the farm and in fact spent the night there. He was invited to do so by both Mr and Mrs Gilmour in order to apply the blister, an operation new to both of them. He slept for the earlier part of the night and rose about 3 a.m. to relieve Christina who was attending to her husband until then. He left about 9 o'clock on Monday morning. Some time on Sunday evening he had another conversation with Christina about her marriage, initiated like the others by herself.

In the next three days John Gilmour's illness completed its mysterious course. The doctor called on Monday and added blue pills to his prescription. He did not comment on Christina's ignoring his request for specimens and did not renew it.

Next day, Tuesday, there were no medical visitors but Mathew Gilmour, who had heard of the progress of the disease, came with Christina's sister Margaret. This time he was prepared to stay and did so, remaining for most of the time in John's bedroom. John was worse than on Saturday and complained very much of pain and thirst.

On Wednesday morning John Muir was sent to Dunlop to

tell Mrs Gilmour senior that John was seriously ill and to ask her to come to Inchinnan. She did not arrive until all was over. Dr William McKechnie arrived in his father's place during the afternoon. He thought John Gilmour was in a dangerous condition, although he seemed to have his wits about him. In spite of being sluggish and drowsy he could answer questions correctly enough. After bleeding him Dr McKechnie left.

From that moment John Gilmour was rarely if ever left alone. His wife and her sister, his father, his cousin Andrew and the servant Alexander Muir were all in and out of his room continuously. The last two heard him express a wish "to be opened". Neither could say whether this referred to the period before or after death. It could have been a cry of intolerable agony or, more sinister, a demand for a post-mortem examination.

Another remark made by the dying man was reported in two different forms. Young Andrew Gilmour heard him say "Oh, if you have given me anything, tell me before I die!" He did not know to whom this was addressed nor could he remember whether Christina was in the room at the time. Alexander Muir heard the phrase "Oh, that woman! If you have given me anything!"

Neither heard a phrase, put by defence counsel in cross-examination, about "being kind to my widow". There is no evidence that any such wish was expressed. But the editor of one of the contemporary reports says that one witness on the Crown list, not called by either side at the trial, heard him use such words within an hour before he died. This was probably Christina's sister Margaret. Unfortunately the evidence is that John Gilmour was "wandering" in his mind for at least an hour before death so that little weight can be given to such a wish. It is equally true that the remark about "giving me anything" was made during the same period so that the dying man's suspicions —if they were suspicions of his wife—were the product of the same "wandering" mind.

John Gilmour died between 6 and 7 o'clock in the evening of Wednesday 11th January 1843.

The funeral took place on Monday 16th January at Dunlop. After the coffin was covered there was erected over the grave a mortsafe—a gaunt ugly iron grating designed to prevent a premature resurrection at the hands of the body-snatchers. The funeral took place eleven years after the passing of the Anatomy Act, 1832, which was meant to put an end to this scandal by providing a legitimate supply of subjects for the dissecting rooms. In fact it was reported in November 1958 that the supply still falls short: there is, of course, no suggestion that the universities should revert to the services of men like Burke and Hare.

However that may be, the Ayrshire farmers of 1843 still feared the resurrectionists. And we shall see that the combined efforts of the blacksmith and the legislature did not secure for John Gilmour's tormented corpse the rest which might have been thought to be its due.

Christina returned as a widow to Town of Inchinnan. She was joined there by her parents-in-law Mathew Gilmour and his wife and all three, with young Andrew, lived together for about two months. About a week after the funeral Christina spent one night in her uncle's house in Paisley and again complained of her misfortune in having had to marry Gilmour. Some time later Robertson visited Inchinnan and learned that Christina had had a letter from her old sweetheart John Anderson. Their correspondence had been interrupted during the short married life but revived soon after its end. It does not seem to have been on other terms than those of simple friendship.

About March Christina went back to her parents in Dunlop. We can easily suppose that the farm servants had not been silent among themselves about the mystery of John Gilmour's death —the packet labelled "Poison" and the dying man's dark hints. But the talk does not seem to have spread beyond that small circle till Christina left the farm. It first came to the ears of Mr and Mrs Gilmour, the dead man's parents, who refused to listen to such gossip. Then it carried to Dunlop where Christina's brother Thomas heard it. Horrified, he reported it to the family.

Christina insisted that her husband's body should be exhumed for expert examination. Alexander Cochran went to see

Mathew Gilmour and both fathers visited the doctors who had been in attendance—presumably the McKechnies and not McLaws. They then went to the Procurator-fiscal to urge him to procure the necessary order from the Sheriff. The Procurator-fiscal, who under the Lord Advocate privately inquires into suspected crimes, was not available but they saw his partner McInnes. (In those days the Procurator-fiscal was not a full-time official as he is now but was at liberty to engage in private legal practice as well.) McInnes advised the two men to go home and wait for eight or ten days when he thought the whole affair would blow over; his view was that it was all nonsense.

Alexander Cochran was not satisfied with McInnes' rather casual assurances. His suspicions were not without foundation for the first rumours of foul play were now supplemented by others that the body was going to be exhumed. He therefore took steps to get Christina out of the way. It is only fair to say that from all accounts this was entirely against her will. She protested sensibly enough that flight would inevitably be taken as a confession of guilt. Her father was inexorable and Christina could not stand against his will. She was not even allowed to say good-bye to her mother.

About the middle of April her long journey began. Her father's younger brother Robert took her to a house in Fenwick, Ayrshire, some five miles from Dunlop. On the 24th a strange man took her to Carlisle and then to Liverpool, using first the name Jameson and then that of Speirs. From Liverpool she sailed with him as Mr and Mrs Speirs in the brig *Excel* bound for New York.

Soon after she left her father's house the Paisley authorities got busy. On 21st April the Procurator-fiscal applied to the Sheriff-substitute for a warrant to exhume John Gilmour's body. As the body was buried outside his jurisdiction he could not grant such a warrant but made a recommendation to his colleague in Ayr that he should do so. The body was disinterred on 22nd April in the presence of Archibald McKean, wright at Inchinnan, who had acted as undertaker, three doctors from Paisley (McKechnie senior, Wylie and McKinlay), and a surgeon from Stewarton who attended on behalf of Gilmour's family.

The body was examined by Dr Wylie and Dr McKinlay, who

made two reports, one of the autopsy and the other of the chemical analysis to which they subjected certain organs. Both concluded that John Gilmour died of arsenic poisoning. Their opinion was shared and supported by Dr (later Sir Robert) Christison, a medical jurist of European reputation who had held the Chair of Medical Jurisprudence at Edinburgh (at that time the only one in Britain) from 1822 to 1832. So overwhelming was the medical evidence that defence counsel at the trial conceded the cause of death as arsenic poisoning.

News of the result of the exhumation and of the examination of her husband's remains may have reached Christina before she sailed for the United States, for on 28th April she wrote to John Anderson from Liverpool. He gave the letter to her brother Thomas and Thomas gave it to his father. It was then destroyed. According to Anderson, Christina said in it that she would confess she had bought arsenic to take herself but she would not admit having given any to John Gilmour. She also complained about having been sent away; she herself would have stayed until the whole thing was settled.

Neither her father nor her brother remembered any reference in the letter to arsenic. All they recalled was her regret at being sent away. Christina herself later denied any knowledge of the result of the exhumation.

Superintendent George McKay of the Renfrewshire rural police had meantime traced Christina's purchases of arsenic. When he learned the result of the chemical analysis he went to Dunlop to interview her but she was gone and no one at the farm could or would give him any information. It was not until well on in May that, armed with a warrant for her apprehension on the charge of murdering her husband, he traced her first to Carlisle and then to Liverpool *en route* for New York.

We do not know who chose the brig *Excel* for Christina's voyage to America and freedom though we may take it that it was not herself. The choice of sail instead of steam had its disadvantages. The passage was protracted by rough weather and Christina was seasick for most of the time. Her provisions were of so little use that she gave most of them away to other passengers, including some children who had taken her fancy. Moreover "Mr Speirs" proved a nuisance. We cannot search his motives too closely and he may have been moved merely by a desire for artistic verisimilitude; but he did try to presume too much on the fictitious relationship of husband and wife and Christina had to appeal for protection to the captain.

There was another and more important disadvantage in sail against steam. Probably the thought of extradition entered the heads of the Cochran family no more than it did Crippen's as he sat watching the sparks crackle round the wireless transmitter of the s.s. *Montrose*. But just as Inspector Dew waited for Crippen off Quebec so Superintendent McKay waited for Christina in New York.

McKay's pursuit was more remarkable than Dew's. Dew sailed from Liverpool a mere three days after Crippen and Ethel Le Neve sailed from Antwerp. McKay sailed from Liverpool a fortnight after Christina left the same port. He was in New York on 2nd June applying for a warrant for her extradition. But he had to wait until 21st June before the *Excel* at last, weatherbeaten and weary, made her landfall. It was a fine tribute to the Cunard s.s. *Arcadia* in which he sailed.

When at last the brig was signalled McKay went to meet her in a Custom-house boat. He had found to his dismay that the newspapers had widely reported his arrival and its purpose and he was afraid that if he waited until the *Excel* arrived in harbour Christina would somehow be warned and enabled to make her escape.

The Custom-house boat met the *Excel* off Staten Island and McKay went on board. At first Christina tried to deny her identity but soon abandoned the attempt. McKay was not depending on description only: he had visited the Gilmours at Inchinnan and recognised her in spite of the ravages of the voyage. That had been on Friday 6th January—a day packed with incident, when John Muir found the "Poison" packet and brought Dr McLaws and when Christina visited her uncle in Paisley and first complained to him about her unfortunate marriage. McKay's visit, however, seems to have had to do with other matters.

Christina was arrested and instructed Thomas Warner, counsellor-at-law of the New York Bar, to oppose the demand for extradition. This was the first case in which extradition was sought under the Ashburton Treaty concluded in Washington on 9th August 1842, less than a year before. It therefore attracted a good deal of publicity, which was perhaps not ungrateful to Warner. He was not reluctant to play to the gallery.

According to one report Christina said later that "the people who acted for her must have been indebted to some unknown and irresponsible informer for the facts which were urged in her behalf. . . . The sweetest sound she ever heard was that which told her she was returned to her native country." This is a singular piece of ingratitude to Warner's tireless, if tiresome, efforts and it does not fit the facts: Christina must have co-operated in the production of some of the evidence at least.

About 24th June Christina was brought before United States Commissioner Sylvanus Rapalyea (a delightful name with its odour of snuff and villainy) whose duty it was to investigate the demand for extradition. Article X of the treaty provided that a fugitive could be surrendered only upon such evidence of criminality as, according to the law of the place where he was apprehended, would justify his commitment for trial. If the commissioner was satisfied of this he would issue a certificate to the proper executive authority so that the necessary warrant might be issued.

But before the commissioner could consider this question, Warner raised a preliminary matter. His client, he said, was insane; she could not be tried or committed for trial and therefore could not be surrendered to the British authorities. The commissioner, apparently with the agreement of the lawyers on both sides, appointed a number of doctors to examine Christina in prison and adjourned the proceedings until Wednesday 12th July.

On that date Warner moved that all the witnesses should be excluded except the one actually giving evidence. This would have been in conformity with the contemporary Scots practice, as we shall see at the trial, but his motion was refused. Evidence was taken on that day and on Saturday 15th July: the reason for the interval was illness on the part of Warner.

B

In all, seven doctors of the official panel were called, but two did not answer the summons. All had visited Christina several times and all at first suspected that she was of unsound mind. On their later visits, however, with one exception they changed their minds and came to the conclusion that she was feigning insanity. From Dr Rogers' evidence it appeared that they all had held a meeting at which they discussed the case and came to a joint conclusion.

Warner regarded Dr Nelson as his best witness. He reported a conversation between Dr Rogers (who had already given evidence) and Christina when the doctor asked "Will you go home? Will you go back to Scotland? I shall sign an order if you say you will go."

"Aye," replied Christina, "I will go."

"You know if you go back you will be tried for the murder of your husband and you will be hanged."

Christina made no reply.

"If you go I will sign the order," repeated the doctor.

"Aye, but how can I go?"

"You will be sent as you came, in a ship."

"Oh," answered Christina with feeling, "I dinna like a ship —it is so long—so long in crossing—I would rather go in a coach."

Dr Nelson also told how each time he saw Christina her hands had been scarified by a pair of scissors: she explained that it was pleasant to see the flies come and lick up the blood. She also claimed to see her grandmother lying on the bed in her cell. "If she were not deceiving," said the witness sagely, "the fact of this imagination of seeing her grandmother, who was dead, would imply a diseased mind."

He was asked for his general conclusion as to the state of her mind.

"*On the supposition that she was not deceiving*, I was of opinion until my last visit that she was not capable of taking good care of herself although capable of taking moderate care. On the final visit I thought I discovered evidence of more intelligence than that evinced on former occasions although still of a very low degree. She appears capable of distinguishing to a certain extent between right and wrong. . . . She is conscious of what is passing around her but not to the same extent as a person of ordinary intelligence."

"Is there any particular in which you differ from the witnesses already examined?"

"It appeared to me that the witnesses examined before me were under the impression that she was deceiving them; that may be so but I have no fact authorising me to swear that."

Warner's top card was a very low one. Dr Nelson seems never to have applied his mind seriously to the question whether Christina's unsoundness of mind was real or feigned.

After three of the five official doctors had given evidence Warner proposed to call a Dr Cumming, who had not been on the commissioner's list. In spite of a fiery accusation that there were attempts to stifle the truth, the commissioner upheld the British Government's objection to any medical witnesses being called. Warner rather sulkily proposed to call a considerable number of witnesses who had known the prisoner since childhood. He did not say whether they were already in the United States or if he would ask for an adjournment for them to be brought from Scotland. In the event it did not matter, for the commissioner decided that he would hear only the evidence of the doctors whom he had named.

After Drs Hoffmann and Cheesman had failed to answer the summons, Lord, for the British Government, moved that the preliminary investigation into the state of the prisoner's mind should come to an end. The commissioner, he thought, had enough evidence to let him decide.

Not unexpectedly Warner demurred. He still maintained his right to call further witnesses to speak about Christina's early life. The commissioner thought that it would take too much time to go into the examination of more witnesses.

"And is a month's time, sir," angrily asked Warner, seizing his opportunity, "of greater importance than the right and interest of the prisoner?"

The commissioner's temper was rapidly going also. "Sir, I don't need a month's time to make up my mind. I have made it up already—that this woman is not insane."

And that was the informal way in which he intimated his decision on the important preliminary question, in the middle of what reads like a brawl between himself and Warner, with Lord intervening from time to time. When things quietened down, Lord proposed to lead evidence relating to the charge of murder.

Warner asked for an adjournment until Monday on the ground of illness. This may have been only tactical but he had been confined to bed two days earlier and his forensic activities had been exhausting. No objection was taken. Perhaps his motion was heard with relief by all concerned.

On the afternoon of Monday 17th July 1843 Superintendent George McKay was called to give evidence of criminality. He knew the late John Gilmour and identified the prisoner as Mrs Gilmour, whom he had seen at the farm. He heard of John Gilmour's death at the time it occurred.

Warner at once objected that this was hearsay. The witness must speak only about facts within his own knowledge. The commissioner upheld the objection and ruled that the witness must confine himself to legal evidence. Warner's victory, however, was short-lived: he had to renew his objection frequently as the witness told of his pursuit of the prisoner. Each time the objection was taken it was upheld. But Lord, for the British Government, and the witness were to be deflected neither by the objections nor by the commissioner's ruling.

That ruling caused some press criticism. The *New York Courier* commented: "There is no moral doubt that Mrs Gilmour is the person accused and scarcely less doubt that her husband came to his death by poison administered by her, and yet, under the rules of evidence claimed by her counsel and conceded by the commissioner, no direct evidence could be adduced on these points."

[The whole point of the ruling was that only direct evidence was permissible and not that form of indirect evidence known as hearsay.]

The *Paisley Advertiser* of 12th August said that the commissioner's attitude was "very extraordinary and directly at variance with the spirit, if not the letter, of the Ashburton treaty for the mutual surrender of criminals. It was never, surely, contemplated that the American Executive were to judge of the guilt or innocence of fugitives from justice. All they can rationally ask or expect, before giving them up to their own government, is satisfactory proof of their identity. . . . Should [the commissioner] decide against her surrender, it will cause, we suspect, another hitch between the English and the American Governments."

McKay's evidence came to this: he had heard of John Gilmour's death and never saw him in life after 11th January 1843. He saw his body when it was exhumed. A few days later Dr Wylie showed him some white powder, which he said was arsenic from Gilmour's stomach. (Warner's righteous indignation at this piece of hearsay evidence may be imagined.) Reports of death by foul play circulated in the district and the prisoner absconded. He traced her (every step in the journey being objected to by Warner) to Liverpool and eventually to the brig *Excel*, on board which, as we know, he accosted and arrested her, in spite of her denial that she was Mrs Gilmour.

In cross-examination he admitted that he was an officer of the Renfrewshire police and had no authority beyond the county boundary. He was not an "officer, minister or authority" of the British Government. [The point was that power to requisition the surrender of a fugitive was given by the treaty to "ministers, officers and authorities" of the two contracting Governments and that McKay, not being such an officer, had no power to make a requisition.]

McKay further admitted that he knew nothing of his own knowledge about Christina's criminality. The rest of the long cross-examination left matters much as they were.

No further evidence was called and Warner argued strenuously that McKay's evidence was quite insufficient. There was no legal evidence that a murder had been committed at all. If there was a murder, there was no evidence that the prisoner was guilty. The body from which the poison was taken was not properly identified. Even if it were John Gilmour's, however, there was nothing to show that he had not taken the poison himself. Warner also attacked the validity of the warrant for Christina's arrest and that of the treaty.

After hearing Lord, the commissioner said he would need several days to make up his mind. He was obviously not going to allow himself on this important question to be dragged into another undignified squabble with Warner.

Four days later on 21st July he issued a certificate that sufficient evidence had been adduced, according to the laws of the
State of New York, to justify Christina's apprehension and
committment for trial. The way was now clear for her surrender
to the avenging McKay.

At least so it appeared. But Warner, though he had lost a
battle, had not yet lost the war. No sooner had the commissioner
issued his certificate than he applied to the New York City
recorder for a write of *habeas corpus.* In his application he
argued that the treaty concluded between the two countries on
9th August 1842 had not been made effectual or acted upon by
Congress. Put in this bald way the point seems a bad one. Under
the constitution of the United States it is for the President with
the advice and consent of two-thirds of the Senate to make
treaties. Congress is not concerned. But in the appeal which
Warner was to make to the President the point was more
elaborately stated. The judiciary power of the United States, he
said, was vested in the Supreme Court. Lower Courts, and *a
fortiori* mere commissioners, could act only where jurisdiction
had been expressly conferred on them by Congress. Congress
had given no powers under the treaty to Commissioner Rapalyea. Therefore, as a matter of judicial machinery, the commissioner had no authority to issue his certificate. This certificate,
if recognised as valid, would be binding on the President. Accordingly "the said Christina, in the peculiar circumstances
under which she is arrested, by an officer acting without the
authority of law and without right of appeal or revision of said
Rapalyea's proceedings, is exposed to unlawful and tyrannical
privations of her unquestionable right to dwell in this land of
freedom and under the protection of its laws."

Secondly, the commissioner, not being a Judge of the United
States, had no jurisdiction.

Thirdly, no legal proofs of criminality had been adduced before the commissioner.

The recorder allowed the writ and made it returnable on
26th July. In the meantime Warner went straight to Washington, where he addressed a petition to the President of the United
States, John Tyler, claiming his intervention in favour of Christina. This petition was on much the same grounds as those

stated in the *habeas corpus* application but Warner thought out some new arguments on his way to the capital.

First, no proper requisition had been made under the treaty.

Second, the treaty was ineffective in that Congress had taken no legislative action on it.

Third, the treaty was bad because no legislative action had been taken on it by the Parliament of Great Britain, which alone could divest subjects of that kingdom of their right to personal liberty in a foreign country. In yet another appeal Warner was to sound a faint echo of the Boston tea-party—no extradition without representation: Christina had not given her consent to this deprivation of liberty through her representatives in Parliament. This seems a slightly better point than the attack on the validity of the treaty because of no legislative action by Congress. Great Britain required ratification by Parliament to make the treaty effective and so it was not binding on Great Britain until 22nd August 1843 when the Royal Assent was given to the necessary Bill. It could be argued, on the view that the treaty was a contract between the two powers, that until it was binding on both it was binding on neither.

As a new point, Warner argued that the treaty applied to male fugitives only and not to females.

After a few variations on the theme of no proper requisition, Warner attacked the commissioner's proceedings as marred by the admission of incompetent evidence and the rejection of exculpatory evidence which he had proposed to lead on behalf of the prisoner.

The writ of *habeas corpus* was returnable in New York before Warner returned from Washington. His junior associate, Greasley, asked for an adjournment, which was opposed by the British Government and refused by the recorder. After argument the recorder decided that he had no jurisdiction. He was a state officer only and could not review proceedings by a federal officer such as he held the commissioner to be. He observed with a certain naivety that the only reason he had issued the writ in the first place was that on the facts as stated to him he would have been subject to a fine of $1,000 had he not done so.

One barrel had misfired. There still remained the petition to

President Tyler. On 9th August the Secretary of State, by inference, rejected this appeal by issuing a warrant for Christina's
surrender to "George McKay, *an officer of the Government of
her Britannic Majesty.*" The State Department obviously
thought that McKay had been too modest about his status. It
may be remarked that the warrant bore to be in response to a
requisition made by the British Minister in conformity with the
provisions of the treaty. So Warner's constitutional technicali-
ties were swept aside.

According to a dispatch in the *Paisley Advertiser* of 19th
August, the matter was considered by the whole U.S. Cabinet,
who referred to the Attorney-General for his opinion. It was
reported that the British Minister took part in the Cabinet discussion and offered to make good any defects in the evidence.
His offer was refused.

Still the fight was not over. The next step was to apply to the
judges of the Second Circuit of the Southern District of New
York (the Court from which Rapalyea held his commission) for
a writ of *habeas corpus* and this was done on 11th August. The
judges were federal judges and the objection which the recorder
had upheld against his jurisdiction would not apply. This application repeated the earlier arguments. Even now, however,
Warner opened up new territory by complaining that the warrant for Christina's surrender was issued by the Secretary of
State under the great seal of his department in the absence of
the President from the seat of government (it was August and
President Tyler may have been, like some of his successors, an
enthusiastic fisherman or even golfer). The warrant should have
been signed by the President and given under the seal of the
United States.

Next day, 12th August, Judge Samuel R. Betts refused the
application. In a succinct opinion he dealt summarily with
Warner's arguments.

"I am of opinion that the tenth article of the Treaty of
Washington concluded August 9th, 1842, is under the second
subdivision of the sixth article of the constitution of the United
States in force as a subsisting law of the land; and is accordingly
to be observed and executed by the judicial authorities of the
country.

"I am of opinion that a Commissioner appointed by a Circuit Court of the United States, pursuant to the Act of Congress in that behalf, is by force of the Act of Congress of August 23, 1842, empowered to perform the functions pointed out by the tenth article of the said treaty.

"I am of opinion that it is not competent for a Judge of the United States in vacation to revise on *Habeas Corpus* the adjudication of such commissioner as to the efficiency of proof of criminality of a party charged before him.

"I am of opinion that a writ of *Habeas Corpus* cannot be rightfully allowed for the purpose of enquiring into the legality of a warrant emanating from the executive branch of the Government, intending to surrender a person, duly committed to a Marshal of the United States, to the authorities of Great Britain under the provisions of the tenth article of the said treaty, before the party shall be thereby actually transferred to and detained in such British custody within the United States.

"I accordingly refuse to allow the *Habeas Corpus* prayed for in this case."

And that, even for Thomas Warner, was that. There was perhaps a hint at the end that an application might be granted after Christina had been handed over to Superintendent McKay. But the hint fell on deaf ears, deafened perhaps by too much banging of the head against a series of stone walls.

It is difficult and indeed presumptuous for one not versed in the laws of the United States and particularly those of the State of New York to comment on the extradition proceedings. The standard of proof is that of the place where the fugitive was found, so that only New York law has any bearing on the rightness or wrongness of Rapalyea's decision on criminality. But some things can be said. He was amply justified on the evidence in deciding that Christina was not insane. All the doctors who seriously considered the question agreed, at least after their later visits, that her apparent insanity was feigned. That opinion may have been right or it may have been wrong. But the evidence was all the one way and the commissioner could have reached no other conclusion.

It may be, however, that other evidence should have been admitted. This is a question for determination by the local law.

Both parties or their lawyers seem to have agreed in advance to refer the question to a neutral panel of doctors named by the commissioner. There is nothing repugnant to general ideas of justice in this course. If that is so, then the motion for additional evidence on behalf of one party was rightly rejected. But was the agreed procedure properly followed? In the first place the doctors met and conferred so that instead of giving personal and independent opinions they may have been giving an agreed common opinion, perhaps thrust on the group by the more forceful members. Then two of the doctors, when called to give evidence, did not appear and their evidence was not heard. There was therefore a partial failure in the agreed procedure and this might have justified further departure from it by calling new witnesses.

It is this stage of the investigation that makes one doubt the assertion, already quoted, that "the people who acted for her must have been indebted to some unknown and irresponsible informer for the facts that were urged in her behalf." The symptoms of insanity were not reported by informers. They were facts which the doctors themselves observed in Christina's behaviour. Unless the doctors were united in perjury, Christina herself acted the part of a mad woman and did so well enough to deceive the experts for at least one visit. Warner may have let his professional zeal run away with him in multiplying appeals. But on the issue of insanity Christina cannot stand aloof and say that she had nothing to do with it.

When the issue of insanity had been decided against her there remained the all-important question of her criminality. Frankly I find it difficult to follow the commissioner here. He ruled, and we must take it that he did so correctly, that the only competent evidence was evidence of facts within the personal knowledge of the witness. In spite of this, McKay, the only witness, gave evidence which was mainly hearsay. Shorn of what other people had told him, it came to this: he identified the prisoner as Mrs Gilmour, whom he knew. He did not see her husband alive after 11th January 1843. He was present when a body, identified as John Gilmour's by the name plate on the coffin, was exhumed on 22nd April. One of the doctors who was at the exhumation later showed him a white powder. After enquiries he sailed to the United States. When the brig *Excel* arrived, he went out to meet her and arrested the prisoner on board.

From such evidence, if the commissioner adhered to his ruling that only legal evidence was admissible, it is very difficult to see how he found that criminality was made out at all. It can only have been by paying heed to the hearsay evidence that he found a *prima facie* case. That might be fair enough by New York law. The commissioner may have been entitled to rely on the evidence of a responsible police officer reporting the results of official enquiries made by him or under his direction. But that was not the basis on which he directed the evidence to be given. A change of mind perhaps while he was considering his decision? It is possible, but all that the outsider can do is to record the commissioner's decision and his own doubts.

In the Oscar Slater extradition proceedings in 1909, five lay witnesses were examined and sworn depositions from a number of others read.

On 16th August 1843 McKay received Christina into his custody for extradition to her native country for trial. A late difficulty struck him. His prisoner would have to be kept under constant watch. The situation was embarrassing for a male officer with a female prisoner. Happily he found an elderly woman (curiously enough called Cochran, Christina's maiden name), who wanted to return to her native Paisley. McKay paid her fare and she agreed to sleep with the prisoner. The two women were locked in a private stateroom each night, Miss (or Mrs) Cochran keeping the inside key, while McKay watched outside. During the days Christina was allowed to mix with the other passengers—seventeen cabin and two hundred steerage.

When Christina was delivered to him McKay very properly told her she must not say one word to him about the alleged murder of her husband as he might be called as a witness to her words. As he gave no evidence of any statement made by her on the voyage we may take it that she kept a discreet silence. We are told she said nothing about the case to her female attendant. The *Glasgow Herald* of 15th September 1843 says that

none of her fellow-passengers made any allusion in her presence
to the delicate situation in which she was. "Generally speaking,
she did not manifest much concern about the awful position in
which she was placed; occasionally she appeared gay and
dressed herself out to the best advantage; but at times she gave
way to gloomy apprehensions and burst into tears. The impression left generally in the minds of the passengers, however, was
that she was callous and unconcerned about her position."

The party reached Liverpool on Monday 11th September
after a voyage of twenty-six days with headwinds nearly all
the way. Christina did not have much luck with her sea travel,
though on her return voyage she was seasick on only one night.
Still she must have wished that she could have travelled by the
coach for which she asked Dr Rogers.

On Tuesday morning, after a night in prison, she sailed with
her attendants for Greenock on the steamer *Achilles*, which
arrived next morning. She was taken by train to Paisley and
lodged in the prison there.

On Thursday 14th September she appeared before Alexander
Campbell, Sheriff-substitute at Paisley, and made a judicial
declaration. This was long before an accused person could give
evidence. The judicial declaration was the only way in which
her story could be put before the Court. It was not always to
the advantage of a prisoner to make such a declaration. It held
the same kind of dangers as giving evidence, though perhaps to
a lesser degree. Only the presiding magistrate (almost invariably
the Sheriff) should put questions.

Christina's declaration was a long one. She gave her age as
twenty-three; in fact she was two months short of her twenty-
fifth birthday. She could remember neither the date of her
marriage nor that of her husband's death.

A great deal of what she said need not be repeated as it describes her husband's illness quite consistently with the other
accounts. Some passages are of special interest. There is perhaps
a half-hearted suggestion of suicide: John Gilmour "never intimated to me in any way that I was the cause of his ailment; but
he said to me shortly before his death that I had broken his
heart. I suppose that he said this because I had told him often
before that he had broken mine and that I could not be to him

as a wife ought to be and the reason of this was well known to him, being that I had been in a manner forced to marry him. While my husband was confined to bed under said illness, I was the only female who attended him."

The passages dealing with the arsenic transactions are important and deserve full quotation.

"I acknowledge that one morning in the course of my husband's illness I walked to the town of Renfrew and there bought from one Wylie, a druggist, some arsenic, for which I paid him some few halfpence, I do not remember how many. He questioned me before he gave it, as to what was my name and what I was going to do with it, and wanted me to write down my name; but I don't think he asked me, or at least I do not recollect of his asking me, where I staid. I told him my name was Robertson, and I think I said Margaret Robertson, but I am not sure of that, and told him it was to poison rats. I took home with me the arsenic, which was wrapped in a paper and had the words 'Arsenic, Poison' on the back of the paper, and I kept it in my pocket among some halfpence till the string came off the paper and a little was spilt among the halfpence, which I discovered by finding some of the halfpence white when I took them out but this I did not discover until after I had returned to my father's house, after my husband's death. The paper of arsenic had never been opened by me from the time I bought it. I first of all put the arsenic, when I got it from the druggist, into a small bag that I carried, and which was made of black silk, or black velvet, I cannot remember which, and when I reached home I took it out of the bag and put it into my pocket, where it remained as aforesaid, unopened. I rather think that I had dropped the bag before getting into the house with it, and that it was brought to me by one of the servants. When I had got back to my father's house, after my husband's death, I missed my packet, which used to lay at my bed head. It was on the morning when I returned to my father's house that I missed it and I found after that that my mother had got it, for she questioned me about the paper and its contents, and what I was going to do with it. I at first was not disposed to tell her what it was, but she told me herself that it was arsenic, and I told her I had got it because they were all tired of me, and would not let me have peace, nor let me sit beside them, as if they thought I was not good enough, nor let me remain by myself, as if that was avoiding their company. I did not tell my mother when or where I had bought it. The truth was, I was made unhappy before I quitted my father's house on my marriage and I had procured the arsenic, thinking that I would put an end to myself with it.

"I further declare, that previous to my purchasing the said arsenic at Renfrew I had procured another paper of it which my servant Mary had bought me at my desire, and I think she bought it in Paisley, but whether this was before or after the commencement of my husband's illness I do not remember. Mary told me that the man from whom she got it said that he must know for whom it was got, and for what purpose, and that she had told him. I had said to her that it was intended for rats, but after I had heard from her what the druggist had said, and what she said about the danger of it I burned it before her face in the furnace fire of the boiling-house, and this I did upon the same morning that she had brought it to me. I am sure that it was the same parcel that she brought to me that I had so burned, and I had never used any part of it in any way nor even opened the parcel at all. My feeling and intention were the same when I bade Mary buy this arsenic as when I bought the subsequent parcel myself, but I was frightened with what she told me about its sudden effects in producing death at once, and I therefore destroyed it. And the fact was also that attempts had been making to catch a rat that came to the jawhole[1] of the house, and it was for that reason that I mentioned to her that it was for the rats. I never gave to my husband, either during his illness or immediately before it, any thing either of meat or drink but what he expressly asked for; and I never gave him arsenic or any other poisonous thing."

Finally she denied any knowledge of the result of the exhumation. "I have never heard that on my husband's body being disinterred and examined by medical men they found arsenic in the bowels, but if this be the case I cannot account for it. He got none from me and I am not aware that he got any from any body else."

·　　　　·　　　　·

[1] Cesspool.

A year and a day after John Gilmour's death, on Friday 12th January 1944, Christina Gilmour entered the dock in the High Court of Justiciary in Edinburgh, there to stand her trial for murdering him by repeated administration of arsenic. Her judges were Lord Justice-Clerk Hope, Lord Moncreiff and Lord Wood. Another Judge, Lord Fullarton, sat on the bench as a spectator. Lord Advocate Duncan McNeill, later to become Lord Colonsay, conducted the case for the prosecution assisted by two advocates-depute, David Milne and Charles Neaves (later Lord Neaves). The defence counsel were Thomas Maitland (later Lord Dundrennan) and Alexander McNeill.

Long before the trial began at 10 o'clock the courtroom was crowded, many people having made the journey from Renfrewshire and Ayrshire. The prisoner wore a deep mourning dress of silk, with a heavy veil which concealed her features until she threw it off on sitting down with her face to the bench.

The indictment, lengthy like all of the times, was read out and the prisoner pleaded Not Guilty in a voice variously described as "low but firm" and "so weak as to be scarcely audible". The Lord Advocate then moved that the medical witnesses might be allowed to remain in court during the examination of the other witnesses, a course which he said was "not unusual and might in this case be advantageous". It will be remembered that, at the extradition proceedings, Christina's counsel had unsuccessfully moved that the witnesses should be excluded while others testified.

The Lord Justice-Clerk refused the motion. "It would certainly be more satisfactory to the Court if this course were not followed; and I, for my part, cannot assent to it. ... In our courts the practice of late years has been opposed to such a proceeding."

Evidence was led for the prosecution. As I have used this for the narrative of events from 26th December 1842 onwards, it is unnecessary and would be tedious to repeat it here. No evidence was led for the defence and the proceedings ended about 7 p.m. with the reading of the prisoner's declaration. The Court adjourned until next day, Saturday, at 9 a.m.

At that hour the courtroom was again crowded. Before calling on the Lord Advocate to address the jury for the Crown, the Lord Justice-Clerk had a complaint.

"I am exceedingly sorry to be informed that some of the doorkeepers have been taking money for admission. Such conduct is discreditable to the court. The doors of a court of justice are open to all who are willing to come in till the court is full and there ought to be no other let or hindrance but the want of room." An enquiry would be held and care taken to see that it did not happen again.

The Lord Advocate then addressed the jury. The first question they had to consider was whether death had been caused by poison at all. He reviewed the evidence, which we need not do as counsel for the defence conceded the point, and invited the jury to conclude that death was caused by arsenic, not in a single dose but in repeated doses.

The next and most serious inquiry was, how was the arsenic administered. It must have been administered by someone, either the deceased himself or some other person. There was not the slightest reason to suppose that the deceased had poisoned himself. In all cases of death by poison the administration was sure to be secret and not in the presence of witnesses, so that the theory of suicide could always be put forward. But that possibility did not mean that the theory was true. The jury were not to adopt it unless they saw in the evidence some rational ground for doing so. Here there was no such ground, and the nature of the illness contradicted the supposition. If John Gilmour had voluntarily taken poison, he would not have done so in small doses perseveringly repeated so as to cause a lingering death, but in such a quantity as would have killed him at once. If he had been found secretly acquiring poison and at the same time complaining of the misery of his marriage with the pannel (prisoner), the theory might have had some plausibility: but the proved facts were all against this view.

There was as little ground for suspecting accident. The deceased had arsenic in his possession before his marriage but he was not proved to have kept it after that event. In any case there was no evidence that anything was taken, about the start of his illness, from the chest in which the poison was kept, in which way an accident might have been caused. The circumstances of the illness, and especially its protracted course, were also against the theory of accident.

The jury had therefore to account for the administration of the poison in some other way. It was his painful duty to ask them to conclude that it was administered by the pannel. Direct evidence was not to be expected in any case of poisoning; but in no case was there less chance of direct evidence than when the poison was administered to a husband by his wife, in a house where no servant attended within doors, where the wife had charge of everything, where she prepared the food and was constantly about the person of her victim. The proof had to be circumstantial.

The first circumstance on which he relied was that the pannel had arsenic in her possession at the time when it must have been administered. Three packets were traced into her possession, the first procured on Tuesday 27th December 1842 and the second and third on Friday and Saturday 6th and 7th January 1843. He analysed the evidence to distinguish between the packet found by John Muir in the black bag and that bought by "Miss Robertson" from Wylie in Renfrew. When she left home on the Friday morning the prisoner told Mary Paterson not to tell the other servants that she had gone; she also said she was going to get something for her husband. But there was no proof that she got anything except the contents of the black bag. Next day she bought more arsenic, giving a false name and a false excuse, from Wylie in Renfrew. The repeated acquisition of poison pointed to repeated administration.

How was all this arsenic accounted for? The first packet was said to have been burned; but all Mary Paterson said was that the burned packet was like the one she had given the pannel. If the poison was meant for the destruction of rats, why was it destroyed? If, however, it was bought to poison her husband, the pannel had a very good reason at least to pretend to destroy it: Mary Paterson had told her the druggist knew for whom it had been bought.

There was no evidence to account for the disposal of the second packet. The pannel said the third packet was kept in her pocket until her mother found it, but there was no corroboration for this improbable story.

The jury had also to consider how the pannel accounted for the acquisition of so much arsenic. First she said it was to kill rats; then she said it was to commit suicide. People who bought arsenic secretly and suspiciously could always allege they meant to commit suicide. But it was incredible that the pannel would have acquired the repeated quantities traced into her possession or that the idea of suicide could have been working in her mind when her husband was seriously ill. She could not have bought poison day after day without some attempt to use it.

"This, then, is our first position against the pannel: that at the time when arsenic was administered to her husband, as the medical evidence proves, in repeated doses, she is in the possession of arsenic; she acquires it on different occasions, secretly and under false pretences; she does not satisfactorily account for the disposal of it; and her alleged purpose in acquiring it is not supported in evidence."

The second circumstance for the consideration of the jury was that the pannel had every possible opportunity of secret administration. She was the sole attendant on her husband: whatever he took she prepared and gave to him.

Means and opportunity being established, was there any motive? No motive could be adequate for such a crime, but there was evidence of a motive which had proved sufficient with minds not well regulated—an ill-fated marriage. "She could not restrain herself in regard to it nor maintain upon the subject even that reserve which common propriety might have dictated. The matter seems to have taken possession of her mind. Her dissatisfaction at it was extreme; so extreme that, according to her own account in her declaration, she could not bear it any longer and actually meditated self-destruction in order to terminate her distress. Her deliberate statement is that she acquired poison for the purpose of dissolving the unhappy union between herself and her husband, which to her had become unbearable. There were two ways in which that union might have been dissolved by the use of arsenic—either by poisoning herself or by poisoning her husband. She is not poisoned—her husband is. By a most extraordinary chance, the cup which she mixed for herself has not been quaffed by her, but by some unknown and mysterious hand was conveyed to the lips of husband. Can you doubt then the purpose for which she procured arsenic or the purpose to which she applied it? The union is thus dissolved, and immediately on its dissolution she begins to correspond with the person to whom she was formerly attached and who seems never to have been absent from her mind during the whole progress of these disastrous events. All the circumstances, in short, of this melancholy case concur in establishing the guilt of the prisoner."

Certain minor circumstances pointed to the same conclusion. The first purchase of arsenic was on Tuesday 27th December. The illness began the next Thursday but no doctor was sent for until Friday of the next week. There was the interview between the pannel and her uncle on the Friday when, whether she expected her husband to be alive then or not, she put off the suggested visit of the doctor until the Saturday. When Dr McKechnie did call, the pannel disregarded his instructions to preserve the stuff vomited. There was the flight to America under a false name. There was also the remarkable statement in her letter to Anderson that she would admit the purchase of arsenic intended for herself, but not for her husband.

"In short, you have all the elements which you can require to enable you to decide in a case upon which depend the issues of life or death. Considering that the acquisition of the poison, the repeated acquisition of it, at the time and under the most suspicious circumstances, is proved against the prisoner, that no satisfactory account is given by her of its disposal, that she had the most ample opportunities of administering it, that you are presented with a probable motive for the perpetration of this horrid crime in the acknowledged alienation of her heart from her husband, that there is a total absence of any suspicion even or surmise of any other person near or about the deceased having acquired arsenic, or having had opportunity of administering it, or any motive for doing so, I feel that in all the circumstances of this case I have no alternative but to ask you to find by your verdict that the poison which caused the death of John Gilmour was administered by no other hand than that of his wife, the prisoner at the bar."

The Lord Advocate bowed to the jury, then to the bench and resumed his seat. He had built up a strong case in logic, an appeal, properly, to the head and not to the heart. If Christina had followed him closely, she must have been anxious but she gave no sign. Indeed throughout the whole trial she is said to have sat "with apparent indifference if not with apathy". This is not unusual: many persons in the dock on a charge of murder seem unconcerned, even bored, as the case against them is gradually built up or knocked down, the case on which their lives depend. The impersonal solemnity of the proceedings seems to have a mercifully anaesthetising effect.

It was now the turn of Thomas Maitland for the defence. The press described his speech as "beautiful". It is not reported verbatim: even if it had been, oratorical beauty is an elusive quality to preserve in print: in a summary it is bound to disappear.

"I cordially join with the Lord Advocate in reminding you that you are here dealing with a question of life and death. In criminal courts this is never a question of probability or of inference but of strict legal evidence. Unless the public prosecutor has made guilt certain and innocence impossible, you cannot convict."

He conceded that John Gilmour died of arsenic poisoning. But he did not admit that death was caused by repeated doses. One of the medical witnesses gave his opinion that death was caused by a single dose administered shortly before death and even Professor Christison admitted that a single dose might cause a protracted illness.[1]

Maitland left the point there and went on: "But the great question in this case is whether the commission of the crime charged has been brought home to the pannel by legal and conclusive evidence. It is admitted by the prosecutor that the proof which he has adduced is entirely circumstantial, but it is contended that in such cases direct evidence is not to be looked for. I feel confident, however, that you will not be disposed to make the pannel suffer for any imperfection in the evidence against her. You have before you a female, belonging to a respectable family, brought up under her father's roof and continually under his care till the period of her marriage. Even the

---

[1] The first witness referred to was Dr McKechnie senior, who thought that death was due chiefly to a dose given after his visit and that it was possible that a dose had been given before that visit. Professor Christison's evidence was that a single dose might produce a long illness but that it was more likely to be due to repeated doses.

Lord Advocate, had he an opportunity of reply, could not dispute that the accused, whose character was proved to have been of the most innocent and mild description, was not likely to have committed so revolting a crime."

From the argument from character Maitland went on to consider motive, which was essential in such a case. Had any motive been established sufficient to account for the perpetration of such a crime? The jury were asked to believe that she was actuated by remorseless hatred toward her husband. Before they could do so they had to be satisfied that a cause existed for such hatred. There was no evidence to justify such a view and the prosecutor was driven to rely on the pannel's statement that she had some secret and unexplained sorrow in connection with her marriage. But when her uncle reminded her of her duty and her marriage vows she received his advice kindly. She was attentive to her husband and showed no signs of excitement before or after his death.

"According to the theory of the prosecution this young and gentle female had for thirteen days been employed in gradually but constantly perpetrating the murder of her husband. Human nature in such circumstances must have exhibited traces of guilt. The pannel, if now justly accused, must have shown, during the commission of the crime, some remarkable symptoms of excitement and confusion. Look to the whole history of this domestic tragedy—scan it from its opening to its close—and say if the conduct of the pannel betrayed in any respect consciousness of guilt."

Her behaviour was all that could have been desired of the most affectionate wife. She went for a doctor as soon as she could overcome her husband's reluctance. If she was guilty, she must have been unwilling to permit access to her husband; but all who wanted to visit his sickbed were freely admitted. Everything in her conduct was inconsistent with guilt.

He argued that only two packets of arsenic had been traced to his client's possession. The witnesses were mistaken about dates and assigned to Friday 6th January events which did not take place until Saturday 7th. These two packets were satisfactorily accounted for; the first was burned and the second lay unopened in her pocket until after her husband's death.

Possession of poison was insufficient to warrant even a suspicion against the pannel. It was accounted for by her explanation that she meant to commit suicide. If her marriage was unhappy, that was no motive for murder. "A broken heart may lead to suicide but not to murder."

Suicide by the deceased was a less extravagant theory than murder by the pannel. He had as much reason for wanting to put an end to the unhappy marriage. And there was even a strong probability of accident. John Gilmour had arsenic, a white powder, in his possession. Other white powders were given to him as medicine. Who could say that the proof was strong enough to exclude even the reasonable possibility of accident?

After a careful analysis of the evidence (the reports do not show how Maitland performed this difficult task but merely say that he did so), he wound up: "In conclusion, I cannot do better than quote the words of a great pleader, while addressing the jury in a case of similar mystery and in circumstances not unlike the present. 'This case could never, under any view, be considered but as one of a most painful and afflicting character. If proved the pannel's guilt was of a most unpalliated kind. They will either return her to society as innocent or condemn her to the death as a most foul and detestable murderess. It was altogether incredible from its extreme atrocity. There was no motive—no provocation—and yet they were called upon to believe that, under pretence of administering relief, she inflicted a death of agony and torture and stood by unmoved, while her helpless victim was descending to an unpitied grave. He was anxious to put them on their guard against yielding to the honest indignation which imputed guilt like this was so apt to excite. There was no cause by which good men were so often hurried into erroneous judgments. It was a natural, laudable, instinctive feeling which roused the human mind to indignation on the bare suspicion of so enormous a crime having been committed, and which made it prone to punish. But they would fortify themselves against this feeling and dispassionately weigh the evidence that was before them. In itself it was hardly a credible case which involved in itself so many unheard-of aggravations. They should rather cling to an opposite supposition by which they might arrive at a more natural conclusion.'

"Lay this striking passage to heart", continued Maitland, "and apply it to this case. It may be a dark history on which I have been able to throw little light. You may not be satisfied that this unhappy lady is guiltless of her husband's blood—nay, you may suspect or even be inclined to believe that she is guilty. But as I stated at the outset this is not the question at issue. You are sworn to say upon your oaths whether guilt has been brought home to her by legal and conclusive evidence; and applying this test I feel confident that you can arrive at no other verdict than that of 'Not Proven'."

It was a wise move not to overstate the defence case but to leave in the ears of the jury the frank admission that there were grounds for suspicion. Fifteen hardheaded Scots would not have been impressed by a claim that complete innocence had been proved. In the earlier part of his speech Maitland had come near to making this claim. But the final impression is of supreme importance and from that point of view it was a good peroration.

Would it have been as successful had he been more specific about the quotation which was its foundation? That quotation came from the speech of Francis Jeffrey (better known perhaps as the editor of the *Edinburgh Review*, but still in his day a leading counsel and later a Judge) in the case of Mrs Mary Smith, tried for poisoning a female farmservant in 1827. She was acquitted on a verdict of Not Proven. But to say the least the verdict was questioned at the time. The presiding Judge pointedly remarked that it was the jury's verdict, not his. She was the woman of whom Sir Walter Scott wrote in his diary that she was clearly guilty when he criticised "that bastard verdict, Not Proven". "It was a face" he wrote "to do or die, or perhaps to do to die. Thin features, which had been handsome, a flashing eye, an acute and aquiline nose, lips much marked, as arguing decision and, I think, bad temper—they were thin and habitually compressed, rather turned down at the corners, as one of a rather melancholy disposition."

Henry Cockburn, later Lord Cockburn, who was Jeffrey's junior, tells us that when Sir Walter left the court after the

acquittal his remark was "Well, sirs, all I can say is that, if
that woman was my wife, I should take good care to be my
own cook". Cockburn himself referred to his old client as
"guilty but acquitted. . . . She was like a vindictive masculine
witch."

But the source of the quotation was not given nor were the
jury told of the comments on the case by these eminent men.
They were not invited to draw too close a comparison between
the cases. No more does counsel, quoting "Who steals my purse
steals trash" in order to enhance the value of an injured reputation, remind the jury that those words were spoken by Iago at
his most hypocritical.

Finally the Judge's charge. This lasted for four and a half
hours, or half as much again as both counsel's speeches together.

Lord Hope began by saying that the jury alone had the power
of judging the innocence or guilt of the pannel. If the evidence
led them to think that the pannel was not guilty, they were to
be regardless of the consequences and without hesitation or
doubt or scruple return a verdict of innocence. If on the other
hand the evidence was such as led them to hold the prisoner
guilty, they would be sustained against all possible feelings of
anxiety by knowledge that they were doing their duty faithfully.

After reading the indictment he continued: "The prisoner is
accused of a crime which can only be explained by that deprav-
ity of human nature the mystery of which man cannot penetrate.
The charge is that, a few weeks after marriage, the young female
at the bar—educated in the house of a respectable Scottish
farmer, coming from a part of the country the inhabitants of
which are well known to be of the highest respectability—
coming, I would say, from the very sanctity of her father's house
and within a few weeks after her marriage, had with the utmost
deliberation, cunning and coolness, conceived and executed the
deadly purpose of poisoning her husband."

He reviewed the evidence minutely (we are spared this in all
contemporary reports). If they were satisfied from the evidence
of the essential foundation of this heavy and serious charge,
namely that John Gilmour died from the effects of arsenic, and
if they were satisfied that none of the substances given to allevi-

ate his illness could reasonably be supposed to contain poison, they would come to that part of the case which must exercise their grave and serious deliberation. If his death was caused by poison, that poison must have got into his body entirely intentionally or accidentally.

"A fair and reasonable probability of accident—I don't say a mere possibility—is always of importance in this part of the case to a jury that is anxious to discharge its duty." Was there anything in the case to lead to the view that the poison was mingled and sold accidentally? [This theory of accident through grossly careless dispensing seems to have been his Lordship's own.] Then might Gilmour not have got it in the house? He had poison, in all probability, in the autumn. It was not improbable that some of the poison was still in his chest. But that chest had been removed before his marriage into his own room. Was there any appearance of his having been careless in its use? If it was administered by accident, was anyone else affected by the food which poisoned him? If kept in his bedroom, was it mingled with his ale or porter, or was it left in any chest where bread or cheese was kept? None of these suppositions appeared in the evidence. "You will look over the whole of the case. . . . You will attend anxiously and vigilantly to every probability which can show that the administration of poison was the effect of accident."

If they were not satisfied of that, a great deal more had still to be proved before they could fasten on anyone the charge of administering it intentionally. They had to consider whether he might have taken it himself. If so there was nothing else to consider. Accident and suicide must both be left aside before they were called upon to consider whether it was intentionally given to him by his wife. "Now I say here that *we must not take the statement as proved that she was forced into this marriage by her parents*. [Italics mine: the jury were being told to disregard her own reiterated statement.] I am glad for her sake that this material fact is awanting; for, had that been proved, you would have had less difficulty in believing that the evil which is in the human heart might have rebelled against the fate which was forced upon her in spite of her declared opposition, than that she might have committed the deed under feelings of disappoint-

ment and regret at having been induced to enter into a marriage
of which she subsequently repented."

An important question was whether Gilmour "knew of the
attachment of his wife for another, that the marriage was
against her inclination and that her heart was alienated from
him. There was apparently no object of a pecuniary nature in
the circumstances of the match; for she, the daughter of a small
but respectable Ayrshire farmer, was married to the son of a
neighbouring tenant in the same circumstances of life apparently as her father. Is there then any proof that John Gilmour
sued and got his wife, knowing that her affections were not
placed upon him, or is there proof that he afterwards found it
out? Correspondence with Anderson he could not detect, because Anderson swears that no letters passed between them
during her husband's life. Her father and brother were both
examined; but neither of them was asked any question on the
subject, and there is no evidence that John Gilmour knew what
is stated in the declaration of the pannel. She says that she often
told him he had broken her heart; and that he, in his turn, said
she had broken his. But no one in the house appears to have
seen any unkindness on his part, and no one has stated that she
complained of his being unkind, but it appears that she spoke
to Mary Paterson with regret. But he is not shown to have
known of this. And you will consider, if that were so, would he
have gone to the place where she formerly lived, to meet her
friends, unless indeed it were to keep up the appearance of
attachment where none in reality existed? Is he shown to have
been a person of such character—a man of such strong and
nice sensibilities—that his hearing of a country girl having had
a previous attachment to another would lead him to commit
suicide? Is there anything in any speech or act of his, anything
that his father heard, or anything that has been stated by any of
the witnesses, to induce you to think that was the state of mind
on his part? On the contrary, it is proved by her father and
others that there was no unkindness on his part towards her. Is
there any appearance of depression on his part? Is he seen to
abandon his occupation—to go about like a broken-hearted
man? Does he complain to that respectable and excellent witness, Mr Robertson, to whom, though his wife's uncle, he must

have felt that he could safely disclose the state of his mind? Nothing of the sort. Then look at the character of the disease and its progress. Is it likely to be the sort of death that a person resolved upon suicide would choose—that he would suffer a slow and lingering process of disease, especially if you adopt the opinion that his death was caused by repeated doses?"

Lord Hope had summed up against accident and against suicide. He now came to the theory of murder.

"These are all matters for your anxious consideration. But though you are not satisfied with either of these views, still there is much evidence required to bring such a charge home to you, that the poison was intentionally given to him by his own wife."

It was not enough to find arsenic in her possession and that she had opportunities of administering it. They must consider the circumstances under which she got it, how it was disposed of and the purpose for which it was got. It was material that the prisoner was not suspected during the life of her husband, that she conducted herself so as to avoid all suspicion.[1] In a case like this, direct proof was not indispensable. The case of Nairn and Ogilvie in August 1765 was probably the only one in which the accused was seen to mix the poison in the food in which it was administered.

"It is a sad and fearful alternative that is presented to us by her own statement in her declaration that she bought the poison traced into her possession for the purpose of dissolving her marriage by taking it herself, especially when the mysterious result is that her husband dies of the same kind of poison and that she lives. Still, that statement may be true and the pannel be innocent and you, who are the only recognised judges of the facts of the case, may say that without any proved act on her part of administering the poison, your minds revolt from the notion that she committed the crime charged against her. Still, with all these great and strong improbabilities, there are strong and weighty facts proved; and it will be for you to say what is the result after you have given them all the weight you can.

"But if, after all, you feel that there is still doubt—that there

[1] John Muir's discovery of the poison in the black bag? John Gilmour's dying words?

is still mystery—that there is less proved than you expected to have heard in such a case—if you think that her conduct during her husband's last illness is inconsistent with the charge—if you do not believe that she could have conducted herself in the way she is described to have done on the supposition that she administered the poison and witnessed its slow and agonising effects—that she could not have conducted herself with that cool and collected deportment to which Dr McKechnie speaks —that she could not have gone through that extraordinary scene without any suspicion in the mind of any human being, except for the finding of the bag—if she could see the father and brother of Gilmour, especially if they knew that the marriage was not according to her will, and still they had no suspicion—if there is not a single act of hers like the conduct of a person that is conscious of guilt attending upon her husband (laying aside, of course, at present the purchase of the poison)— if you think that no human being could have gone through such a scene without exciting suspicion in the minds of her relatives, or of the doctors, or of Mr Robertson, to whom she detailed her complaints and who saw no want of attention on her part—if you think that hers was not the conduct of a person engaged in poisoning her husband and that doubt is left in the case, that there are still mysteries unexplained, I will not tell you that you must give, for I know that you will give, the full benefit of that doubt or obscurity to the individual who is charged with the perpetration of this dreadful crime.

"You will now retire to consider your verdict; and the result you come to I feel will be—nay, I have a perfect confidence that it will be—the truth of the case. For of the truth of the case, in a question of the guilt or innocence of a person who is charged in a Court of Justice, there is no test that I recognise superior to the judgment of an intelligent jury who deliberate under the sanction of their oaths on the question that is submitted to them."

The charge was over. Lord Justice-Clerk Hope had accomplished the not inconsiderable feat of summing up against every theory that had been advanced—accident, suicide and (in the final catalogue of doubts) murder. The jury returned after an absence of nearly an hour with their verdict: "The jury, after careful and mature deliberation upon the evidence brought before them in this case, are unanimously of the opinion that John Gilmour died from the effects of arsenic; but they find that the charge is Not Proven against the pannel at the bar as libelled."

This verdict was greeted by "very decided expressions of approval from part of the audience". The Lord Justice-Clerk strongly censured this conduct, observing that, if applause were allowed, the next thing would be that, when a jury gave in a verdict contrary to the feelings of the audience, they would be hissed for the conscientious discharge of their duty. If any of the persons responsible had been identified, they would have been send to prison for a great contempt of court.

The Court rose at 5.40 p.m. Crowds waited outside. To deceive them, a hackney coach was ostentatiously driven up to the main entrance as if to wait for Christina. She and her friends were thus able to walk out quietly by a side door.

She returned to her native Ayrshire and lived to the ripe age of eighty-seven. In her latter years she lived at Stewarton, "a charming old lady, serene and beautiful, famed through the district for her singular piety."[1] Sometimes she would moan in the querulous tones of age "My case, my case; it was not proven, not proven, ye ken."

She died on 14th December 1905, nearly sixty-two years after her trial. In her death certificate she is described as the widow of "Matthew" Gilmour. Sixty-two years is a long widowhood to preserve the memory of six weeks' unhappy marriage.

In cold logic, as we read in dead print the evidence in the case, it is difficult to see why Christina was acquitted. It becomes easier when we read the truncated reports of the speeches and charge which are available: more so when we consider the full implications of the word "beautiful" as applied to Maitland's speech. Oratorical beauty must have the quality of persuasiveness. And it is even easier when we read the Lord

[1] William Roughead, Locusta in Scotland. in *Glengarry's Way* (W. Green and Son, 1922).

Justice-Clerk's peroration. The jury left the jury-box with doubts ringing in their ears and their hour's discussion did not resolve them.

It must be remembered that a jury is not a mere logical machine. Logic and reasoning must, of course, play their part in reaching a verdict. That is why stress is so often laid on the idea of the fifteen or twelve reasonable men and women who form the jury. But the logical process is not their sole function. Before logic begins to operate other more intuitive processes take place. A jury sees and hears the witnesses, it does not merely read a dry and edited report of what they said. The written record is the raw material for the logic of posterity. A jury's logic is exercised on something rather different. There is the indefinable sense that witness A is exaggerating, that B is holding something back, that C is hostile to the prisoner while D is falling over backwards trying to help her. These feelings result in a trimming of the literal meaning of the evidence, almost imperceptible perhaps with any one witness but in the aggregate giving a very different impression of the whole.

And even in 1844, when the prisoner could not give evidence, she was under the close observation of the jury, who could see, as the press who reported her impassivity could not see, her face. That was another piece of material for their logic to work on and it is material which cannot be available to us who criticise at a later date.

Nor is this all. When we think of the reasonable men who form a jury, we sometimes tend to overstress the adjective "reasonable" and to translate it, not quite accurately, as "reasoning" or "logical". The noun is also important. A jury must be composed of men (and today women)—that is, human beings with human sympathies and a working knowledge of human nature. Their task is, as has been said, to temper law with common sense.

What may have affected the jury in favour of Christina Gilmour? First, her apparent character—meek and mild and perhaps (though this is sheer guesswork) giving the impression of a nice douce respectable lassie caught up in a bewilderment of events she could not control. Although there was no evidence other than her own repeated statement that she had been forced to marry John Gilmour—and, indeed, the Lord Justice-Clerk had been glad for her sake that this was so—the jury might have accepted her account and found it to be, not a motive for murder on her part, but a ground for sympathy on theirs. I have already suggested that paternal approval from Alexander Cochran might have been indistinguishable in Christina's mind from paternal compulsion. And, though Alexander was not asked in the witness-box about the marriage preliminaries, the jury saw and heard him and could judge of his character.

In particular they heard him give evidence about the unfortunate voyage to America. His evidence in chief ended with the bald statement "I advised her to go away". In cross-examination this was amplified: "She was not very willing to go away. I made arrangements for sending her off. I employed my brother Robert to make the arrangements with a man of the name of Simpson to convey her away. I am sure she did not know she was going to America when she left. I did not go with her. I paid all expenses."

In her declaration Christina said: "When I was sent away, I was not informed where I was to go. . . . I received no information as to the cause of my leaving except from my sister Elizabeth; and, on my enquiring if it was on account of the reports that had been going about as to my husband's death being blamed on me, she said it was. On my telling her that my going away would cause people to think I was guilty, she told me I would be back in a few days and that people would say that I could not stand such reports. And my father obliged me to go away without even speaking to my mother."

The two accounts hang together. Alexander Cochran was a very determined man, used to getting his own way. And if he insisted on Christina's flight, may he not also have insisted on her marriage? No doubt in those days, father was the undisputed head of the household. But even so the idea of force in the marriage—not necessarily physical or direct force, but an exceptionally strong moral compulsion—may have won some sympathy from the fifteen men in the jury-box for the one young woman in the dock.

Then there was John Anderson, the preferred but dutifully rejected sweetheart. In his cross-examination he paid tribute to Christina's character: "She was of a very gentle, mild, fine disposition. Not a person of a violent temperament in any way." But in his examination in chief, in dealing with Christina's destroyed letter to him dated 28th April 1843, he had said: "She said she would confess she had bought arsenic to take herself, but she did not admit she had administered it to Gilmour." Later he stressed that the words "did not admit" were in the letter. This evidence was not corroborated by Christina's father and brother, who also read the letter. It is inconsistent with Christina's declaration that, even in September 1843, she knew nothing of the discovery of arsenic in her husband's body.

The jury may have disbelieved John Anderson. They may have thought his evidence to have been the wicked invention of a spiteful, because unsuccessful, lover. They may even have been right. John Anderson may have been the one exception among the witnesses who, as the contemporary report says, "told the facts with remarkable accuracy". At least, rightly or wrongly, the jury may have thought so. If so, there was another powerful reason for sympathy. It is true that this view does not altogether consist with Anderson's tribute to her character. But the evidence is reported in narrative and therefore edited form, and not as question and answer. We cannot tell how many questions were needed. It may have been extracted only against considerable reluctance.

Speculation—of course it is. Any attempt to fathom a jury's collective mind is and must always be. But it may go some way towards explaining an otherwise mysterious verdict.

It does not prove innocence. That is not my purpose.

Nearly one hundred years later, in June 1940, there occurred a similar case, in which Lord Justice-Clerk Aitchison, without reference to Lord Justice-Clerk Hope's charge in Christina's case, gave very similar directions to a jury.

Mrs McMillan, another farmer's wife, was charged with (1) the attempted murder of her husband by repeated administration of arsenic during two periods in 1937 and (2) his murder, also by repeated doses of arsenic, in the end of 1939 and early 1940, and in particular by a dose on 5th January 1940.

In 1937 Robert Drennan McMillan was a strong, healthy farmer. In that year he suffered from two illnesses which were diagnosed by his doctor as due to arsenic poisoning. He had in his own possession arsenic used for killing rats. None was traced to the accused.

McMillan died on 6th January 1940, the medical evidence being that his death was due to a series of increasing doses of arsenic over a long period. Two particularly large doses were thought to have been administered, one about the end of December 1939 and the other about 5th January 1940. One single witness said that he supplied arsenic in December 1939 to the accused "to kill rats", but there was contradictory evidence and the accused herself denied any such purchase.

The Crown could suggest no motive. The McMillans were apparently a normal married couple and there was no proof of any ill-will between them. While her husband was ill, the accused was in every way an attentive wife. This fact was used against her to support the argument, also used in Christina Gilmour's case, that she had every opportunity to administer the poison.

The Solicitor-General's argument was short and simple. Suicide and accident were both excluded. Therefore the case was one of murder. The accused was the only person with an opportunity of administering the final dose on 5th January. Therefore she must be convicted.

Lord Aitchison, however, did not take this simple view. In his opinion the method of exclusion, on which the Crown relied, called for the greatest caution in its application, especially in a murder trial. After reviewing the evidence bearing on the theories of accident and suicide and pointing out that no conviction was possible unless these were excluded, he continued: "On the other hand, if you come to the conclusion that suicide and accident are reasonably excluded, that does not mean that you must necessarily convict. . . . If you look at it in abstract logic, it seemes very simple and convincing to say, 'Well, there are your alternatives—suicide, accident, murder. You rule suicide out and you are left with two. And you rule accident out

C

and you are left with one, and that is murder.' I suppose logically there is no answer to that. But is it really sound? Is there not another alternative? Is there not this alternative, that the thing is unexplained? When you are dealing with a grave criminal charge of this kind, must you not take into account what I will call the fourth alternative, and that is that the thing is just left in mystery? As I said to you before, you are not bound as a jury to say affirmatively that this was suicide, or that it was accident, or that it was murder. You may be entitled to say, 'Well, to tell the honest truth, we have done our best, and, notwithstanding the evidence of exclusion, we feel unable to come to any positive conclusion, we just do not know what the truth is.'

"... I have not been able to get very much help from any of our law books, but I have this feeling about it, that, if you do not apply the method of exclusion with very great care, you run a risk of putting upon the accused the burden of explaining things. Now, the burden of proof in a criminal case is never on the person accused, and if you could simply proceed by a process of exclusion ... it might be coming very near to saying it is for the accused to explain something that may be inexplicable."

Later he gave the jury an express direction in law: "Even if you reject the theory of suicide and the theory of accident, in the absence of proved motive you cannot find a verdict of guilty against the accused unless you can find some clear positive evidence definitely incriminating the accused and connecting her with the crime charged."

After a reference to the case of Madeleine Smith, he reiterated the need for the jury to be positively satisfied of the guilt of the accused. The verdict, as in Christina's case, was Not Proven.

It is an odd coincidence that Mrs McMillan's junior counsel, Mr Hector McKechnie, was the greatgrandson and grandson of the two Doctors McKechnie who attended John Gilmour. He was not so fortunate, however, seven years later as senior counsel for Peter Withers, who was convicted of murder in Ayr. He appealed, his ground of appeal including a complaint that the presiding Judge, in charging the jury, had not given Lord Aitchison's direction in Mrs McMillan's case.

Lord Justice-General Cooper did not find it necessary to consider whether the direction had been warranted by any special features in the McMillan case. He deprecated its use, however, as laying down a general rule for which there was no prior authority. He referred to Lord Aitchison's "fourth alternative": "With the greatest respect, I cannot accept that formulation. If 'the thing is unexplained' or 'just left in mystery', that is merely another way of saying that the process of elimination of alternatives cannot have been exhaustive and complete. But where the process of elimination of alternatives is exhaustive and complete, it offers as reliable a process of reaching a just conclusion upon evidence as any mental process within the reach of human faculties. If in weighing evidence juries are not to accept the conclusions to which 'logically there is no answer', then there is no possible basis upon which they can proceed."

The appeal was dismissed and logic reinstated. But in these two judicial pronouncements we can see, reflecting the different temperaments of the two Judges, the two ways of looking at the jury, as "reasonable *men and women*" on the one hand and "*reasonable (i.e. reasoning)* men and women" on the other, to which I have already referred. Lord Cooper's view, of course, as the view of the appellate Court, is that now accepted in Scots law.

(II)

MADELEINE HAMILTON SMITH

Never the time and the place
And the loved one all together.
Browning

THIRTEEN years after Christina Gilmour left the dock a free woman, her place was taken by the most famous and fascinating of all who have ever benefited, or suffered, by a Not Proven verdict. Her name was Madeleine Hamilton Smith.

The cases have many points in common. Indeed there are times when Christina's seems a rehearsal, or perhaps "try-out" is the more appropriate term, for the later trial that has shadowed it into Limbo.

Consider the background. Madeleine and Christina were each the eldest of a family (six Smiths, five Cochrans) large enough by modern standards but moderate for their times. Both families were respectable and comfortably situated for their stations in life. It is perhaps significant of the social temper of the age that we can picture each family using the word "respectable" with some pride of itself; we can picture the Smiths (Papa was a wealthy architect) using the word condescendingly of the Cochrans, as Judge and counsel did at Christina's trial; but it is difficult to think of the Cochrans using it of the Smiths.

In each family the father was undoubtedly the head of the household. We have seen Alexander Cochran's power over his daughter. Of James Smith it is enough to say that even Madeleine, with her great independence and strength of mind, stood in fear of him. When she wrote to her lover in a hysterical appeal for silence "my father's wrath would kill me; you little know his temper", the cry was one of real terror, with only a minimum of her habitual dramatic exaggeration.

Each girl enjoyed a good, or at least expensive, education. Each went to boarding-school, Christina at nearby Paisley and Glasgow and Madeleine near London. Christina may have had the better of it: the more fashionable the school for young ladies the more worthless seems to have been the education provided. But Madeleine had enough intelligence and taste to overcome this disadvantage. Her reading was extensive. She enjoyed history—Gibbon, Macaulay, Hume, Alison and Bacon are among the authors she studied with pleasure. She also read the magazines of the day, including *Blackwood's* (her favourite) and *Chambers' Journal*.

Each was intended to be a good wife to a good man of her own class, as could be said of practically all their contemporaries. In each case the white crystals of arsenic proved a barrier to parental plans.

At the beginning of 1855 Madeleine was a lively young woman of nineteen. She had just left school and was taking over from her mother the management of the household. Her duties were light. The Smiths kept six servants and there was no need for drastic economy. Her time was conventionally occupied in social activities. There were visits to be paid and received with Mama and there were balls where she and her immediately younger sister Bessie met and flirted with young officers on their romantic way to the disease and muddle of the Crimea. It was an age when it took a great deal of determination on the part of a young lady to make her mark. Florence Nightingale did so; so in another way did Madeleine Smith.

When walking or taking carriage exercise with Mama, Madeleine and Bessie had to recognise and bow to accepted acquaintances. Other faces became familiar by frequent observation. One was that of a heavily moustached and whiskered young man who sometimes looked at the Smith girls with bold admiration.

He was Pierre Emile L'Angelier. His father had settled in Jersey as a refugee from France during the revolution of 1830 and set up in business as a nurseryman. When he died, Emile became an apprentice to a seedsman in Jersey and at the age of seventeen took a similar position with Dickson and Company in Edinburgh. In 1847 he went to France and was there during the 1848 revolution. He was a member of the National Guard. The details of his service are unknown, but the fact that he served added a romantic touch to his stories when he eventually returned to Scotland.

That return was not a happy one. He seems to have come back

at the instance of someone who has survived only as "the lady from Fife". But she became engaged to another and L'Angelier, who had no prospects and indeed for a time no employment, made several attempts or rather gestures at suicide.

He at last obtained employment with a nurseryman in Dundee. In 1852 he went as packing-clerk to Huggins and Company in Glasgow at a wage of ten shillings a week. He held this post until the end of his life, by which time his remuneration had increased to £50 a year.

James Smith himself seems to have been a self-made man who married an architect's daughter. L'Angelier, however, had not qualified for such a prize by making something of himself. He was not yet eligible from the Smiths' point of view. Money should marry money and not be thrown away on fortune hunters, especially of foreign extraction. The Smiths, however, were highly eligible to a young man like L'Angelier, who wanted to improve his position. He may have been genuinely attracted as well by the vivacity of the two girls. Madeleine in particular was a lively flirt; but it was apparently to Bessie that L'Angelier passed his first surreptitious note. It came into Madeleine's possession somehow; it may have been addressed to both.

About March 1855 L'Angelier was introduced. It was not, however, an introduction designed to meet with the approval of the Smith parents. He was friendly with a fellow-employee at Huggins' warehouse and through him came to know his two nephews, Charles and Robert Baird, the latter a boy of seventeen. Their parents knew the Smiths and L'Angelier pestered Robert to bring about the desired introduction. Without an introduction the affair could not have progressed beyond bold or languorous glances in the street. Robert, with the social diffidence of youth, thought the introduction would come better from his uncle; but his uncle refused to have anything to do with it. Robert then asked his mother, with as little success, to invite Madeleine to their house one evening so that he could ask L'Angelier. It was left to Robert himself to introduce L'Angelier in the street to both Madeleine and Bessie.

From time to time the two sisters met and walked in the street with L'Angelier, but soon the Smith family left for their country house, Rowaleyn, at Row or Rhu, near Helensburgh. The acquaintance was left to ripen through a secret correspondence into friendship and love, then wither into coolness and fear—perhaps hatred. We can plot its development as on a graph from Madeleine's letters. We do not have L'Angelier's, except for two drafts or scrolls, which were not allowed to go before the jury, and one press-copy, which was. Each acted prudently, Madeleine in destroying his letters, L'Angelier in keeping hers, in spite of her repeated requests, even in the innocuous early stages of the correspondence, that he should destroy them. Madeleine's prudence may have come upon her only at a late date. She told him once that she had been re-reading his letters; and even when the affair was building up to its climax she offered to return all his letters in exchange for her own. True, she may not have had them at the time and the promise may have been an empty one. But let us give her the benefit of the doubt.

The course of true love did not run smooth. That was an added attraction to Madeleine, as she admitted in one of her letters. In April 1855 her father learned that his two eldest daughters had been seen walking with a gentleman unknown to him. He was very angry. Bessie, probably feeling herself slighted by L'Angelier's obvious preference for Madeleine, supported him. Madeleine retorted that L'Angelier had been introduced and that she saw no harm in it. We are not told how the argument developed but no doubt it was a lively scene.

About a fortnight later Madeleine wrote to L'Angelier proposing that "for the present this correspondence had better stop". In the same letter she told him how he should address his reply and quoted a song, "There is a good time coming, only wait a little longer". The correspondence continued.

That summer L'Angelier proposed and in September Madeleine was bold enough to ask her father for his consent. The result might have been expected. Madeleine could never have deceived herself. Wealthy architects' daughters did not marry packing-clerks with ten shillings a week, or even £50 a year.

Dutifully she wrote a farewell note urging L'Angelier, with her characteristic attention to detail, to burn all her letters. She had done so before but probably thought there was no harm in repeating the instruction. As we know, there was as little good.

About the same time she wrote to Miss Perry, an elderly maiden lady and friend of L'Angelier's, whom she had only recently met. "Emile will tell you I have bid him adieu. My papa would not give his consent, so I am in duty bound to obey him. Comfort dear Emile. It is a heavy blow to us both. . . . Think my conduct not unkind. I have a father to please, and a kind father too. . . ." It was a letter skilfully designed to suit the recipient's conventionally romantic and sentimental mind.

L'Angelier's answer is probably represented by one of the drafts which the jury was not allowed to see. But we are not so thirled to the ruling of the Court. The difficulty is that this scroll bears the date 19th July 1855, but L'Angelier may have been using old paper which for some reason bore that date. Its angry reproach is out of context with the reasonably smooth course of the July correspondence.

He took a high moral tone. "You have deceived your father as you have deceived me. You never told him how solemnly you bound yourself to me, or if you had, for the honour of his daughter he could not have asked you to break off an engagement as ours. Madeleine, you have truly acted wrong. . . . You desire and now you are at liberty to recognise me or cut me just as you wish—but I give you my word of honour I shall act always as a Gentleman towards you."

In spite of this promise there was a sinister passage near the end: "Think what your father would say if I sent him your letters for a perusal. Do you think he could sanction your breaking your promises. No, Madeleine, I leave your conscience to speak for itself."

The threat was less terrible than it was to become; but it was there. And L'Angelier was tacitly admitting that, in spite of all appeals, he had not destroyed her letters. If she noticed this, the romantic side of her nature, which comes out so clearly in her dramatisations, was probably pleased rather than otherwise.

The correspondence did not stop. The reason was less L'Angelier's threat than the fact that he did not go as he had half thought of going to Peru in order to better himself. He remained in Glasgow. The Smiths returned to Glasgow for the winter. Meetings could be arranged.

On the afternoon of 3rd December 1855 we find Madeleine writing to L'Angelier as "my own darling husband" and signing herself "thy own thy ever fond thy own dear loving wife thy Mimi L'Angelier". From this time she used the words "husband" and "wife" regularly. But in nearly every letter she referred to marriage in the future; for example in the same letter of 3rd December she wrote "My own sweet beloved, I can say nothing as to our marriage, as it is not certain when they may go from home, or when I may go to Edr. it is uncertain. My beloved, will we require to be married (if it is in Edr.) in Edr. or will it do here? You know I know nothing of these things. I fear the Banns in Glasgow, there are so many people know me. If I had any other name but Madeleine it might pass—but it is not a very common one. But we must manage in some way to be united ere we leave Town."

Clearly the words "husband" and "wife" were used proleptically, or perhaps merely as forms of endearment. Madeleine did not think of herself as a married woman. What she contemplated was a regular marriage celebrated in church after due calling of banns, banns called with as much secrecy as the law permitted. But there was no marriage ceremony that winter and in the spring the Smiths again left Glasgow for Rowaleyn. Sometimes L'Angelier travelled by boat to Helensburgh (with careful directions from Madeleine about how to avoid Papa if he were to be on the same steamer) and they snatched a secret meeting in the woods.

And there in the woods on the night of 6th June 1856[1] the lovers, as lovers will, anticipated the rites of the church. Next day (at the amazing hour of 5 a.m.) Madeleine wrote an exulting letter, tempered with a few conventional expressions of regret: "My own, my beloved husband. . . . Beloved, if we did wrong last night it was in the excitement of our love. I did truly

[1] Some writers give this important date as 6th May: we have a letter from Madeleine making an appointment for that date. But in the Appendix to the report of this trial in the *Notable British Trials Series* there is a note that the envelope for this letter (itself undated) bears two post-marks, one that of Helensburgh dated 7th of an illegible month and the other that of Glasgow bearing the date 14th June 1856. I can myself corroborate the illegibility of the month in the Helensburgh postmark. The part of the back of the envelope where the Glasgow postmark was set has been torn off.

love you with all my soul. I was happy, it was a pleasure to be with you.... Am I not your wife. Yes, I am. And you may rest assured after what has passed I cannot be the wife of any other but dear, dear Emile. No, now it would be a sin.... I did not bleed in the least last night—but I had a good deal of pain during the night. Tell me, pet, were you angry at me for allowing you to do what you did—was it very bad of me. We should, I suppose, have waited till we were married. I shall always remember last night. Will we not often talk of our evening meetings after we are married.... Adieu again, my husband. God bless you and make you well. And may you yet be very, very happy with your Mimi as your little wife. Kindest love, fond embrace, and kisses from thy own true and ever devoted Mimi, Thy faithful Wife."

L'Angelier's reply, of which we have only the legally inadmissible scroll, was a masterpiece. "My dearest and beloved wife Mimi. Since I saw you I have been wretchedly sad. Would to God we had not met that night—I would have been happier. I am sad at what we did, I regret it very much. Why, Mimi, did you give way after your promises? My pet, it is a pity.... We did wrong. God forgive us for it. Mimi, we have loved blindly. It is your parents' fault if shame is the result; they are to blame for it....

"I do not understand, my pet, your not bleeding, for every woman having her virginity must bleed.[1] You must have done so some other time. Try to remember if you never hurt yourself in washing, &c. I am sorry you felt pain. I hope, pet, you are better. I trust, dearest, you will not be ———. Be sure and tell me immediately you are ill next time and if at your regular period. I was not angry at your allowing me, Mimi, but I am sad it happened. You had no resolution. We should indeed have waited till we were married, Mimi. It was very bad indeed....

"For Gods sake burn this, Mimi, for fear anything happening to you, do dearest."

Apparently Mimi did. But L'Angelier seems to have been so proud of this monstrous epistle that it is one of the few of which he kept any record.

---

[1] Am I alone in thinking this is about as nasty a remark, in spite of what follows, as any in this letter? Other commentators seem to overlook it.

During the rest of the summer L'Angelier visited Row and met Madeleine in the woods and sometimes in her bedroom. Occasionally there were vows of chastity which were meant to prevail until after the church ceremony which both had in mind, but these were of short duration and passionate nature triumphed.

As early as the middle of June rumours began to link Madeleine's name with that of William Harper Minnoch, a much more desirable suitor. Madeleine never lacked courage and she herself reported the rumours to L'Angelier. Needless to say she denied them, with many protestations of her dislike of "this Mr M". The dislike, however, grew less and less. "I did tell you at one time that I did not like William Minnoch, but he was so pleasant that he quite raised himself in my estimation." She still protested herself free from any ties, but L'Angelier was not unnaturally disturbed by the progress Minnoch was making in the liking if not affection of his "wife".

It did not help matters when the Smith family returned in November 1856 from Row to Glasgow. They had lived in India Street; they were now to live at 7 Blythswood Square, only some ten minutes' walk from L'Angelier's lodgings. It was even nearer William Minnoch. The Smiths' house (now the College of Agriculture) was at the corner where Mains Street (now Blythswood Street) runs down from the Square to Sauchiehall Street. It occupied the ground floor and basement. Minnoch's house was above part of the Smiths'. It was entered from the first door in Mains Street—on to which looked the basement bedroom occupied by Madeleine and her young sister Janet. This proximity did nothing to allay L'Angelier's growing suspicions, nursed as they were by constant reports of an intended marriage between Madeleine and the very eligible Minnoch with his rumoured £4,000 a year.

Although Madeleine had returned to Glasgow, meetings did not become easier. There were no convenient woods and it was more difficult to arrange a surreptitious entry into the house. The front door in Blythswood Square was in normal circumstances out of the question. The lower sills of Madeleine's bedroom windows were about eighteen inches below the pavement of Mains Street and only some six inches distant from it. Unfortunately, like the other basement windows, they were barred by stout iron stanchions and could be used only as a posting box for hand-delivered letters—for which Madeleine carefully prescribed brown and not white envelopes to make detection more difficult. Even without the bars, however, L'Angelier could hardly have entered by these windows without either attracting attention from the street or disturbing Janet, who shared Madeleine's bed.

There were two doors on the basement floor. One opened on to the sunk area that formed a dry moat between the front of the house and the pavement of Blythswood Square. It was under the bridge of steps that led to the front door, so that it was out of sight of watchers from the ground floor. But the stairs which led down to the area from the pavement were in full view of the drawing-room windows. The other basement door gave access to a small back area and then to a lane that ran from Mains Street behind the Blythswood Square houses. This approach lay under Mr Smith's bedroom windows.

Both basement doors were kept locked at night and so were the gates into the front and back areas. Anyone inside the basement, however, could easily open either door, as the keys usually remained in the locks. The key of the front area gate was kept by the houseboy and that of the back area by the housemaid, Christina Haggart. She had been an accomplice of Madeleine for some time. Letters posted by L'Angelier were usually addressed to her. On one occasion at least she and the cook stayed out of their bedroom while Madeleine entertained her lover there. Christina Haggart had a fellow-feeling. At the time she was being courted by Duncan Mackenzie, whom she married in March 1857. So enthusiastic about helping Miss Madeleine was she that Mackenzie grew suspicious of L'Angelier's object in visiting Blythswood Square and had to be reassured by a letter from Madeleine herself.

A police officer patrolled both Blythswood Square and Mains Street by night. His friendly myopia was bought by L'Angelier for a couple of cigars.

But all Christina Haggart's sympathetic help and the police-man's tolerance could not give cover to an approach to the house across the lighted pavements. And the basement doors were noisy, adding to the strength of the defences. L'Angelier gained entrance on only a few occasions. But he did at times dally with Madeleine at her bedroom window. Once at least, as she admitted in her declaration, she handed him out a cup of cocoa. In the main, however, their "quite a small romance", as she called it in one of her cooler letters, had to be continued by correspondence.

Madeleine's letters, even before her return to Glasgow, show her growing frustration and the weakening of her passion. Con-tinued renewal of physical proximity, if not contact, was essen-tial to her. Absence did not make her heart grow fonder. The phrase "quite a small romance" is dangerously significant of her calmer feeling. And meanwhile William Minnoch was quietly, respectfully and persuasively pressing his claims, with all the added opportunities that parental approval and a house next door gave him.

As usual, we can only guess L'Angelier's reactions from Madeleine's answers to his letters. But she seems to have gone out of her way sometimes to bait him with references to the expensive way of life to which she was accustomed and her pleas that she was prepared to face poverty with him ring sadly false. For example, how could L'Angelier appreciate this, as one item in the Smith family budget for their youngest son? "James is liking school very much—only, poor boy, he com-plains of not getting enough sugar or Butter—fancy, he pays £80 for board alone—it is far too much for such a boy—Is it not." L'Angelier must have asked himself how a woman with such a family background could seriously contemplate keeping house on an income of that very amount of £80, which Made-leine had said she would find enough for their needs.

Madeleine's letters grew cooler and shorter. Minnoch's court-ship, never ardent or passionate, prospered like the man him-self.[1] On 28th January 1857 he proposed to Madeleine and was

---

[1] "My attentions to her, I understood, had been such as to make her quite aware that I was paying my addresses to her." (*Evidence of William Minnoch at the trial.*)

accepted, although no arrangements were made about the wedding date. At that time Minnoch was as ignorant of her relations with L'Angelier as John Gilmour had been of Christina Cochran's feeling for John Anderson.

Less than a week before that engagement Madeleine wrote to L'Angelier in rather warmer terms than she commonly used at this time and suggested March for their wedding. She never told L'Angelier of her engagement to Minnoch.

Early in February an opportunity occurred to break, as she hoped, with L'Angelier. He returned one of her letters. Her reply deserves full quotation for the calmness with which she seized her chance.

"I felt truly astonished to have my last letter returned to me. But it will be the last you shall have an opportunity of returning to me. When you are not pleased with the letters I send you, then our correspondence shall be at an end, and as there is coolness on both sides our engagement had better be broken. This may astonish you, but you have more than once returned me my letters, and my mind was made up that I should not stand the same thing again. And you also annoyed me much on Saturday by your conduct in coming so near me. Altogether I think owing to coolness and indifference (nothing else) that we had better for the future consider ourselves as strangers. I trust to your honour as a Gentleman that you will not reveal anything that may have passed between us. I shall feel obliged by your bring me my letters and Likeness on Thursday eveng. at 7—be at the Area Gate, and C.H. will [take] the parcel from you. On Friday night I shall send you all your letters, Likeness, &ca. I trust you may yet be happy, and get one more worthy of you than I. On Thursday at 7 o'C. I am, &c. M.

"You may be astonished at this sudden change—but for some time back you must have noticed a coolness in my notes. My love for you has ceased, and that is why I was cool. I did once love you truly, fondly, but for some time back I have lost much of that love. There is no other reason for my conduct, and I think it but fair to let you know this. I might have gone on and become your wife, but I could not have loved you as I ought. My conduct you will condemn, but I did at one time love you with heart and soul. It has cost me much to tell you this—

sleepless nights, but it is necessary you should know. If you remain in Glasgow or go away, I hope you may succeed in all your endeavours. I know you will never injure the character of one you so fondly loved. No, Emile, I know you have honour and are a Gentleman. What has passed you will not mention. I know when I ask you that you will comply. Adieu."

L'Angelier was distressed by the calm brutality of this letter, as well he might have been. Nothing that had passed before had prepared him for anything so final. He told his friend Tom Kennedy, cashier at Huggins', with tears in his eyes that Madeleine had asked for her letters back. Kennedy advised him to return the letters and be done with it: the lady was not worthy of him. L'Angelier replied with a threat to show all the letters to her father. Kennedy again urged him to give the letters up, to which L'Angelier said "No, I won't; she shall never marry another man as long as I live."

Then, as though fey, he added: "Tom, it is an infatuation; she shall be the death of me."

So far as Madeleine was concerned, however, he took no steps in response to her letter. On 9th February she wrote curtly: "I attribute it to your having cold that I had no answer to my last note. On Thursday evening you were, I suppose, afraid of the night air. I fear your cold is not better. I again appoint Thursday night first same place, Street Gate, 7 o'clock. M.

"If you can not send me or bring me the parcel on Thursday, please write a note saying when you shall bring it, and address it to C.H. Send it by post."

The absence of any self-justification from this short note suggests that L'Angelier's silence had done something to restore Madeleine's slightly wavering self-confidence. She felt herself now in supreme control of the situation. But this time L'Angelier replied at once. We can all too easily infer the terms of his letter from Madeleine's hysterically abject reply of 10th February.

"Monday Night. Emile, I have just had your note. Emile, for the love you once had for me do nothing till I see you—for God's sake do not bring your once loved Mimi to an open shame. . . . Emile, write to no one, to Papa or any other. Oh, do not till I see you on Wednesday night—be at the Hamiltons at 12, and I shall open my Shutter, and then you come to the Area Gate, I shall see you. It would break my Mother's heart. Oh, Emile, be not harsh to me. I am the most guilty, miserable wretch on the face of the earth. Emile, do not drive me to death. When I ceased to love you, believe me, it was not to love another. I am free from all engagement at present. Emile, for God's sake do not send my letters to Papa.... Will you not—but I cannot ask forgiveness, I am too guilty for that.... Pray for me for a guilty wretch, but do nothing. Oh, Emile, do nothing. 10 o'c To-morrow night one line, for the love of God.

"Tuesday morning. I am ill. God knows what I have suffered. My punishment is more than I can bear. Do nothing till I see you, for the love of heaven do nothing. I am mad, I am ill."

L'Angelier replied at once and Madeleine wrote again on Tuesday night in fawning, but still hysterical, gratitude. "Emile, I have this night received your note. Oh, it is kind of you to write to me. Emile, no one can know the intense agony of mind I have suffered last night and to day. Emile, my father's wrath would kill me; you little know his temper. Emile, for the love you once had for me do not denounce me to my P/. Emile, if he should read my letters to you—he will put me from him, he will hate me as a guilty wretch.... I did love you, and it was my soul's ambition to be your wife. I asked you to tell me my faults. You did so, and it made me cool towards you gradually. When you have found fault with me, I have cooled—it was not love for another, for there is no one I love. My love has all been given to you. My heart is empty, cold—I am unloved. I am despised. I told you I had ceased to love you—it was true. I did not love you as I did—but, oh, till within the time of our coming to Town I loved you fondly. I longed to be your wife. I had fixed Feby. I longed for it. The time I could not leave my father's house I grew discontented, then I ceased to love you. Oh, Emile, this is indeed the true statement.... While I have breath I shall ever think of you as my best friend, if you will only keep this between ourselves. I blush to ask you. Yet, Emile, will you not grant me this, my last favor. If you will never reveal what has passed. Oh, for God's sake, for the love of heaven, hear me. I grow mad. I have been ill, very ill, all day.

I have had what has given me a false spirit. I had to resort to what I should not have taken, but my brain is on fire. I feel as if death would indeed be sweet. Denounce me not. Emile, Emile, think of our once happy days. Pardon me if you can, pray for me as the most wretched, guilty, miserable creature on the earth. I could stand anything but my father's hot displeasure. Emile, you will not cause me death. If he is to get your letters, I can not see him any more. And my poor mother. I will never more kiss her—it would be a shame to them all. Emile, will you not spare me this—hate me, despise me—but do not expose me. I cannot write more. I am too ill to-night. M."

About this time (the exact date is not clear) Madeleine sent the houseboy to buy prussic acid, which she said she wanted for her hands. The druggist refused to supply it and no more was heard of prussic acid. In the context of these letters it is not unlikely that, as Peter Hunt has suggested,[1] she wanted it for herself in case L'Angelier carried out his threat to send her letters to her father. But it is also possible that she meant to use it on L'Angelier if she got the chance to do so.

They met at this critical point in their affairs. And suddenly the crisis seemed to disappear. On Saturday 14th February— only four days after the last letter—Madeleine wrote: "My dear Emile, I have got my finger cut, and cannot write, so, dear, I wish you would excuse me. I was glad to see you looking so well yesterday. I hope to see you very soon. Write for me next Thursday, and then I shall tell you when I can see you. I want the first time we meet, that you will bring me all my cool letters back—the last four I have written—and I will give you others in their place.

"Bring them all to me. Excuse me more, just now it hurts me to write; so with kindest and dearest love, ever believe (me), yours with love & affection, M."

This letter was far from being as passionate as her earlier ones. "Affectionate" is the appropriate term. The letters which followed were warmer. Once more we read the old endearments —"my love my pet my sweet Emile", "dearest love of my soul", "with fond and tender embraces", "my dear and very beloved sweet little Emile". Only the words "husband" and "wife"

[1] *The Madeleine Smith Affair* (Carrol and Nicholson, 1950).

were now missing from her letters and she no longer signed herself "Mimi L'Angelier".

On 19th February—five days after she had written to
L'Angelier for the return of her "cool" letters in exchange for
others—Madeleine went with William Minnoch and his sister
to the opera. The piece they saw, as Sir Compton Mackenzie
has discovered, was *Lucrezia Borgia*. One would give a lot to
know Madeleine's reactions. They returned about 11 p.m. The
cab stopped at 7 Blythswood Square and Madeleine entered the
house. The Minnochs went home, round the corner to Mains
Street.

About 8 o'clock next morning L'Angelier's landlady knocked
at his door but he received no answer. She knocked again and
he called to her to come in. He had been very sick during the
night and said he had been taken ill on the way home the
previous night, with a violent pain in his bowels and stomach,
so that he thought he would have died. From that time he was
never really well, although he was able to go back to work at
Huggins'.

On Saturday 21st February Madeleine went to Murdoch
Brothers, chemists in Sauchiehall Street, and bought one ounce
of arsenic. The price, sixpence, was charged to her father's
account, along with the more innocuous purchase of two dozen
soda water. She signed the register as required by the recent
Arsenic Act of 1851 and told the druggist that she wanted the
poison for the garden and the country house—to kill rats and
destroy vermin about the flowers. This was untrue. Campsie, the
gardener at Rowaleyn, never got arsenic from her and indeed
never used it; phosphorus paste was good enough for the rats at
Row. In her judicial declaration Madeleine admitted the purchase and admitted that the rats were not her target. She really
wanted to use the arsenic as a cosmetic wash. While she was at
school a pupil teacher, Augusta Guibilei, who as the daughter
of an actress might have been expected to know the secrets of
beauty culture, had discussed the use of arsenic for this purpose. At the trial Miss Guibilei denied any such discussion:

there had, however, been a discussion of a magazine article which told how the Swiss mountaineers ate arsenic to improve their breathing on the hills, with incidental improvement to their looks.

Articles on the arsenic-eating habit appeared in *Chambers' Journal*, which was one of the periodicals read by Madeleine, in December 1851, June 1853, and February and July 1856.

The arsenic sold by Murdoch was mixed, in obedience to the statute, with one ounce of soot to the pound of arsenic, a process which one would have expected to make it unattractive for cosmetic use. Madeleine said, however, that she did use it, diluted with water, on her face, neck and arms. The maid Christina Haggart never noticed the water in Madeleine's basin to be peculiarly black.

In the early hours of Monday 23rd February L'Angelier suffered a recurrence of his mysterious illness. This time he was off work for eight days. Dr Hugh Thomson was called in and treated him for a bilious fever. It did not occur to him at the time that he was suffering from an irritant poison, but the symptoms were such as he would have expected if he had known that such a poison had been taken. He thought smoking might have something to do with it and advised his patient to give it up.

On 2nd March L'Angelier dined with his old friend Miss Perry. He told her of his two illnesses and could not give any cause for them. A week later, however, he said to her: "I can't think why I was so unwell after getting that coffee and chocolate from her." Miss Perry understood that he was referring to two different occasions and that by "her" he meant Madeleine. Later he said: "It is a perfect fascination my attachment to that girl; if she were to poison me I would forgive her"—a sentiment for which Miss Perry rebuked him.

At the beginning of March the Smiths were going to go to Bridge of Allan for a few days. Madeleine wrote to L'Angelier, urging him to go to the south of England, perhaps the Isle of Wight, while they were away. He had meant to go to Bridge of Allan himself but she begged him not to. "I hope you won't go to B. of Allan, as P/ and M/ would say it was I brought you there, and it would make me to feel very unhappy. Stirling you need not go to as it is a nasty dirty little town."

L'Angelier wrote back that his doctor had ordered him to
go to Bridge of Allan and that he could not afford to travel 500
miles to the Isle of Wight and 500 miles back. "What" he asked
"is your object in wishing me so very much to go south? I may
not go to B. of A. till Wednesday; if I can avoid going I shall
do so for your sake." It is clear from this letter that his suspicions were only temporarily lulled by the renewal of the
correspondence; he asked for an explicit answer to his question
—was she directly or indirectly engaged to William Minnoch?
    She denied it.
    6th March was the day set for the Smiths' departure for
Bridge of Allan. Before they left, a school friend of Madeleine's,
Mary Jane Buchanan, called. There was an old promise between them that whichever was first engaged to be married
should ask the other to be bridesmaid and Madeleine had
written to tell Mary Jane of her engagement to Minnoch. When
Mary Jane arrived Madeleine was out but she soon came back.
Her visitor could not wait so, as there were several matters to
discuss about the proposed wedding, Madeleine offered to walk
with her for part of the way home. Their route lay along
Sauchiehall Street. As they passed Currie's chemist's shop,
Madeleine said "Oh, just stop a minute. I want to go into this
shop. Will you go with me?"
    Mary Jane and Madeleine went into the shop, where Made-
leine bought sixpenceworth of arsenic. Again the ostensible
purpose was the slaughter of rats, this time at Blythswood
Square. The assistant, Haliburton, recommended phosphorus
paste as safer, but Madeleine said that she had used that unsuccessfully and insisted on arsenic. The family were going from
home so that it would be quite safe to lay it down. She signed
the register and was supplied with an ounce of arsenic mixed
with indigo. As they left the shop, Mary Jane laughed at the
idea of a young lady buying arsenic. Madeleine said nothing
but laughed too.
    Believers in her guilt will remember the laugh that was heard
from the upper floor in the Borden house at Fall River, Massa-
chusetts, on 4th August 1892.
    So Madeleine went to Bridge of Allan on 6th March armed
with an ounce of arsenic—for cosmetic purposes, as she stated

in her declaration. L'Angelier stayed in Glasgow for a few days, then went to Edinburgh.

On 12th March William Minnoch visited the Smiths at Bridge of Allan and formally proposed. The wedding date was fixed as 18th June. On his return to Glasgow Madeleine wrote him a prim little note which is worth quoting for its contrast with her letters to L'Angelier.

"My dearest William, It is but fair, after your kindness to me, that I should write you a note. The day I part from friends I always feel sad. But to part from one I love, as I do you, makes me feel truly sad and dull. My only consolation is that we meet soon. Tomorrow we shall be home. I do so wish you were here to-day. We might take a long walk. Our walk to Dumblane I shall ever remember with pleasure. That walk fixed a day on which we are to begin a new life—a life which I hope may be of happiness and long duration to both of us. My aim through life shall be to please you and study you. Dear William, I must conclude, as Mamma is ready to go to Stirling. I do not go with the same pleasure as I did the last time. I hope you got to Town safe, and found your sisters well. Accept my warmest kindest love and ever believe me to be, yours with affecn., Madeleine."

On Tuesday 17th March the Smiths returned to Glasgow. So did L'Angelier. He asked his landlady if there were any letters for him and was disappointed to find that there were none. He left Glasgow again on Thursday 19th March and went to Bridge of Allan—*via* Edinburgh, where he asked at the Post Office for a letter but did not get one.

There is no evidence that he and Madeleine met on any of the three days they were in Glasgow together, 17th–19th March. Indeed they seem not to have met after 5th March, before the Smiths went to Bridge of Allan. L'Angelier seems to have kept away from that inland spa.

On Wednesday 18th March Madeleine bought another ounce of arsenic from Currie. She told him that she had found eight or nine large rats lying dead and wanted to repeat the dose. These rats were mythical; no one but Madeleine ever claimed to have seen one, far less eight or nine, alive or dead.

On Thursday 19th March Madeleine and her parents dined

with William Minnoch. Before she went, she said, she used the second ounce of arsenic she had bought from Currie as a face wash.

On Sunday 22nd March L'Angelier returned unexpectedly to his lodgings in Glasgow from Bridge of Allan. About 9 o'clock he left with the pass-key which he needed if he was going to return late. But when he came back, about 2.30 a.m., he was too ill to use it and had to ring for admission. In spite of prompt medical attention from Dr Steven, he died about 11 o'clock on Monday morning. His own doctor, Dr Thomson, was summoned, but neither he nor Dr Steven could find any natural cause of death. At the request of the dead man's employers they carried out a post-mortem examination. That examination and a chemical analysis which followed showed conclusively that death was due to arsenic poisoning. About 88 grains (one-fifth of an ounce, or at a modest estimate over twenty times the fatal dose) was found in his stomach. The experts judged that probably more than twice that amount had been swallowed: perhaps half an ounce.

When news of L'Angelier's death reached Huggins' warehouse, the warehouseman Stevenson went at once to his lodgings and made a search of his effects. Some letters were discovered, one in his vest pocket beginning "Why, my beloved, did you not come to me? . . ." There was also a memorandum book in L'Angelier's handwriting. Stevenson took these away with him to the office and began to read the entries in the memorandum book. Meanwhile L'Angelier's desk had been opened and other letters found. The clerks began to read them to discover, if possible, his mother's address.

M. August de Mean, chancellor to the French consul, heard of the death through Amadee Thuau, a young man who lodged with L'Angelier. He had been a friend of L'Angelier but had dropped his acquaintance when he married: he thought L'Angelier an unsuitable companion for a married man because of his levity. At some stage L'Angelier had asked de Mean for his advice; de Mean told him that he should formally ask Mr

Smith for his consent: that was the most gentlemanly way to go about things.

When he learned of L'Angelier's death he thought it right to go to Mr Smith, whom he knew, and tell him about the correspondence between Madeleine and L'Angelier, so that he could take steps "to exonerate his daughter in case of anything coming out". This presumably referred only to the danger of scandal if the letters got into the wrong hands. At Mr Smith's request he went to Huggins' warehouse and asked for the letters. Huggins himself was not in the office and the clerks refused to give up the letters without their employer's consent.

A day or two later de Mean saw Madeleine in her mother's presence. He told her that L'Angelier had, according to his information, come from Bridge of Allan at her express invitation the Sunday night before he died. Madeleine said she had written to him making an appointment for Saturday, not knowing that he was at Bridge of Allan. De Mean then urged her to tell the truth about her meeting with L'Angelier, if one took place on Sunday night. If she had been seen, her denial would look suspicious. Madeleine insisted there had been no meeting. "I swear to you, M. de Mean, that I have not seen L'Angelier, not on that Sunday only, but not for three weeks."

On Tuesday 25th March Drs Thomson and Steven made a guarded preliminary report on the post-mortem examination. Their observations justified a suspicion of death by poison but they were careful to state that it might have resulted from natural causes. The warehouseman Stevenson told the Procurator-fiscal of the doctors' findings, not to start any criminal proceedings but simply to let him know that a foreigner had died suddenly. Next day, however, he began to feel uneasy and at the Procurator-fiscal's request handed over some of the letters. It was probably after this that de Mean had his interview with Madeleine in her mother's presence.

Next day Janet, Madeleine's thirteen-year-old sister, woke in the morning to find that Madeleine was not in bed with her as usual. Minnoch called at the house later that morning. Someone guessed that Madeleine had gone to Rowaleyn and Minnoch with one of her brothers went by train to Greenock in pursuit. They boarded the steamer for Helensburgh and Row and found

her on board—a neat piece of interception, if hardly as spectacular as that of Christina Gilmour by Superintendent McKay.
The three completed the journey to Rowaleyn, then returned to
Glasgow by carriage. How Christina would have envied her successor!

Meanwhile rumours continued to spread. William Minnoch,
like the faithful Dobbin he was, called regularly on the Smiths.
On Saturday Madeleine told him that she had written a letter
to "a Frenchman" to get back some letters she had written to
him earlier. On Tuesday morning she referred to the report that
L'Angelier had been poisoned and remarked that she "had
been in the habit" of buying arsenic as it was good for the
complexion.

That afternoon Madeleine was arrested.

The trial began in the High Court in Edinburgh on Tuesday
30th June 1857. In accordance with the practice of the day
three Judges were on the bench. Lord Justice-Clerk Hope,
whom we have already met at Christina Gilmour's trial, presided, this time with the assistance of Lord Ivory and Lord
Handyside. The prosecution was conducted by Lord Advocate
Moncreiff (later Lord Justice-Clerk), Solicitor-General Edward
Francis Maitland (later Lord Barcaple) and Donald Mackenzie,
advocate-depute. Maitland was a younger brother of Thomas
Maitland, who defended Christina Gilmour and was now on
the bench as Lord Dundrennan. The defence was conducted by
the Dean of the Faculty of Advocates, John Inglis, one of the
greatest lawyers ever to adorn the Scottish bar and later, as
Lord President, the bench. He was assisted by George Young
(later Lord Young) and Alexander Moncrieff.

The court was crowded. It was not often that the dock was
occupied by a young lady of such good social standing and all
were eager to catch a glimpse of the already legendary Madeleine Smith. For the benefit of the many who could not obtain
admission the newspapers of the day printed their impressions
and artists busily sketched in court for the illustrated papers.
Some descriptions of the accused were critical—even severely

so. But people rarely appear at their best in the dock in a criminal court. And Madeleine's principal attraction was probably her vivacity, a quality that was not displayed during the trial. Then observers noticed her ostentatious unconcern. She entered the dock, in the immortal phrase of an anonymous reporter for the *Ayrshire Express,* "with the air of a belle entering a ballroom".

Her fiance William Minnoch also contrived to behave coolly in the witness-box in spite of the embarrassing position in which he, a thoroughly conventional and respectable man, found himself. He did so by firmly refusing to look at the prisoner in the dock; she, on the other hand, gazed calmly at him. The general impression given by the two during this episode of the trial was such as to suggest to one contemporary that "they might have taken up house at the North Pole without much inconvenience to either".

The Smith family were not called as witnesses, except for young Janet who appeared for the defence. The parents retired to Rowaleyn and took to their beds when the publicity grew too great for them to face.

The indictment contained two charges of administering arsenic to L'Angelier with intent to poison him on (1) Thursday or Friday 19th or 20th February 1857 and (2) on Sunday or Monday 22nd or 23rd February. The third charge was that of murdering him by the same means on Sunday or Monday 22nd or 23rd March. The alternative dates were necessary because of the late hours at which Madeleine and L'Angelier were supposed to have met. The meetings could not be assigned with any certainty to one side or the other of midnight.

But did the meetings ever take place? That was and still is the great question in the case. But before we come to consider it there are one or two minor points which may be discussed.

First, the medical evidence. This left no doubt that L'Angelier's death was due to arsenic, although the two earlier illnesses were of uncertain causation. But where did the arsenic come from?

The medical evidence for the Crown was distinguished. As well as the two doctors who carried out the preliminary post-mortem examination, there was Dr Frederick Penny, Professor of chemistry at the Andersonian University, Glasgow, whose evidence won a tribute from the Lord Justice-Clerk: "Certainly, Dr Penny, more satisfactory, lucid or distinct evidence I never heard." This may have been said to soothe the witness's feelings: he had arrived late and been publicly rebuked for delaying the start of the trial by so doing. But it was none the less well deserved.

Then there was, inevitably, Dr Robert Christison, who gave evidence at Christina Gilmour's trial. Almost from the date of his appointment as Professor of Medical Jurisprudence in 1822 at the age of twenty-four, no poisoning trial was complete without him. At first he appeared for the defence. In that capacity he so impressed Hope, then Solicitor-General, that he became, in his own words, "unacknowledged standing medical counsel for Her Majesty's interest". His fairness and accurate preparation were appreciated by both sides. Indeed it is noticeable when one studies the trials of the period that before his rise to fame most of the controversy in poisoning trials was about the cause of death, while afterwards his evidence on that issue was rarely challenged.

The only serious dispute at Madeleine's trial was as to the source of the arsenic found in L'Angelier's body. You will remember that the first ounce of arsenic (Murdoch's) had been mixed with soot and the second and third (Currie's) with indigo. No trace of either colouring substance was found in L'Angelier's stomach: the experts did not look for such traces, as their attention was not directed to the point. They thought, however, that soot or indigo would have left visible traces. It was very difficult to remove either from arsenic. But the indigo used by Currie was not true indigo, but waste, which had already been used by dyers, and this did not possess the same properties.

A minor point arose from the great quantity (88 grains) of arsenic found in the stomach. The defence contended that this pointed to suicide rather than murder, as it could not have been swallowed unknowingly. The doctors thought that it could have passed unobserved in a thick fluid like cocoa. [It may be observed that L'Angelier set up a record by this figure of 88 grains. He did not hold his pre-eminence for long: in two undoubted cases of murder in England (Dodds in 1860 and Hewitt in 1863)

the amounts recovered were 150 and 154 grains. But the Edinburgh jury of 1857 could not foresee these cases and they do not
take away from whatever force the defence argument may have
had.]

These matters, however, were little more than side-issues. The
main question was, did the meetings take place? This is a
question which we may find easier to answer than did the jury.
They were not allowed to see a memorandum book kept by
L'Angelier in which he noted engagements kept—not merely
future engagements, for the jottings are in the past tense. We
may, however, look at it.

Let us first, however, consider each alleged meeting in the
light of the evidence which was before the jury and then consider the effect of the memorandum book.

The first charge related to the night of Thursday/Friday
19th/20th February. First, there was a letter from Madeleine to
L'Angelier dated Saturday 14th February: "Write for me next
Thursday, and then I shall tell you when I can see you." It was
posted between 8.45 a.m. and 12.20 p.m. and would have been
delivered in normal course of post the same day between 1.30
and 3 p.m. [We can only wonder at and envy the efficiency of
the Post Office services of those days.] If L'Angelier received
that letter in the ordinary way, he would have had time to arrange a meeting for the night of the 19th.

On 17th February L'Angelier dined with Miss Perry and told
her he expected to see Madeleine on the 19th. She did not see
him again until 2nd March when he told her he had been very
ill on a date which she was able to calculate as 19th February.
He did not say, however, that he did in fact see Madeleine on
that date. It was unfortunate that Miss Perry was only able to
calculate the date as the 19th after that date had been suggested
to her by the official who was taking her statement in preparation for the trial.

The evening of 19th February was the evening on which
Madeleine visited the opera with William Minnoch and his
sister. She arrived home about 11 p.m.

On 23rd February L'Angelier consulted Dr Hugh Thomson. His tongue was furred and he was complaining of vomiting and purging. The doctor understood he had been suffering in this way for a day or two but had been taken worse on the night of 22nd/23rd February. [This evidence therefore has a bearing on each of those first two charges.] The symptoms might have been those of poisoning by some irritant, but at the time he did not suspect any such cause.

Mrs Jenkins, L'Angelier's landlady, put the second illness about 22nd February and the first one "eight or ten days before".

Amadee Thuau, a fellow-lodger, could not remember dates. He said, however, that L'Angelier, on the morning of his first illness, told him he had seen "the lady" the night before and had been unwell in her presence.

On this evidence the Lord Justice-Clerk seemed to think that the jury would probably hold that L'Angelier and Madeleine met on the night of 19th/20th February. This is doubtful. It rests almost entirely on L'Angelier's statement to Miss Perry that he expected to see Madeleine that night, with some help from Thuau: but the evidence of both witnesses originates with L'Angelier. There was, however, a more important obstacle to conviction on the first charge. There was no evidence, in spite of a thorough search of druggists' registers, that Madeleine had arsenic in her possession on this night, nor was there sufficient evidence to prove that L'Angelier's illness of the 20th was caused by arsenic.

Accordingly the Lord Justice-Clerk directed the jury to find the accused Not Guilty on the first charge.

This charge was not of itself of great importance. But it had been included in the indictment to paint a picture of a deliberate and persevering course of poisoning. The charges, said the Lord Advocate, "hang together; they throw light up on each other; they are not unconnected acts of crime. Our case is that the administration with intent to poison was truly part of a design to kill."

In view of that connection, if the first charge could not be established, an important part of the picture was missing. This weakness in the Crown case was eagerly seized on by the Dean

of Faculty. "I give my learned friend the option of being im-
paled on one or other of the horns of that dilemma, I care not
which. Either L'Angelier was ill from arsenical poisoning on
the morning of the 20th or he was not. If he was, he had received
arsenic from other hands than the prisoner's. If he was not, the
foundation of the whole case is shaken."

The failure of the first charge was complete and this may
have been a major factor in Madeleine's ultimate acquittal. It
must be remembered, however, that, in framing the indictment,
the Crown had before them L'Angelier's memorandum book
and that they undoubtedly contemplated that it would be before
the jury. The Judges ruled otherwise. If it had been admitted as
evidence, what would have been the result?

First, the relevant entry:—

> "Thurs. 19 Feb. Saw Mimi a few moments was very ill
> during the night."

Was that entry accurate? We cannot test it except by the
other evidence to which I have referred. But where independent evidence is available, it goes to support generally the accuracy of the memoranda in the book. It is therefore reasonable
to assume that this entry is accurate. If so, it supports the view,
hinted at in Madeleine's letter of 14th February and what
L'Angelier told Miss Perry on the 17th, that a meeting took
place between Madeleine and L'Angelier on the night of 19th/
20th February. It also supports the evidence of Miss Perry and
Dr Thomson about the date of the first illness against Mrs
Jenkins' recollection that it was about the 13th. It does not, of
course, prove in any way that Madeleine had arsenic in her
possession on that date or that L'Angelier's illness was due to
that poison. But it links the meeting and the illness in point of
time; and the illness showed the same kind of symptoms as
irritant poisoning.

There was still, however, insufficient evidence for a conviction in the absence of proof that Madeleine possessed the means.
But the case would not have been as deplorably weak as it
turned out to be at the trial. The adverse effect on the other
charges would have been less. The temporal connection between
the meeting and the illness, emphasised by the very simplicity of
the memorandum, must have cast a dark cloud of suspicion

about the rest of the case. *Post hoc ergo propter hoc* may be frowned on by logicians, but it can have a powerful effect on the minds of jurymen.

By the date of the second charge, Sunday/Monday, 22nd/ 23rd February, Madeleine had obtained arsenic. This was the ounce of arsenic mixed with soot which she bought from Murdoch Brothers on Saturday 21st February and intended, according to her two statements (one in the shop and the other that of her declaration), for either the rats at Row or her own cosmetic use.

There is no doubt about the date of L'Angelier's second illness, with its vomiting, purging, pain in the stomach and bowels, and thirst. That was in the early hours of Monday 23rd February. Mrs Jenkins said at first "about the 22nd" but later said "on a Monday morning about 4 o'clock". According to her he was off work for eight days. Dr Thomson was consulted on 23rd February. Tom Kennedy, the cashier at Huggins', agreed that L'Angelier was off work for a week beginning 23rd February. The evidence is all to the same effect. The illness began on 23rd February, a day and a half after Madeleine had bought arsenic. And the symptoms could have been, though they were not necessarily, the symptoms of arsenic poisoning.

But did L'Angelier meet Madeleine on the night of 22nd/23rd February at all? On Saturday 21st, he told Mrs Jenkins that he was not very well and did not intend to go out on Sunday. He did not ask for the pass-key which he needed to return late to his lodgings. Sometimes his fellow-lodger Thuau let him in if he was late, but Thuau did not think L'Angelier was out the night before the second illness.

Neither Miss Perry nor Tom Kennedy can help very much about a meeting on this date. In discussing his first illness with Miss Perry on 2nd March, L'Angelier said that he could not attribute it to any cause. On 9th March he seems to have referred to two illnesses and said "I cannot think why I was so unwell after gettting that coffee and chocolate from her." If this refers to his illness of 23rd February, it may be evidence of a meeting

D

on the night of the 22nd, but it would have been very unsafe to place much reliance on such a slender piece of evidence in a murder trial.

He did not tell Tom Kennedy where he had been or what he had been doing before his illness of the 23rd.

There was only one other piece of evidence before the jury about a meeting on the night of 22nd February. This was not very satisfactory. It was a letter from Madeleine, dated simply "Wednesday" and found in an envelope with an almost indecipherable postmark. In it she said: "I am so sorry to hear you are ill. I hope to God you will soon be better—take care of yourself—do not go to the office this week—just stay at home till Monday.... You did look bad Sunday night and Monday morning." The Lord Advocate argued forcefully that internal evidence proved this letter to have been written on Wednesday 25th February 1857. The Sunday and Monday referred to were therefore the 22nd and 23rd. In reply the Dean of Faculty treated the internal evidence in a somewhat cavalier fashion and argued that the letter could have been written on any Wednesday during the whole course of the correspondence. On the whole the internal evidence supports the Crown theory.

At the trial there was one witness who contradicted the theory. A Post Office official claimed to have seen the letter "R" in the postmark. That letter does not occur in any Post Office abbreviation of "February". On the other hand it is possible to-day, with a strong lens and a good deal of faith, to decipher faintly the figure "2" and the letters "FE". This can only be, if a Wednesday in 1857, Wednesday 25th February. But, of course, that evidence was not before the jury.

The Lord Justice-Clerk did not direct a Not Guilty verdict on this charge but he did hint strongly at his own opinion that the evidence was insufficient. The foundations of the Crown case were sapped.

There are three entries in the memorandum book which have a bearing on the second charge:—

> "Sun. 22 Feb. Saw Mimi in Drawing Room. Promised me
> French Bible. Taken very ill.
> Tues. 24 Feb. Wrote M.
> Wed. 25 Feb. M wrote me."

If this had been admitted as competent and accepted as accurate, it would have closed an awkward gap in the Crown case. It serves to establish the meeting of the 22nd—the Smith parents at least were apparently from home, or the meeting could never have taken place in the drawing-room. It links the meeting and the illness in time. It shows a letter from L'Angelier to Madeleine on Tuesday 24th February: that was obviously how she learned that he had been ill. And it is at least consistent with the Lord Advocate's contention that the letter of "Wednesday" was written on Wednesday 25th February 1857.

There was, of course, still no certain evidence that the second illness, any more than the first, was due to arsenic poisoning. But there was a meeting between a woman who had arsenic in her possession and a man whose continued existence was at least highly inconvenient to her; almost immediately after that meeting the man was taken ill, with symptoms which could have been caused by arsenic. Might the jury not have drawn the inference that they were so caused and that the arsenic was administered by Madeleine?

Between the date of the second charge and that of the final charge of murder there is an interval of one month. For most of that time the two had no opportunity of meeting. The memorandum book mentions two meetings only, on 4th and 5th March, when they seem merely to have exchanged notes.

From 6th to 17th March the Smiths were at Bridge of Allan, where Minnoch formally proposed on the 12th. For part of this time L'Angelier was in Edinburgh. The Smiths and L'Angelier were all in Glasgow, though apparently no meeting took place between Madeleine and L'Angelier, from 17th to 19th March. On 19th March L'Angelier went to Bridge of Allan.

Before she went to Bridge of Allan, as we have seen, Madeleine bought her second ounce of arsenic, this time from Currie in Sauchiehall Street. On 18th March, after her return to Glasgow, she bought another ounce. Why did she need that third ounce? Had she used or lost or destroyed the ounce bought on 6th March? And if she used it, how did she do so?

The Crown theory was that she bought the first ounce from Currie and took it to Bridge of Allan to give it to L'Angelier if he should dare to visit her there. When he did not do so she destroyed it and had to buy more when she returned to Glasgow. With all respect to the Lord Advocate, this is an unconvincing theory. It is not in accordance with Madeleine's character. Her letters show that, once she had decided on a course, she stayed on that course until she reached the end—or at least until she definitely decided to leave it. She was also shrewdly practical. It does not sound like the determined, practical Madeleine that she should waver in her intention to poison L'Angelier (assuming that she had such an intention) or that she should destroy one ounce of arsenic only to buy another almost at once.

It may therefore be that she used the first ounce of arsenic from Currie's for cosmetic purposes. The waste indigo which was used to colour it could have been easily removed, according to the experts, from the white crystals of arsenic.

But if she used one of her three ounces for cosmetic purposes why should she not have used them all in the same way? The Crown could not have conceded even the possibility of cosmetic use without virtually giving up the whole case. They therefore had to propone the theory of destruction.

Madeleine said she used the third packet, that bought on 18th March, as a wash before going with her parents to dine with William Minnoch. There was, of course, no corroboration of her declaration to that effect. Nice young ladies did not use, or did not admit to using, cosmetics. But from many sources it is clear that the use of arsenical face washes was not uncommon in the nineteenth century.

On Sunday 22nd March L'Angelier came back to Glasgow. He left his lodgings at 9 o'clock and returned at 2.30 next morning, too ill to use his pass-key. He died the same morning of arsenic poisoning. Madeleine had arsenic in her possession a few days before his death and there was only her own story in her declaration to account for her disposal of it. But the great question once more was, had the Crown proved a meeting between her and L'Angelier on that night?

There is no doubt of the date of L'Angelier's return. We have the evidence of Mrs Jenkins, of the guard on the 3.30 train from Stirling to Coatbridge that afternoon, and of a fellow-passenger, Thomas Ross, with whom he walked from Coatbridge into Glasgow. He was also seen in Glasgow by at least two other witnesses.

It is almost as clear that his return was unexpected and was probably for the purpose of meeting somebody. Mrs Jenkins said he told her he meant to return to Bridge of Allan by the first train next morning. Thuau, who left Glasgow on the Saturday afternoon or evening, did not expect him to return. On Friday 20th March L'Angelier wrote to William Stevenson, the warehouseman at Huggins', saying that he meant to be home "not later than Thursday morning".

The Crown case, of course, was that he returned to meet Madeleine and that he did so. The foundation of the first part of this theory was a letter from her which was found in L'Angelier's pocket after his death by Stevenson, who remarked at the time that this explained his presence in Glasgow. It was in an envelope addressed to him in Glasgow and postmarked 21st March. It would have been normally deliverable between 1.30 and 3 p.m. the same day. Before he left Glasgow Thuau forwarded it to Bridge of Allan, where it was received about 10.30 on Sunday morning. It was collected from the Post Office there, presumably by L'Angelier.

The letter read: "Why my beloved did you not come to me. Oh beloved are you ill. Come to me sweet one. I waited and waited for you but you came not. I shall wait again to-morrow night same hour and arrangement. Do come sweet love my own dear love of a sweetheart. Come beloved and clasp me to your heart. Come and we shall be happy. A kiss fond love. Adieu with tender embraces ever believe me to be your own ever dear fond M."

In her declaration Madeleine admitted sending this letter. She expected a visit from L'Angelier on Saturday 21st, but he came neither that night nor the next one. Her explanation of why she sent the letter is interesting, if unlikely: "For several years past Mr Minnoch, of the firm of William Houldsworth & Co., has been coming a good deal about my father's house, and about a month ago Mr Minnoch made a proposal of marriage to me, and I gave him my hand in token of acceptance, but no time for the marriage has yet been fixed, and my object in writing the note before mentioned was to have a meeting with M. L'Angelier to tell him that I was engaged to Mr Minnoch."

"If that was her only object," asked the Lord Justice-Clerk, "could she not have told him so in writing? On the supposition that that was her object, her language was most unaccountable. According to that, it was to clasp him to her bosom, and tell him she was engaged to another man—a very odd mode of making known her engagement."

Had L'Angelier been the unenterprising type of suitor that John Anderson had been to Christina Gilmour, the theory could have been advanced that Madeleine was using her engagement to Minnoch as a spur to encourage him. The meeting then, if it ever took place, might have been like the one where John Anderson, like a gentleman, relinquished his claim, to Christina's undying disappointment. But such a theory, of course, is wildly at variance with all the facts.

The Crown case was that L'Angelier's sudden return was caused by Madeleine's urgent appeal. He told Mrs Jenkins "The letter you sent brought me home". From that the argument ran that the two met, at the bedroom window or elsewhere, and that Madeleine handed him a cup of cocoa heavily laced with arsenic. Whether or not she told him of her engagement to Minnoch it was unnecessary to discuss.

The defence attacked each stage of the argument in turn. First, the Dean of Faculty picked on a phrase in a letter written by L'Angelier to Thuau on Monday 16th March from Edinburgh. "Je ne [? n'ai] point de lettres de Mr Mitchell, j'aurais bien voulu savoir ce qu'il me voulait."

"Now we don't know anything of Mr Mitchell," said the Dean, "and the Crown has not told us; but apparently L'Angelier was expecting letters from this Mr Mitchell when he was in Edinburgh. He was anxious to receive them, and anxious to know what Mitchell wanted; and who can tell what letters he received at Bridge of Allan on Sunday morning? Who can tell whether there was not a letter from this Mitchell? and if so, who can tell what it contained?"

An interesting and subtle theory; but does it hold water? We know of one letter L'Angelier received at Bridge of Allan that Sunday morning, the one from Madeleine. It was sent on by Thuau in a covering letter which began "Je trouve cette lettre" —no mention of more than one. It cannot be argued that Mitchell's letter, if there was such a document, was sent direct to Bridge of Allan or directed to him there from Edinburgh. That would not explain L'Angelier's remark to Mrs Jenkins. Undoubtedly the Lord Advocate had the better of this argument. Indeed the Lord Justice-Clerk told the jury that there was no doubt on the evidence that Madeleine's summons had brought him back.

In the next stage of the argument the defence were on stronger ground. The Crown could not positively prove an actual meeting and had to argue that it was inconceivable that L'Angelier, having returned for an assignation with Madeleine, should not have met her.

First, the evidence: Mrs Jenkins said that L'Angelier left her house about 9 o'clock with the pass-key. Soon afterwards, he was seen walking slowly eastwards in Sauchiehall Street, in the direction of Blythswood Square, and some four or five minutes' walk away. At 9.20 he called at a house in Terrace Street, St Vincent Street, which lies another five minutes' walk south and a little west of Blythswood Square, to ask for a Mr McAlester who lodged there. McAlester was out when L'Angelier called and after a little talk with the servant he went away again. We are not told in what direction he went. On his way to Terrace Street, he must have passed within a hundred yards of Blythswood Square, or he may have walked through it without any great deviation from his direct route. The same is true of his way home, if he went directly from Terrace Street. But he was not seen again, so far as the evidence goes, until he returned home about half-past two next morning.

It was "incredible, impossible", said the Lord Advocate, that, having come from Bridge of Allan to meet Madeleine, he did not do so. And in this way he waved aside a considerable amount of negative evidence.

The houseboy, William Murray, attended family prayers with the rest of the household at 7 Blythswood Square about 9

o'clock. He went to bed at 10. A sound sleeper, he heard no
sound until morning. Christina Haggart had been ill that day
and kept her bed until 5 or 6 o'clock. Her fiance, Mackenzie,
arrived between 7 and 8 and stayed in the kitchen while Christina went upstairs to prayers. He left about 10 and Christina
went to bed. The cook, Charlotte McLean, joined her nearer
11 than 10 o'clock. The policeman, Thomas Kavan, was on his
beat in Blythswood Square that night. None of these witnesses
saw L'Angelier that night. None of them even heard anything
out of the way. Janet, Madeleine's young sister, who shared her
bed, said that she and Madeleine both went downstairs to bed
about 10.30 and took about half an hour to undress. Madeleine
was in bed before Janet fell asleep, which was not long after
going to bed.

This is all, of course, negative evidence and does not prove
positively that no meeting took place during the five hours between L'Angelier's call at Terrace Street and his return to his
lodgings. It must be remembered that almost certainly similar
evidence could have been brought for evenings on which there
was in fact a meeting. But it covered one and a half hours of
the missing five and leaves L'Angelier's movements for that
period in utter mystery.

In attacking the Crown contention that a meeting took place,
the Dean first of all reverted to the shadowy Mr Mitchell. "Why
have we not McAlester here to tell us what he knew about him
[L'Angelier] or whether he expected him? Could McAlester
have told us anything about the Mitchell of the letter? Could
not McAlester have explained what was the errand on which
he had come from the Bridge of Allan? Why do the Crown
leave all these different things unexplained on this, the last and
most important day in his history?"

The probable answer is, of course, that McAlester did not
expect a visit from L'Angelier that Sunday night. L'Angelier
may have left his lodgings eagerly, unthinkingly, about 9 o'clock,
then realised that during family prayers any call at Blythswood
Square would be useless—worse than useless, as he might be
seen and Madeleine unnecessarily compromised. A visit to his
friend McAlester might have seemed a way of filling in the time
which must pass before they could meet in safety. But the value

of the Dean's rhetorical questions lay in this, that they were not mere general assertions that L'Angelier might have been anywhere, doing anything, that night: they were linked, however tenuously, with the evidence of the call on McAlester and with a suggestion that arose, however faintly, out of L'Angelier's letter to Thuau.

But the Dean did not omit a fiery, general attack on the Crown case. "Now, gentlemen, from half-past nine till half-past two o'clock—at least five hours—he is absolutely lost sight of; and I was startled at the boldness of the manner in which my learned friend the Lord Advocate met this difficulty. He says it is no doubt a matter of conjecture and inference that in the interval he was in the presence of the prisoner. Good heavens! Inference and conjecture! A matter of inference and conjecture whether, on the night he was poisoned, he was in the presence of the person who is charged with his murder! I never heard such an expression from the mouth of a Crown prosecutor in a capital charge before, as indicating or describing a link in the chain of the prosecutor's case.[1] It is absolutely new to me. I have heard it many a time in the mouth of a prisoner's counsel, and I dare say you will hear it many a time in mine yet before I have done, but for the prosecutor himself to describe one part of his evidence as a piece of conjecture and hypothesis is to use an entire and most startling novelty—and yet my learned friend could not help it. It was honest and fair that he should so express himself if he intended to ask for a verdict at all. For he can ask for this verdict on nothing but a set of unfounded and incredible suspicions and hypotheses."

Suspicions and hypotheses, inference and conjecture? Yes, the Crown case included all these. But unfounded and incredible? Hardly; one can almost feel the jurymen shifting uneasily on their narrow benches at this exaggeration of debate. But the Lord Justice-Clerk in his charge reinforced the doubts that the Dean had, perhaps without their noticing, introduced into their minds. "You must keep in mind that arsenic could only be administered by her if an interview took place with L'Angelier; and that interview, though it may be the result of an

---

[1] To do the Lord Advocate justice, the Dean did not hear the expression in this case either.

inference that may satisfy you morally that it did take place, still rests upon an inference alone; and that inference is to be the ground, and must be the ground, on which a verdict of guilty is to rest. Gentlemen, you will see, therefore, the necessity of great caution and jealousy in dealing with an inference which you may draw from this."

The third stage of the Crown case, that at this hypothetical meeting on Sunday night Madeleine gave L'Angelier the fatal dose, need not detain us long. The Crown assumed that, if the meeting was proved, that was enough to prove the administration. The Lord Justice-Clerk took much the same view. Only the Dean disputed it.

His argument was that L'Angelier was already suspicious of Madeleine and would have been the last man to take poison at her hand. But the Crown case demanded that he should have taken not merely arsenic but an amount hitherto unprecedented in a murder case. It was impossible that, if he had taken the half-ounce suggested by the experts, he would not have noticed the gritty, undissolved crystals passing over his throat; it was incredible that, when his illness came upon him again, he should not have remembered the two previous occasions when he was ill after taking coffee or chocolate from her; yet he never breathed a word of suspicion to anyone.

The counter-argument for the Crown was the common-sense one that Madeleine, having failed twice, was anxious on the third critical occasion to make absolutely sure.

In addition to attacking the Crown case, the defence suggested that L'Angelier took the poison himself, either suicidally or accidentally, in the form of an overdose in the course of his practice of arsenic-eating. There was evidence that, after his disappointment in love from the "lady in Fife", he had attempted suicide. He made to jump from a high window—but waited until someone else was present to prevent his doing so. He picked up a knife—but he did not try to use it and was easily disarmed. He talked of throwing himself from the pier at Leith or over the Dean Bridge in Edinburgh—but did nothing about it. It is no easier to believe in his genuine suicidal intent than it is in Christina Gilmour's.

He was also given to talking about arsenic as an aid to endurance in horses and claimed that he ate it himself to improve his complexion. In order to support a vague case of drug-taking in general, the defence produced evidence that L'Angelier used to pick up handfuls of poppy seed in the seedsman's shop in Dundee and thrust them into his mouth, saying that they were far nicer than filberts. There were also three druggists on the road between Coatbridge and Glasgow who said that, one Sunday night in March (or it may have been April), a man (who was not unlike photographs of L'Angelier) came in and bought 20 to 25 drops of laudanum (or at least some medicine) which he swallowed in the shop. But even if L'Angelier did indulge in this unlikely and slightly comic laudanum-crawl on his eager way from Coatbridge to keep his tryst with Madeleine, it does not explain the presence of 88 grains of arsenic in his stomach. And, although there were several bottles of more or less innocuous medicines in his room, there were no signs of arsenic.

We cannot be sure what effect the defence evidence had on the jury. It did not impress the Lord Justice-Clerk.

"Probably none of you will think for a moment that he went out that night, and that without seeing her, and without knowing what she wanted to see him about if they met, he swallowed above 200 grains of arsenic on the street and that he was carrying it about with him. Probably you will discard that altogether, though it is very important, no doubt, if you come to the conclusion that he did not swallow arsenic; yet, on the other hand, gentlemen, keep in view that that will not of itself establish that the prisoner administered it. The matter may remain most mysterious—wholly unexplained; you may not be able to account for it on any other supposition; but still that supposition or inference may not be a ground on which you can safely and satisfactorily rest your verdict against the pannel.... The great and invaluable use of a jury, after they direct their minds seriously to the case with the attention you have done, is to separate firmly—firmly and clearly in their own minds—suspicion from evidence."

The jury retired. When they returned to deliver their verdict, Lord Hope, no doubt mindful of the scene that had greeted Christina Gilmour's acquittal, expressed the hope that there would be no demonstration. Silence was maintained while the chancellor, or foreman, announced the verdict: on the first charge, Not Guilty by a majority; on the second charge, Not Proven; and on the third charge, Not Proven by a majority. Madeleine was dismissed from the bar. There was one notable absentee from the crowd who congratulated her: John Inglis sat at counsel's table in the well of the court, his head slumped in his hands. Probably he was exhausted.

During the scene which followed the announcement of the verdict the Lord Justice-Clerk's eye fell on a young man in the front of the public gallery who was shouting and brandishing a newspaper. He called one of the officers and instructed him to apprehend the offender. He was brought to the bar after Madeleine had left the dock. Lord Hope gazed at him sternly through his spectacles for a few moments. The young man looked as though he was calculating the years of penal servitude that lay before him.

But the affair ended in anti-climax. "This Court has ordered you to its bar as an offender against its rules; but after looking at you we do not think you are worthy to stand even in that position. You appear a very stupid person. Foolish, silly fellow, go away!" And go away he did, with the jeers of the other spectators ringing in his ears.

Meanwhile Madeleine had been taken down several flights of stairs to the rear entrance to the Parliament House in the Cowgate, where a cab waited. A wardress was dressed to resemble her and sent out from the front of the building among the waiting crowds. Madeleine rode in her cab to Slateford to join the Glasgow train. She did not altogether escape notice. At Slateford another cab drew up behind hers and an emissary of Madame Tussaud made her an offer for the scarf she was wearing. I have been unable to find whether she accepted the offer or not. She certainly refused the many offers of marriage which she claimed to have received as a result of the notoriety of the trial. These offers and the Slateford incident add weight to the comment of the *Examiner* after the trial: "After what passed between her and the deceased L'Angelier, her composure, in our view, wears the aspect of heartless callousness. But that will not prevent her taking her place amongst the celebrities, being run after by crowds, stuck in printshop windows and illustrated newspapers, and modelled in wax. Nay more, she will have scores of candidates for her hand. The passion for notoriety is the insanity of the age throughout the civilised world."

The verdict was generally accepted as inevitable. Madeleine herself was disappointed by it. But a long debate began, one that has not ended yet. Was she guilty or innocent? Did L'Angelier commit suicide? Did he swallow arsenic by mistake —not once but three times? If so, where did he get it? Above all, how was it and whose fault was it that these two people reached a situation where death seemed inevitable? L'Angelier was blamed; Madeleine was blamed; her parents were blamed; society's over-rigid rules were blamed; so was its laxity; and one Scottish patriot blamed Madeleine's English education for her un-Scottish behaviour. The reader can choose almost any theory: he will find some support. Fundamentally, however, Madeleine's misfortune was to be born in an age whose conventions did not suit her sensuous nature. She took a frank pleasure in sex: that, for a woman of her times, whether married or not, as Miss Tennyson Jesse has pointed out, was outrageous. It was also her misfortune to be attracted by a man whom she could never have married without losing the life to which she was accustomed and which, in spite of occasional boredom, she enjoyed. And it was her misfortune that she tired of him before he tired of her, or at least before he was prepared to let her go.

But was she guilty? We are never likely to know. It is about as certain as any statement about a jury's reasoning can be that the verdict was due to the Crown's failure to bring the time and the place and the loved one all together. In the circumstances there must always be a doubt. And yet a positive finding of Not Guilty—virtually Innocent—would have involved a series of strange coincidences. If ever a case called for the Not Proven verdict, it was Madeleine Smith's.

From a general impression of the evidence most people seem to believe in her guilt. The longer it is since I have read the evidence the more convinced I am of guilt. But any detailed study of that evidence reveals great gaps in the Crown case; and an accused person is always entitled to escape through these gaps.

The strength of the Crown case, as presented, lies in the question, how could she hope to extricate herself from the position in which she found herself—threatened with blackmail through her letters? Paradoxically, one strong point in the defence is that L'Angelier's death was not the way out; that death inevitably resulted in the discovery and disclosure of the very letters which she had to keep a secret. Of course, it may be said that many murderers do not think far ahead; she may have killed L'Angelier as a first step, to remove the human blackmailer without thinking of how to get rid of the weapons that still lay in his armoury.

But were the letters Madeleine's real danger? Or was L'Angelier himself a greater threat?

Earlier I drew attention to the use in Madeleine's letters of the words "husband" and "wife", coupled with references to marriage in the future, indicating that she did not consider herself married and looking forward to a church ceremony. But in Scotland there were other forms of marriage, irregular but none the less legally binding. Madeleine may or may not have had these in mind but the question calls for consideration.

There were three forms of irregular marriage in all. Today only one remains and we can ignore it. That is marriage by habit and repute, where a man and woman live together as husband and wife and are generally recognised as such and believed to be married. To build up this reputation takes time and publicity. Both were lacking in the L'Angelier-Smith relationship.

Then a man and woman could simply declare themselves to be man and wife. No witnesses were necessary, though if a dispute rose in the future about their marital status witnesses were obviously useful to prove the case. But all that was needed was a declaration of consent to present marriage as opposed to a promise, or statement of future intention. As Madeleine's letters are full of references to future marriage and they are our only evidence, we can pass over any idea that she had contracted a marriage in this way, in spite of Nigel Morland's argument for it in *That Nice Miss Smith*.[1]

But there was a third form of irregular marriage, more insidious in its action. When a man and woman promised to take one another in marriage at a future date and after that promise, and in reliance on the engagement, the woman allowed sexual intercourse to take place, that fact of itself constituted marriage. The presumption (or fiction) was that at that moment the parties gave their consent to present instead of future marriage. Both were bound in wedlock from that time onward. And, although from the nature of things it was usually the woman who brought an action to have the marriage judicially declared to exist, it was competent for the man to do so.

This third form of irregular marriage—by promise *subsequente copula*—is highly relevant in considering Madeleine Smith's status. From her letters and L'Angelier's scroll which I have quoted above, there is abundant written evidence that promises to marry had been interchanged. The first requisite existed.

That the second requisite also existed is quite clear from the letters, which show conclusively that on the night of Thursday 6th June 1856, in the woods beside her father's house of Rowaley, Madeleine Smith surrendered her person (as the too passive phrase goes) to her affianced lover. It does not matter who took the initiative. Conventionally both parties attributed that to L'Angelier:[2] but the seduction was almost certainly mutual.

There is then a promise of marriage followed by intercourse. That, however, is not yet enough to constitute marriage. The intercourse must not merely follow the promise in point of time; it must be permitted on the faith of the promise. The Courts have on the whole taken a very reasonable view and held that, unless there is something to suggest the contrary (for example, that the woman was as free of her favours with other men), it was permitted for that reason. There do not seem to be any facts to justify taking the L'Angelier–Smith case out of the general presumptive rule. So we can proceed on the footing that

[1] Frederick Muller, 1957.

[2] Madeleine: "Were you angry at me for allowing you to do what you did?" **L'Angelier**: "Why, Mimi, did you give way after your promises?"

Madeleine allowed the intercourse only because of the promise to marry.

The essence of marriage by the law of Scotland is consent. The foundation of even an irregular marriage of this kind is presumed consent. Now, supposing that Madeleine did not know of the legal doctrine, as seems to be the case from the terms of her letters with their references to marriage as a thing of the future, can she be said to have given her consent, actually or as matter of presumption, to present marriage? In 1933 it was held that such ignorance meant that there was no marriage because there was no consent.

But the law in the middle of the nineteenth century was not so clear as it was to become later. In 1823 it had been suggested, on the highest judicial authority, that it made no difference to the legal situation that the woman was unaware of the result on her status when she allowed her lover to consummate the promise to marry. If she learned later of the legal rule, she could then have the marriage judicially established. On this basis Madeleine would have been able, had she so wished, to have herself declared to be, in law as well as in her own signature, Mimi L'Angelier. More important is the fact that L'Angelier could have invoked the aid of the Court to the same result. It is true that this was not expressly determined until 1931. But, if there is a marriage, that marriage must in logic be binding on both parties or on neither. It is difficult to justify the view that some legal writers have held, that only the woman could bring an action to have a marriage declared on this ground, except on the theory that she had a personal privilege to hold the man at her disposal for as long as she chose.

Peter Hunt in *The Madeleine Smith Affair* quotes evidence (not adduced at the trial) that L'Angelier believed that he was married to Madeleine and he may well have been right in this belief.

At the risk of adding to the confusion, it may be said that, where the conduct of the parties as a whole shows that they did not regard themselves as married, the presumption of consent will be displaced and there will be no marriage. Both L'Angelier's and Madeleine's letters refer to marriage as having yet to take place. That is not necessarily conclusive. There have been several cases where such references have been more or less tacitly taken to be to a regular church ceremony and it has been assumed that a woman is entitled to such a formal and public ceremony as well as the more private proceedings that led to the irregular marriage.

All that can be said, without a tedious citation of authority inappropriate to this book, is that Madeleine Smith very probably became Madeleine L'Angelier in the woods at Row on 6th June 1856. If this is so, it was a marriage which could be undone only by death or divorce. Even if Madeleine had learned of the law and only believed there was a danger that a Court would hold her to be married (and the dropping of the words "husband" and "wife" after the reconciliation of February 1857 may suggest the realisation of this danger), the only ways of escape must have seemed the same to her mind—death or divorce. Divorce was out of the question.

If L'Angelier were in law her husband, he and not the letters would be the major obstacle to a settled married life with Minnoch. Discovery of the letters might—indeed would—cause scandal. But they might not be discovered. And if they were discovered only after her marriage to Minnoch the scandal might be allowed to lie, a skeleton in the family cupboard (even with the door ajar), and a brave or brazen face might prevent its excessive interference with the solid and expensive security which was her object. But a husband alive when she married Minnoch could bring the whole thing about her ears at any time. The marriage with Minnoch would be shown for what it was, no marriage but a crime calling for severe punishment. If she were, or even might be, as she had so often signed herself, Mimi L'Angelier, Emile must die. He showed no sign of doing so naturally; then she must help nature.

Had this case been argued before the jury, it could have done nothing, of course, to make good the failure of the Crown to prove the critical meetings between Madeleine and L'Angelier. But it might have strengthened the Crown case by meeting in advance one criticism made by the Dean of Faculty: "What possible motive could there be—I mean what possible advantage could she expect from L'Angelier ceasing to live, so long as the letters remained? Without the return of his letters she

gained nothing. Her object—her greatest desire—that for which
she was yearning with her whole soul was to avoid the exposure
of her shame. But the death of L'Angelier, with these letters in
his possession, instead of ensuring that object, would have been
perfectly certain to lead to the immediate exposure of everything that had passed between them."

It is a perfectly valid point and one that has troubled many
who have studied the trial. But it was not met as I have suggested it could have been met, although it was not altogether
overlooked by the Lord Advocate. In addressing the jury he
said, in dealing with one of the attacks that was going to be
made on L'Angelier: "In other circumstances, and had matters
not gone so far between these unfortunate persons, it might have
been considered a dishonourable and ungenerous thing in a man
in L'Angelier's position to take that line of conduct. But
whether it was or no is not material to the matter in hand. I
must say, however, that in the position in which the prisoner
and L'Angelier stood, I do not see how he, as a man of honour,
could allow this marriage with Mr Minnoch to take place and
remain silent. *It may be doubted whether they were not man
and wife by the law of the land. It is needless to discuss this
question. There certainly were materials in the correspondence
to show that this view might be maintained by L'Angelier had
he chosen to do it.*"

That was the only reference in argument to what I am persuaded lies at the root of the whole case.

Christina Gilmour and Madeleine Smith: did they murder
their husbands or did they not? Each had the means and each
had a motive, Madeleine's being much the stronger. Christina
had the opportunity as well; we do not know about Madeleine.
They were fortunate in the Judge who presided. He strongly
suggested to each jury that Not Proven would be the appropriate verdict. Tradition says that Lord Justice-Clerk Hope was
unpopular with the bar because of his arrogant nagging of counsel: but no one could call him a hanging Judge—neither Christina nor Madeleine nor the anonymous young man with the
newspaper.

They were also—particularly Madeleine—fortunate in their defenders. Thomas Maitland's speech received great praise at the time but it has been forgotten—overshadowed like his client by his successor. John Inglis' speech for Madeleine has few if any rivals in any country. It is one of the rare forensic speeches that preserve some (though not all) of their magic when read in black print on white paper, without the speaker's personality to add force to the sheer logic of his argument. Its closely knit reasoning and its superbly balanced appeals to the emotions of the jury have been analysed time and time again and I am not going to repeat the process. It is enough to quote in silent contrast the opening sentences of the two speeches.

First, Maitland: "I cordially join with the Lord Advocate in reminding you that you are here dealing with a question of life and death. In criminal courts this is never a question of probability or of inference but of strict legal evidence. Unless the public prosecutor has made guilt certain and innocence impossible you cannot convict."

John Inglis' first sentence passed at once into legend: "Gentlemen of the jury, the charge against the prisoner is murder and the punishment of murder is death; and that simple statement is sufficient to suggest to us the awful solemnity of the occasion which brings you and me face to face."

After their trials both young women lived for many years. I have already told how Christina died nearly sixty-two years after her acquittal, in December 1905. Again she was surpassed by Madeleine, who survived for almost seventy-one years. She died in America on 12th April 1928 under the name of Lena Wardle Sheehy. She had found marriage to her taste, for she married twice after her trial, first George Wardle, an associate of William Morris in London and second an American named Sheehy who died in 1926. The second and third names on her gravestone commemorate her recognised husbands: "Lena" was Bessie's pet name for her. "Mimi" and L'Angelier were both forgotten.

When her second husband died, a film company approached

her with a suggestion that she should take part in a film of her own story. She refused and was threatened with deportation as an undesirable alien. The threat failed. She was then ninety years old, in poor health and going blind.

So far as I know Christina and Madeleine never met. Had they done so, what tales they might have told had their very different characters allowed frank communication between them. But would their memories have served them accurately?

On Christina's death certificate her husband's name is wrongly given as "Matthew". At the end of her life Madeleine referred to L'Angelier as "Louis". Time had brought oblivion.

(III)

ALFRED JOHN MONSON

Oh, dry the starting tear, for they were heavily insured.
W. S. Gilbert

ANOTHER case where both attempted murder and murder were charged was that of Alfred John Monson, who was accused of these crimes in 1893 along with Edward Sweeny *alias* Davis *alias* Scott. In each case the alleged victim was Windsor Dudley Cecil Hambrough. The two crimes were said to have been committed within a few hours of one another, and the accused men were credited with the versatility of using drowning as their first method and shooting as their second. Sweeney (or Davis or Scott) did not appear in the dock; he had got away. His name was formally called by the macer (court officer) and as he did not answer the summons he was outlawed. The trial started on an appropriate note of mystery.

The social background of the Monson trial was very different from the solid respectability of Christina Gilmour and Madeleine Smith. Monson, the black sheep of a good family,[1] and Cecil Hambrough moved in faster circles, where some of good Queen Victoria's subjects dispensed with the staid virtues we associate with her name.

But for the financial embarrassments of Major Dudley Albert Hambrough, Cecil's father, there would have been no trial. He came of age in 1870 and succeeded as life tenant or heir of entail to estates at Ventnor, Isle of Wight, and in Middlesex which, with brick royalties and investment income, produced £4,680 a year. Income tax ranged from 2d to $6\frac{1}{2}$d in the pound. Even so, his income was not enough for the major. By 1885 he had spent fifteen years' income and contracted debts from time to time of £37,000. As security he mortgaged his life interest with

[1] His uncle, Sir Edmund John Monson, was at the time of the trial British Ambassador in Vienna and in 1896 became Ambassador in Paris.

the Eagle Insurance Company and took out life policies for
£42,000. This left him with interest and premiums to pay. In
1886 he borrowed another £2,500: his credit was then exhausted.
Not surprisingly he fell into arrears with the interest and the
Eagle Company foreclosed in 1890. Next year they became
absolute owners of the life interest.

In 1890 the major met Beresford Loftus Tottenham, a financial agent operating under the name of Kempton & Co. at 8
Delahaye Street, London. Just over thirty, he had already enjoyed a variegated career. He served in the 10th Hussars, then
joined the Turkish Army under Baker Pasha, a former commanding officer of that regiment, whose career in the British
Army came to a sudden end in 1875 when he was convicted of
indecent assault on a young woman in a railway compartment.
After Baker Pasha's death in 1887, Tottenham took part in the
suppression of the Cretan insurrection of 1889. He then became
a financial agent and in that capacity took the impecunious
major in hand in order to re-arrange his affairs.

First he tried to re-insure the major's life. The existing
policies were at a high premium and Tottenham's idea was to
insure at a lower rate and then surrender the existing policies for
£5,000 or £6,000. He also planned to buy the life interest back
from the Eagle Company. The scheme failed because the major
could not pass the necessary medical examinations. Nothing
daunted, Tottenham engaged Dr Hambleton to get the major
into a state of health in which he would be accepted as a first-
class life. During the training period he paid the major £7 and
the doctor £3 a week. In security he received two mortgages
over the major's assets, one for £1,500 to cover advances already
made (with, as he put it, a bonus) and the other for £1,000 to
cover future advances and his commission.

Major Hambrough was anxious about the education of his
elder son, Cecil, then a boy of seventeen destined for the army.
About this time Tottenham met Alfred John Monson, an army
tutor, and introduced him to the major, who engaged him to
educate Cecil for his military career. His salary was to be £300
a year "when my financial arrangements are made". Unfortunately that day never came and Monson remained unpaid.

Once in the Hambrough circle, Monson joined heartily in

the business of re-arranging the major's affairs. The major's first reaction was to ask for a regular allowance. He did not get it, but Monson gave him £160—£25 to pay for his two daughters going to Germany, £15 for travelling expenses and £120 to open a bank account. From time to time he also obliged with a sovereign or a cheque for £2 or £3—to such straits was the life tenant of £4,680 reduced.

The major, a practised hand by now, granted further mortgages over his assets (whatever these were) in favour of Monson. In the witness-box he suggested that some of his signatures were forged but, although he knew that Monson claimed to hold mortgages for more than £11,000, he took no steps to challenge them.

Meanwhile Monson was trying to buy the major's life interest from the Eagle Company. The major insisted that Monson was only his agent. He understood that Monson would pay a deposit of £600 and that then he (the major) would have a contract open for completion for a number of months. Monson had other ideas. He was acting for himself. His plan, like Tottenham's, involved re-insuring the major's life, borrowing on the policies and buying the life interests. Then, when Cecil came of age, the entail was to be barred.

About the end of 1891 the Eagle Company agreed to sell to Monson. But he could not pay the necessary deposit and his solicitor, Hanrott, concluded the agreement in his own name. Later Monson proposed to take it over from Hanrott, who repudiated any obligation. After proceedings in the High Court of Justice, Mr Justice Chitty gave Monson the contract. He still, however, could not complete the purchase and again had to turn to Hanrott for help, agreeing to give him a quarter share in the bargain. The deposit was at last paid. But the purchasers could not raise the full price and the transaction fell through in July 1892.

In the meantime Monson's insistence that he was acting for himself had led to a breach of relations early in 1892. The major's solicitor, Morris Natali Fuller, was instructed to obtain a full statement of the payments made by Monson on behalf of the Hambroughs, father and son.

Monson's reply was not helpful. To frighten Fuller off, he

told him that the major was an undischarged bankrupt and had
acted criminally in obtaining credit in that situation. This statement was inaccurate. The major had never been adjudicated
bankrupt. But a receiving order (the first step towards that end)
had been pronounced and an agreement reached with his creditors to pay them 4s 3d in the pound.

Negotiations between Monson and Fuller continued for some
time. Monson stuck to his plan to buy for himself. Fuller proposed that Monson should buy the life interests only under an
agreement to sell later to the major at an agreed profit. No
compromise was possible and the negotiations broke down. The
danger to the major was that, if Monson was absolute owner
of the life interests when Cecil came of age, he and Cecil could
do as they pleased; and by this time Cecil was very much under
Monson's influence. It was not surprising. The major was living
in lodgings in London and often had to move from one place to
another. Life with Monson was outwardly at least more settled
and comfortable.

There was more trouble in 1892. The major wanted Cecil, as
a Hampshire man, to enter the army through the Hampshire
Militia. Monson suggested the Yorkshire Militia but the major
disagreed. He did allow Monson, however, to take Cecil to
York to buy his uniform: Monson explained that his London
tailor would not make it. While they were in York, Cecil was
gazetted to the Yorkshire Militia. In spite of his father's appeals
he did not return south but stayed with Monson.

The major also wrote to Monson urging that Cecil should
return. To one of these appeals Monson replied in a phrase that
took on a sinister colour from the sequel: "I am not your son's
keeper."

Although he had already failed once, Monson was still trying
to buy the life interests from the Eagle Company. There were
now two bidders. On one side were Monson, Tottenham and
Cecil. Hanrott was no longer with them but a new name appeared, that of Adolphus Jerningham. On the other side were
Major Hambrough, Dr Hambleton and Henry Prince, who had
succeeded Fuller as the major's solicitor.

The "Monson syndicate" was virtually a one-man affair—
Tottenham. Cecil was a minor with nothing but his army pay

and £5–£10 from Tottenham. His expectations were in the future. Jerningham was described by Tottenham as "living in expectation of succeeding to a considerable property". What he actually had was doubtful, even to Jerningham. At the time he needed help himself and could not have purchased the life interests. He understood that he was to be associated with the project as "a kind of trustee for young Hambrough". He had private means from house property but did not know how much: all he knew was that it came to him through his marriage. He expected to succeed to a "position of some distinction" but counsel had advised him, he thought wrongly, that his expectation was not a good one.

Monson too was receiving financial help from Tottenham. His position had been insecure for some time. He had no private means and only one pupil, Cecil, for most of the time: and there was little chance of any payment from him. His wife had a prospective interest in £910 if she survived her mother, but that interest had been mortgaged since 1890 and Mrs Monson, like the major, was in arrears with the interest. In August 1892 Monson was adjudicated bankrupt and he was still undischarged at the date of his trial. The recoverable assets were £25, 5s and the liabilities £2,300.

Early in 1893 Mrs Monson recovered judgment in an undefended suit for £800 against Cecil for board, lodging and education. Tottenham bought the judgment for £200 cash. The episode is typical of the shifts by which the Monsons lived and Tottenham sought his profit.

The Monson syndicate does not inspire much confidence. But it still planned to buy the major's life interest, valued by the Eagle Company at £40,000. They could not now insure the major's life. But they had Cecil.

The financial standing of the major's syndicate is not very clear either. The major himself had nothing. Dr Hambleton was only a prospective trustee to hold the estate for the major. Henry Price was a solicitor, not a principal in the business. He did, however, try to win Cecil from Monson by offering to provide him with an efficient military tutor, make him an adequate allowance until he came of age and place a hunter at his disposal.

After a good deal of correspondence, which periodically descended on Monson's side to acrimony, the Eagle Company decided on 29th March 1893 to sell to the major's syndicate. The contract was to be completed by 1st August but this was not done. The company's solicitor was too busy.

Monson and Cecil protested without success. Thus matters stood in the spring of 1893.

In May 1893 Mr and Mrs Monson, their three children and Cecil left Yorkshire, where they had been living, and went to Ardlamont in Argyllshire. This estate lies at the south end of the most westerly of the three claws with which the Cowal peninsula makes to grasp the island of Bute and is a pleasant, if somewhat inaccessible spot, with a white-harled house looking towards Arran.

For some time Messrs J. & F. Anderson, W. S., Edinburgh, had advertised the estate for sale on behalf of its owner, Major John Lamont. In May they let it for the season at a rent of £450 to Cecil Hambrough and Adolphus Jerningham. At least their signatures appeared on the lease as lessees. At the trial Jerningham had said he had never seen the lease, let alone signed it. As it was held incompetent to lead evidence of a crime not charged in the indictment, the Crown was not allowed to lead evidence of forgery. Next year, however, in a pamphlet entitled "The Ardlamont Mystery—Solved", Monson admitted that Jerningham did not sign. He said that Jerningham was "elected" to stand as trustee for Cecil. In this capacity he was about to incur a personal liability of £40,000 "so that a further liability of £500 would be of small consequence to him and he was asked to stand as guarantee for the rent of Ardlamont on behalf of Cecil, to which he readily agreed. Certainly he was aware that Tottenham was providing the funds, as he was being financed by Tottenham to a considerable extent himself."

When the lease was sent to Riseley Hall (Monson's house in Yorkshire), "Jerningham was not available at the time, and therefore his name was signed under a distinct authority given by him, and without any fraudulent intention whatever". In his evidence in a later case, Monson said he signed Jerningham's name himself.

After this shady preamble the Monsons and Cecil took up residence in May. The Monsons' governess Edith Hiron accompanied them. The domestic staff consisted of a cook, a housemaid and a kitchenmaid, who were joined about 10th June by Alexandrina Shand, nursemaid for the younger children. A butler, James Wright, was added to the strength on 9th August and took over the duty of waiting at table from the housemaid. There were also outside servants—gamekeepers, gardeners, joiners and the like, who were paid by the landlords. It was no wonder that Cecil preferred this life to his father's cheap lodgings.

The comfort was, of course, being paid for by Tottenham, who was allowing Cecil £10 a week. He also paid for some extras, including the move to Ardlamont. He wrote: "Herewith cheque for £40, just to go on with. I conclude the moving job can be financed on that, and until the next week am short, as I have to keep a balance at the Bank of England, or they give you notice to close the account. Next week a further remittance shall be sent. I have made the cheque payable to you for facility in cashing, but naturally I don't debit you with this oof, but look on it as a payment made on the general account of the show."

In July Mrs Monson opened a bank account for housekeeping purposes at the Royal Bank of Scotland, Tighnabruaich, with £15.

In the same month Tottenham visited Ardlamont and discussed with Monson and Cecil the purchase of the estate. When he got back to London Monson wrote to him: "I have just returned home, and have seen the agents to-day and fully discussed the question of the purchase here. The existing mortgage on the property is £37,000 at 4 per cent. . . . They eventually agreed to accept £48,000. . . . They are willing to accept £250 as a deposit, on the contract being signed by Mrs Monson, to be limited to June, 1894. [This was the month when Cecil would come of age.] The contract is now being drawn and will be ready in the course of a week or so. . . . I have told C. that the price is £50,000—£1,000 each for division; thus he will have to raise £13,000 to enable him to complete next year."

At the end of July Tottenham wrote to Cecil, enclosing a cheque for £250 to meet the deposit: "I have dated the cheque 10th, because, as you know, I have an awful lot of irons in the fire, and the oof don't always turn up as expected."

Now that Cecil was living in the seclusion of Argyll, Monson set vigorously about insuring his life. His first two attempts, with the Scottish Provident Institution and the Liverpool London and Globe Company, failed because he could not satisfy the companies that he or his wife had an insurable interest worth £50,000, the sum proposed. The nearest he got to submitting evidence was a letter, bearing to be from Cecil to the Liverpool London and Globe Company: "I am requested by Mrs Agnes Maud Monson to write to inform you that she has an interest in my life to the extent of £26,000. I have given her an undertaking to pay her this sum on my attaining twenty-one, if I should live until then. Yours truly, W. D. C. Hambrough."

Monson was in the Glasgow office of the company on 2nd August when this proposal was finally refused. The resident secretary described him as looking "a little disappointed, as anyone would in such circumstances. He did not say anything except 'It is a pity'."

Earlier that day he called at the Glasgow office of the Mutual Life Insurance Company of New York. He told the district manager, McLean, that he "was trustee and guardian of Mr Hambrough, a young gentleman who was coming into a fortune of £200,000, that Mr Hambrough was about to purchase the Ardlamont estate, that Mrs Monson was to advance £20,000 to secure the purchase of Ardlamont, and that he wanted to effect an insurance on Mr Hambrough's life to cover the advance."

McLean had to consult his London office, but in the meantime he arranged for Cecil to be medically examined. Monson asked specifically that the insurance should be carried through by 8th August, as he was going to Edinburgh that day to complete the purchase of the estate.

On the morning of 8th August Monson called again and was given two temporary policies of £10,000 each, subject to head office approval. In exchange he handed over a cheque for £194 3s 4d drawn by Mrs Monson on the Tighnabruaich branch of the Royal Bank. He also handed McLean a letter: "Will you kindly deliver my two insurance policies of £10,000 each to Mr and Mrs Monson, as I have assigned the policies to Agnes Maud Monson for proper considerations received? Mrs Monson will therefore be the person to whom the insurance is payable in the event of my death. Kindly acknowledge receipt of this notice and oblige, yours truly, W. D. C. Hambrough."

Some weeks later Tottenham "accidentally" left with McLean a copy of another letter, this time to Mrs Monson, in which Cecil (if he in fact wrote the original) told her "I am willing that you should hold the policies as security for all moneys due to you from me, and as security against all liabilities incurred by you on my behalf; and in the event of my death occurring before the repayment of these moneys you will be the sole beneficiary of these policies."

From Glasgow Monson went to Edinburgh, where he saw William Hugh Murray, W.S., the partner of Messrs Anderson who handled all matters connected with the Ardlamont estate. In spite of Monson's letter to Tottenham in July, this was his first meeting with Murray and there was no understanding whatsoever about the price. Messrs Anderson had been advertising the estate for sale for £85,000 and wanted to get something at least near that sum. Monson opened the discussion by saying that his commission from Hambrough was to offer not more than £60,000. Murray replied that, as the difference between the two figures was so great, there was no use saying anything more about it.[1]

There the discussion ended. Murray, however, had some other comments to make in his evidence about Monson's report to Tottenham. Had there been any question of a deposit, for example, he would have wanted some thousands; he would certainly not have accepted £250.

In cross-examination for the defence, Comrie Thomson ingeniously suggested that Monson had in fact accurately represented the price to be paid. If the debts of £37,000 [actually £30,000] secured over the estate were allowed to remain as a burden on the estate and were taken over by the purchaser, the seller would, on Monson's figures, receive the equivalent of

[1] A month or so later the estate was sold for £70,000. By then notoriety had brought its value down.

£85,000—relief from £37,000 debt *plus* £48,000 in cash. But
the argument overlooks the final passage of the letter to Tottenham: "I have told C. that the price is £50,000—£1,000 each for
division; *thus he will have to raise £13,000 to enable him to complete next year.*" In other words, Cecil was to find £13,000, of
which £1,000 was to go into the pocket of each of the partners,
Monson and Tottenham, and £11,000—the difference between
£48,000 and the debts of £37,000—to the seller of the estate.

It is no surprise to find Monson and Tottenham both scheming to get what they can out of Cecil. But believers in honour
among thieves will be disillusioned to learn that in this instance
Monson was scheming to get what he could out of Tottenham.
He talked of £1,000 each from Cecil's cheque for £13,000; but
he knew, none better, that this was a fictitious profit. What he
was really looking for in that letter of July was Tottenham's
cheque for the £250 "deposit".

After all, he needed the money. He was trying to insure
Cecil's life and knew that he would have to pay a substantial
premium for a substantial policy. And that was how the cheque
was used. Cecil endorsed it to Mrs Monson. She paid it into her
housekeeping account and then drew a cheque for the premium
due to the Mutual Life Insurance Company of New York.

But Tottenham, it will be remembered, had post-dated the
cheque to 10th August. Almost as soon as he sent it off, he
realised that he had only Monson's word for the satisfactory
negotiations for purchase. He instructed the Bank of England to
withhold payment. As the Royal Bank had rashly honoured
Mrs Monson's cheque for the premium before Tottenham's
cheque was cleared, the account was overdrawn. Monson promised to pay in £1,000 but failed to do so.

According to the evidence, the results of Monson's financial
operations up to 9th August were these: he was still himself an
undischarged bankrupt without means; his wife's bank account
was overdrawn, but she held two temporary policies for £10,000
each on Cecil's life; she also held a letter from Cecil (or so it
appeared) telling her that she was to be the sole beneficiary
under the policies in the event of his death as her debtor.

As Cecil was a minor, by English law (and he was an Englishman) he could not validly assign the policies. All the witnesses

who knew him agreed that Monson knew this, as one of them put it, "as well as any man in England". His understanding of the law of Scotland is not so clear. Tottenham said that he personally thought the assignation was valid by Scots law but that Monson disagreed. There may be some support for this in the fact that, after Cecil's death, it was Tottenham and not Monson who pressed for payment under the policies. The two men were, however, so closely associated that this circumstance is less significant than it might otherwise have been. And, of course, if Tottenham did succeed in making the company pay up, they would have paid in the first instance to Mrs Monson.

But, if Monson thought the assignation was of no value, why did he trouble to hand notice of it to the insurance company?

Monson's understanding is more important than the actual law. If he thought that his wife would receive £20,000 on Cecil's death at any age, even if that belief was wrong, he had a substantial motive for wishing Cecil dead. That would not prove that he killed him, but it would be matter for the jury's consideration. But if his understanding was, correctly, that Cecil could not validly assign the policies until he reached the age of twenty-one, Monson had a very good reason—quite apart from any mere ethical scruples—for not killing him at the age of twenty.

On his return from Edinburgh on 8th August Monson travelled from Glasgow to Greenock with James Donald, a partner of Hanna Donald & Wilson, engineers and shipbuilders, Paisley. Monson had been negotiating with them for the purchase, on Cecil's behalf, of the steam yacht *Alert*. The price was £1,200, to be paid on 10th August.

At Greenock both men embarked on a steamer for Kames, the nearest pier to Ardlamont. During the voyage Donald saw Monson talking to a respectable-looking stranger in his early thirties, slightly built, with a sallow complexion and a small moustache. Monson told Donald that he was "a person from the estate office who was going to see Mr Hambrough".

This description was curious. Monson told everyone else that

E

he was an engineer, Scott, who had come to inspect the boilers of the yacht which he was about to purchase.

Neither statement was true. "Scott" never went to the yacht. He lived as a guest for two days at Ardlamont, although the governess Edith Hiron, with the instinct of her kind, thought he was not quite a gentleman: he talked like a Londoner and dropped his "h's". On 10th August, the day of Cecil's death, he boarded a steamer at Tighnabruaich and was not seen by any of the witnesses again. This was, of course, the mysterious "Edward Sweeney *alias* Davis *alias* Scott" who was charged along with Monson and formally outlawed.

As the evidence relating to his identity is only of minor importance in relation to the crimes charged, it is as well to deal here with the question. Monson told P.C. McCalman, Tighnabruaich, on 10th August that he did not know the man, who had been engaged by Cecil Hambrough to look after the yacht. On 24th August he told McLean of the Mutual Life Insurance Company that Scott came from Stockton-on-Tees and had been engaged by Hambrough. On 27th August he told the constable that he understood that Scott had started business as an engineer in Glasgow but had failed; he was, however, well known in Greenock. Widespread newspaper advertisement by the defence failed to trace him.

His real name was Edward Sweeney and he used the name Davis for his bookmaking business. He had been seen several times in Monson's company in London. About Bank Holiday (7th August 1893) Edward Sweeney left London and returned about a week later. Monson was arrested on 30th August and early in September Sweeney left the lodgings in Pimlico where he had been staying with the rest of his family. In their turn they went away at the end of October, leaving no address.

According to his brother George, Edward said he was going to Bournemouth. The family theory was that he had taken a voyage to Australia for the benefit of his health (literally). George thought Edward was silent because he did not want his mother to worry about his health. He could not explain why complete disappearance should be reassuring.

In his pamphlet Monson explains Scott's position in this way: "I mentioned to Mr Donald, as stated in the evidence, that

Scott came from London, to see Hambrough and myself, on financial business relating to Hambrough; and as this financial business necessitated him coming to Ardlamont, Hambrough and I passed him off as Mr Scott, who had come to take charge of the yacht *Alert* for a week. The question about the boilers which arose through the evidence of Mr Steven, the factor, and Miss Hiron, was perfectly true. Hambrough had been told that the boilers were defective, and he told Scott to go on board and see that the engineer, who lived on board, made a careful examination of the boilers in his presence." Monson's logic and his standard of "perfect truth" were both curious.

It is convenient to refer to this man as "Scott", the name under which he went at Ardlamont. On the morning of 9th August he went with Monson to borrow a boat from Stewart McNicol, the estate joiner, for two nights. Monson explained that they wanted to do some splash-net fishing, which involves the use of a long net, one end of which is tied to a large stone which is made fast on shore. One man rows the boat and another stands in the stern, paying out the net as they go, returning in a semi-circular course to the shore, where the other end of the net is in its turn made fast. The boat remains in the middle of the semicircle and the two occupants splash the water, driving the fish into the net. A good deal of water accumulates in the boat from the splashing and again when, at the end of the day, the net is hauled inboard. Obviously a stable boat is desirable, especially for the man standing in the stern, and Monson told McNicol that his boat, being broader, would be safer than one which Cecil had already hired for the season from Donald McKellar, Tighnabruaich. Monson had in fact borrowed Mc-Nicol's boat twice before, as McKellar's was "a bit of a crank". There had, however, been no accident, though splash-net fishing was one of the regular amusements at Ardlamont.

There was another difference between the two boats. Mc-Kellar's had no plug-hole in it. He did not think it necessary, as it was quite easy to tilt the boat up when it was on shore to get rid of any water. McNicol's had a properly bored plug-hole, stopped with a cork.

After launching McNicol's boat about 11 o'clock, Monson and Scott rowed it to Ardlamont Bay, where they joined the children on the beach. After lunch, Alexandrina Shand, the nursemaid, saw Monson and Scott rowing about in a varnished boat—apparently McKellar's, the one originally hired. The children joined them for about twenty minutes. The two men then rowed by themselves for another three quarters of an hour. Cecil and Mrs Monson were walking on the cliffs to the south of the bay.

Eventually the boat put into shore and Monson left Scott alone in it for about twenty minutes. No one saw what he was doing. He then took off his shoes and socks and pulled the boat up on shore.

That night Monson and Cecil went out splash-net fishing. In the early hours of the next morning they returned to the house, both wet through as a result of a mishap of some kind.

After a few hours' sleep they went out shooting; Scott went with them to pick up any rabbits that might fall to either gun. About 9 o'clock Cecil Hambrough died from a gunshot wound through the head. The death was attributed to accident. On 12th August, two days after the event, the *Glasgow Herald* reported: "*Tragic Occurrence at Ardlamont.* On Thursday Mr Hambro of Ardlamont, Kyles of Bute, was accidentally shot dead while going over the estate. He had his gun slung over his shoulder and while getting over a stone dyke the gun went off and the contents lodged in his head, death being instantaneous. Mr Hambro was about 21 years of age, is said to have been of the firm of Messrs C. J. Hambro & Co., bankers, Broad Street, New York. His trustees recently purchased the Ardlamont Estate on his behalf, and he had just entered into possession."

The paragraph is, of course, full of inaccuracies. One cannot help feeling that it represents, especially in its reference to the New York bankers, the stories which Monson spread about in order to ensure credit for himself and the Ardlamont household.

Officialdom also accepted the death as accidental. But suspicions were roused by the discovery of Monson's insurance transactions and other matters. On 30th August he was arrested and charged with murder. On 30th October he was also charged with attempted murder by drowning.

The trial began on the cold, wet morning of Tuesday 12th December 1893. The Judge was the Lord Justice-Clerk, John Hay Athole Macdonald, Lord Kingsburgh, who had occupied that position for five years and would do so until he resigned in 1915. As Lord Advocate he was responsible for piloting through Parliament the Criminal Procedure (Scotland) Act of 1887, which still largely governs procedure. As a young man of thirty, he had written a treatise on criminal law which (after several editions) is still in daily use.

The prosecution was conducted by the Solicitor-General for Scotland, Alexander Asher, assisted by three advocates-depute —R. U. Strachan, J. A. Reid and J. C. Lorimer. The defence team was Comrie Thomson, John Wilson and W. Findlay. Of all the counsel involved, only one, Wilson, was destined for the bench. This was not due to any lack of ability on the part of the two leaders. Asher was the acknowledged leader of the bar, a man of imposing presence, deep and accurate knowledge of the law and a master at the examination and cross-examination of witnesses, based on meticulous preparation of his cases. He resigned his office of Solicitor-General soon after the trial. In 1895 the Faculty of Advocates elected him their Dean, an office which he held until his death in 1905. He has one unique distinction: his portrait by Orchardson is the only portrait of an advocate to have been hung in the Parliament Hall in Edinburgh while the subject was still alive and in regular practice.

Comrie Thomson was another advocate of commanding presence. Though he fell short of Asher in his knowledge of law, he was the greater jury counsel. White haired and golden voiced, he had the warmer and more human approach; in comparison, Asher seemed remote.

The three principal characters were more or less of an age: Macdonald was born in 1836, Asher in 1835 and Thomson in 1839.

With the two different personalities of the opposing counsel, the stage was set for the traditional clash between the Crown's appeal to the head and one to the heart from the defence. This was in fact the pattern; but the trial disappointed some of the reporters who thronged the court anxious for scenes. The *Sunday Observer*, however, paid a tribute to the "peculiar solemnity and dignity" of the Scottish system: "The mode of swearing the witnesses with the judge himself in his striking robes, standing with his right hand uplifted administering the oath in the ancient Scottish form, is as impressive as any ceremony of the kind can be, and is very different from our own gabble by a subordinate, followed by a kissing of a dirty and greasy book. The manner of the counsel on both sides in the case was in keeping with the solemn scene. They acquitted themselves like men in defence of the respective interests committed to their charge, and the London correspondent who complained that they dealt with each other with silk gloves on, paid them very nearly the highest compliment in his power. There were no 'scenes', no bullying in the style of our own Old Bailey of long ago. . . ."

Although there were no scenes, there was a good deal of interruption to the work of the Court as one hundred press reporters and innumerable members of the public flocked through the building. No money was taken for seats as it had been in Christina Gilmour's case; but disappointed applicants for admission were allowed by the attendants to snatch glimpses of the accused in the dock through the circular glass windows of the doors behind the bench. We are left to guess the effect on the accused of a succession of eyes appearing at an estimated rate of five hundred an hour.

The indictment first charged that Monson and Scott, having formed the design of causing Cecil Hambrough's death by drowning, bored a hole in the side of McKellar's boat and then, having plugged or closed it, induced Cecil to enter it with Monson on 9th August 1893; that thereafter, on 9th or 10th August (the doubt, as in Madeleine Smith's case, was caused by the lateness of the hour), Monson removed the plug when the boat was in deep water in Ardlamont Bay, thus admitting the water and sinking the boat, whereby Cecil was thrown into the sea; and that they did thus attempt to murder him.

As we have seen, although Monson was charged with murder on 30th August, it was not until 30th October that he was taken from Greenock prison across the Firth of Clyde to appear before the Sheriff of Argyll charged with attempted murder. The evidence on the minor charge was not strong: the more serious incident of the next day tended to drive detailed memory from the witnesses' mind; but the charge had to be included in the indictment to admit evidence of a deliberate plot to murder in one way or the other.

Some facts were not in dispute. McKellar's boat originally had no plug-hole. On the morning of 10th August it had a hole —not neatly bored with an auger so that a cork would fit snugly, but roughly cut with a knife and in an unusual position. There was no plug in it. Four days later a knife which could have been used was found by McNicol below highwater mark near where the boats were drawn up. Monson and Cecil went out in a boat some time after 10 p.m. on the 9th and arrived back at the house about 1.30 a.m., thoroughly soaked after being in the water. Monson could swim and was proud of his prowess; Cecil could not.

The theory that Monson or Scot bored or cut the hole in McKellar's boat depends on the evidence of the nursemaid that on the afternoon of the 9th Monson left Scott alone in it for twenty minutes. This part of the beach was quite open to view but no one saw Scott doing anything. He may have been thinking of his ostensible duties as engineer for the *Alert*; or he may just have been listening to the lapping of the little waves at the edge of the sea against the sides of the boat. It was a very hot day.

That was the evidence against Scott. There was none directly implicating Monson. The whole Crown case on this branch of the first charge was that he and Scott were fellow-conspirators.

In his declaration (a prepared and dictated statement) Monson said that Cecil cut the hole. The only support for this was that the knife found by McNicol was like one which Cecil used to carry. Cecil's knife had a ring to attach it to a chain in his pocket; the knife found on the shore had no sign of any ring.

There was no evidence at all that either Scott or Monson "induced" Cecil to embark, apart from the fact that he was in the boat. All the evidence suggested the opposite; Cecil was an enthusiastic splash-net fisher. He was also, according to one witness, a clumsy awkward young man to have in a small boat. This may help to explain how he and Monson came back from their fishing trip wet through.

The only direct evidence of what happened in the boat came

from Monson. His first accounts were given to people whom he met next morning and were all, with one exception, to the effect that when they were out in the boat they struck a rock and the boat capsized: Cecil climbed on to the rock and Monson swam ashore, got the other boat and rescued him.

In his judicial declaration he gave the same story in more detail: "After dinner on the evening of August 9th Cecil Hambrough, who was living in family with me at Ardlamont House, stated that he was going out fishing, and asked me to go with him. I agreed to do so, though I did not care for the kind of fishing intended, which was fishing with a splash-net. Hambrough had hired from a man at Kames or Tighnabruaich a small boat, which he had used on previous occasions for the same purpose. In this boat he and I started. We had on board a considerable length of net, probably about 300 yards, the width being about 14 feet. The nets were piled up in the boat, and were in themselves a considerable load. Hambrough took off his coat and rowed, while I busied myself preparing the nets. I did not steer the boat; there was, in fact, no rudder. While occupied with the nets, suddenly there was a bump, and the boat tilted, and I fell over the side. At the same time the boat capsized, and for a minute or two I was entangled in the nets. Immediately on getting clear I called out for Hambrough, and then saw him sitting on the rock laughing. The boat had struck the side of this rock and tilted over, which, with the load, and piled up as it was with nets, she would easily do. Hambrough, I knew, could not swim, so I told him to wait while I swam ashore and fetched another boat which was there. The sea was a little rough and the night was dark. The distance I had to swim would be between 200 and 300 yards. As I was working with the other boat to get her off I observed Scott, a man who was staying in the house at the time, coming down, and called out to him to run to the house and fetch a lamp, as I could not find the plug or the plug hole in the boat. The tide, I understood, was then rising, so I deemed it wiser not to wait until Scott returned, and, accordingly, pushed off the boat. I knew that, although the plug might be out, there would be time without danger to row to where Hambrough was and back. I pulled off and picked up Hambrough. I told him that I thought the plug was out, but there was then only about 2 inches of water in the boat, and we decided to pull out and pick up the other boat and nets, which were floating about 20 yards or so away. I got out and made fast a line to the capsized boat, and we then hauled the nets in and proceeded to row ashore, but made no progress. Eventually we discovered that the anchor had fallen out of the capsized boat and was securely fastened aground. We then got released and rowed ashore. There we found Scott, who had in the meantime come down with a lamp. By the time we landed, the boat we were in was nearly full of water. We made fast the boats and went to the house. We all went into the smoking-room and a manservant brought whisky and water. I immediately went off to bed, leaving Scott and Hambrough together.

"Both their rooms were near the smoking-room on the same floor. I do not know whether the plug was in the boat we first went out in; neither of us looked to see. The plug hole in that boat, however, was a homely affair. Hambrough complained that it had no plug hole, and that in consequence it was a bother to empty her after he had been out splash fishing, during which a lot of water gathered, and, accordingly, he himself cut a plug hole in the boat. I have no further answer to give to the charge now made against me. It is not true. On the contrary, so far from attempting on that evening to take young Hambrough's life, I consider that I saved it."

Full corroboration of this account was not to be expected in the circumstances. But next morning Cecil's jacket was lying under the seat and this confirmed Monson's statement that Cecil was rowing. He would thus have been facing the stern where Monson was standing with the nets and must have seen Monson remove the plug if he did so in deep water, as the indictment alleged. This would not have mattered if the attempt had been successful; but an unsuccessful attempt must have left the victim suspicious.

There was also the evidence of the butler, Wright, who had been waiting up for the return of the sportsmen. One of the party came in about 1 a.m. for a lamp. All three came in half an hour later and Wright provided whisky and water. The most significant feature of his evidence was this: "The persons whose clothes had been wet put on dry suits and then came down to the smoking-room, where I heard them all talking in a friendly way. They were all in good spirits, and I heard them laughing. I don't know whether they were treating the ducking as a kind of joke."

If this is correct, and there is no reason to doubt it, Cecil at least did not suspect that he had just escaped murder by drowning.

The one different account was spoken to by Dr Macmillan, Tighnabruaich, the first medical man to see Cecil's body on 10th August. After he had seen the place of the shooting, he went back to his trap with Monson. "He said it was very curious that he had had a very narrow escape from drowning the night before. He said he and Hambrough had gone splash fishing, and when about a mile from shore the plug went out of the boat, and they saw it filling, and turned and made for the shore as fast as they were able, and when half-way into the shore the boat came on a sudden rock and capsized, throwing the boat into the water. Mr Hambrough scrambled on to the rock first, and Mr Monson, being entangled with some ropes, was longer of getting on. But when he got on to the rock, being an expert swimmer, and Hambrough not being able to swim, he swam to the shore. He had not gone very far before he was able to touch the ground with his feet, and he brought out the second boat and rescued Hambrough."

Dr Macmillan had no notes of this conversation but relied on his memory. It is probably inaccurate; for one thing, a mile from shore would be a very long way out for splash-net fishing. The longest net actually measured was one about 160 yards long which McEwan, the piermaster at Kames, had lent Cecil. In his pamphlet Monson said that Cecil was experimenting with two nets tied together: this would agree with the figure of 300 yards given in his declaration.

A number of local men gave evidence that there were no rocks on which the boat could have struck. But no detailed charts were produced and there are rocky parts of the coast just outside the bay. It was pointed out that there were no marks on the boat to show that it had struck a rock, but this might have been due to the rock being covered with seaweed.

In his speech to the jury, the Solicitor-General implicitly

abandoned the original Crown theory that Monson removed the plug when the boat was in deep water. He so far departed from the words of the indictment as to suggest that the boat put off without any plug in the hole, which was only about one inch in diameter and would not cause the boat to sink immediately. On this view Monson expected the boat to stay afloat until it reached deep water, when Cecil could be left to drown. Scott was standing by on shore ready to rescue Monson with the other boat if necessary. "The boat providentially filled with water manifestly much earlier than was expected. Both were cast from the boat and immersed in the water, but at a distance which enabled Cecil Hambrough perfectly easily to scramble to the shore, and they returned, accordingly, that night saturated with water, without the scheme which had been devised being effectually accomplished."

Comrie Thomson had little difficulty with this charge. After reviewing the evidence he asked: "If the Crown theory is correct that an attempt of this kind was made by Monson to murder Hambrough, could Hambrough have failed to be aware of it? Is it conceivable that this lad should have been taken out into deep water, that he should have seen the plug withdrawn from the boat, that he should have found the boat sinking, and that he should have been allowed, as my learned friend said yesterday, to scramble ashore, without his suspicions being aroused— without his being absolutely certain that a nefarious attempt had been made upon his life? But if he knew that, would he have gone home and drunk whisky and water with the man who had attempted to murder him? Still less would he next morning have gone out shooting with the man who he knew had tried to compass his death by drowning the previous night. That is a point I urge you to keep in your minds. If an attempt was made to drown, it must have been seen and known by the intended victim, who next morning goes out with a gun in his hand, and with the man who made the attempt upon his life with another gun in his hand. Is that consistent with any possible theory? Does it not carry absurdity on the face of it? I say not merely that the Crown have failed to prove this attempt at murder, but that it has been absolutely disproved by the conduct of the parties interested."

This argument impressed the Judge: "We never heard before of an attempted murder or drowning in which the person against whom the attempt was made never had the slightest idea of anything of the kind, but came home with his companions, had his whisky and water, and laughed and joked, and was on perfectly friendly terms."

In the circumstances it is not surprising that the jury acquitted. The evidence was just not there. They may have been too grudging in not returning a verdict of Not Guilty. The conduct of the people concerned suggests an innocent accident and Comrie Thomson was well justified in asking for this more positive verdict. Had this charge stood alone such a verdict would have been more likely.

But, although the Judge directed them to consider the first charge in isolation, the jurymen probably found it difficult to disregard the sinister coincidence of a drowning accident soon after midnight and a shooting accident a few hours later, even if they were not convinced of the guilt of the accused.

The main charge of the indictment, however, was murder— murder by shooting on the morning of 10th August. Again the choice for the jury was between a crime and an accident.

There was little quiet in Ardlamont House that night. Wright, the butler, went to bed about 2 o'clock, leaving Monson, Scott and Cecil in the smoking-room. When they went to bed we do not know. Monson said he went before the other two.

Mrs Monson, Edith Hiron and the children rose about five o'clock and left the house at six to catch the early boat. Guests were expected on the 12th (at £100 a gun a helpful addition to the household finances). There was shopping to do in Glasgow and the children had to have their hair cut. By this time Mrs Monson knew of the boating mishap; unlike the men, she took a serious view of it.

Wright got up about seven o'clock. Cecil was then in the dining-room asking for a glass of milk and biscuits. Monson and Scott had already gone to the second gamekeeper's house to call for the head-keeper's attendance at ten o'clock, when they proposed to go out shooting. They also asked for a 20-bore gun which Cecil usually carried. Monson himself as a rule used a 12-bore. When they got back to the house, however, Monson said they found Cecil experimenting with amberite cartridges in the 12-bore; and on that morning Cecil used the 12-bore and Monson the 20-bore. This statement, however, was not made until about a fortnight later.

It was a "coarse morning—thunder and lightning and rain", which had started about six o'clock. In spite of this ill omen, the sportsmen were anxious to get to work and did not wait for the head-keeper. Shots were heard from the plantation to the east of the house soon after seven o'clock. Later the three men were seen near the schoolhouse, about a quarter of a mile south of Ardlamont House. Cecil jumped over the wall from the road, picked up a rabbit and gave it to Scott, who had no gun. All three men then walked north along the road until they reached the plantation again, when they entered it. They separated, Cecil going to the right and Monson and Scot staying nearer the road.

The plantation immediately east of the road was known as the old plantation. Further east was a plantation of younger trees, which was on the lower side of the dividing sunken fence. People shooting wood pigeons and rabbits in the wood tended to follow the line of the fence and this was the line Cecil took. Monson said he followed the west boundary of the old plantation. Scott walked between them and to the rear. His task was to carry any rabbits that might be shot. In these positions Cecil was out of sight of his two companions.

About nine o'clock a shot was heard from the sunk fence and Cecil Hambrough died. Monson said that he shouted "What have you got?" When there was no reply he and Scott went over and found Cecil lying in the ditch. They lifted him to the top of the wall and returned with both guns to the house.

At the house Monson first removed the cartridges from the guns. Then, apparently very distressed, he told Wright that Cecil had shot himself and was dead. They went to the sunk fence and were joined on the way by the gardener Whyte and the coachman Carmichael; others came along later. The body was lying on its back on top of the wall, with its left side nearer the young trees, the head towards the north. There was no gun near. Blood was oozing from a wound about the size of a half-crown behind the right ear. While Carmichael went to fetch the doctor, a farm cart came along. Cecil's body, wrapped in a rug, was placed on it and taken to the house.

Between ten and eleven the gardener went back to investigate. He had heard that the body had been lifted from the ditch but, although he looked carefully, he could find no trace of any heavy body having fallen into the coarse grass and ferns which grew there; and Cecil Hambrough was six feet tall and stoutly built. Nor could he find any traces of blood either in the ditch or between it and the place where the head had lain. Here there was a pool of blood in a small hole in the ground: it might have amounted to a kitchen-bowlfull.

About nine inches from the pool of blood, between it and the ditch, Whyte found two small pieces of bone, in the larger of which there were three shot pellets. He showed them to McNicol, the joiner, who was with him, and then buried them in the pool of blood, marking the hole with a turf. Then he followed a track from the body southwards along the top of the wall for about twenty paces; he thought this looked like the track of one man, though other witnesses disagreed. Another track led west from where the body had been and then turned south. The two tracks reunited nearer the schoolhouse. This may corroborate Monson's account of how the men had been walking. But it does not, of course, show in any way whether Monson went across to the sunk fence before or after the shot was fired.

Later Whyte found a cartridge wad with blood on its some two feet from the pool of blood. He showed it to Lamont, the underkeeper, but then for no apparent reason threw it away. It was the only serious error in a very competent piece of detective work. Lamont identified it as coming from a 12-bore cartridge and not a 20-bore. The importance of Monson's statement that he and Cecil exchanged guns that morning is obvious.

Dr Macmillan came from Tighnabruaich about eleven-thirty and was taken to the room where Cecil lay. There was a gunshot wound (the first he had seen in the course of his practice) in the head. He washed away the blood, bound up the head and helped to dress the body. After lunch he interviewed Monson and Scott separately. Their accounts agreed substantially. He then went with Monson and the estate factor to see where the body had been found.

On 14th August he reported to the insurance company that Cecil "had been accidentally shot by his own gun through the occipital bone, the charge entering the brain in a compact mass through an opening 1 inch in diameter." He added an explanatory note: "It seems to me highly probable that deceased was going along carrying a short-barrelled 20-bore gun, with his finger on the trigger, when he stumbled, and, putting out his hands to break the fall, raised the muzzle, lowered the breech, and pushed back the trigger, with results I have described. The injury was caused by the discharge of the gun while his finger was on the trigger."

Two days later Dr Macmillan made a similar report to the Procurator-fiscal: "The wound was exactly what I would expect to find from a charge of small shot fired from a distance of perhaps 12 inches. The shot had not time to spread, as there were no separate pellet marks. I would expect blackening of the edges of the wound from the powder but afterwards ascertained from Mr Monson that they had been trying amberite, a nitro powder. That explains the absence of blackening. The skin or hair was not burned."

So far there was no suspicion of anything but an accident. Scott left, quite openly and with the agreement of Dr Macmillan, by boat that afternoon. On the pier he met the local policeman, McCalman, and gave him as his address the Central Station Hotel, Glasgow.

Some of the shooting guests arrived at Ardlamont on 11th August but there was no shooting until after the funeral. On 12th August Major and Mrs Hambrough arrived. They had heard of the accident from Dr Hambleton, to whom Monson reported it, but did not know it was fatal until they read that news in an evening paper in Glasgow. The major said that Monson told them distinctly that Cecil had the only gun.

On Monday morning, 14th August, the Hambroughs left Tighnabruaich and went to Glasgow. Here the major enquired for Scott without success. As he did so at the North British

Station Hotel, his failure casts no doubt on Scott's veracity. Monson arrived in Glasgow in the evening and the major told him he had not found Scott. Monson replied that Scott was still at Tighnabruaich. It is one of the minor mysteries of the case that, if the major's evidence is correct, Monson told him, both about Cecil's having the only gun and the whereabouts of Scott, a different story from that told to any other person. The change seems pointless. It may be that the major's memory was unreliable and that the state of health which made him a bad insurance risk made him also a bad witness. Or he may have been trying to make the case against Monson blacker than it was by adding a few lies to his score. He was undoubtedly bitter. No doubt he felt, justifiably, that, if Cecil had not disobeyed him by staying with Monson, he would still have been alive. He may also have felt humiliated by the consciousness of debt. In spite of their unfriendly relationship, he had asked Monson for £10 to complete the journey from Glasgow to Ardlamont and allowed him to pay for the whole funeral expenses, including the transport of the coffin from Ardlamont to the Isle of Wight, all the fares to Ventnor and the hotel expenses there. He did say that he asked Monson to send an account of expenses to Prince, his solicitor; but as Prince had no funds belonging to the major, such an approach would have been unrewarding.

Cecil was buried at Ventnor on Thursday 17th August and Monson returned to Ardlamont. On 23rd August he went to Inveraray with two insurance men who wanted to see the Procurator-fiscal. That official understood that Cecil had been uninsured, but Monson told him that the major had insured Cecil's life for £15,000 without telling Cecil. The insurance men, however, told the Fiscal that the amount insured was £20,000 and that either Monson or his wife had an interest. This changed the Fiscal's view of the matter and he visited Ardlamont next day.

Monson was given to prevarication about the insurance. On the day of Cecil's death he told the factor of the policies he had failed to effect; he did not mention the two he had effected. He told Major Hambrough that the only policy was one for £400 in Mrs Monson's name. He told Tottenham first that the insurance was for £8,000, then £10,000 and finally £20,000. And he told two of the referees under the proposals, whom he met at the funeral, that there was no insurance.

At the same meeting with Monson the Fiscal said he heard for the first time of the 20-bore gun; but this can hardly be right, as Dr Macmillan had blamed that gun in his report. The Fiscal had never seen such a gun and asked Monson to send it to him with the amberite cartridges. As Monson did not do so, the Fiscal, on his arrival at Ardlamont, asked Lamont the under-keeper for the 20-bore and the cartridges. Lamont brought the 12-bore and amberite cartridges, saying that Monson had told him there had been an exchange: this was the first mention of any exchange. The Fiscal, his suspicions now thoroughly roused, began a more vigorous investigation.

Dr Macmillan, too, changed his opinion when he learned that there were no amberite cartridges (which cause less scorching and blackening than black powder cartridges) for the 20-bore. The 12-bore, in his view, could not have caused the accident as he had described it in his first report, which he now withdrew. He said in evidence "I had begun to think over the medical part, and I had before me the mistake of taking moral instead of medical evidence. The moral consideration was that I did not credit that a man like Monson could be guilty of so dreadful an act as killing his friend. I began to think over the character of the wound, its position, direction, &c., and I took a gun, and tried it in every direction to see if I could get it into a similar position." His experiments were all conducted with his finger on the trigger.

On 30th August Monson, who had been under close police watch, was arrested. Next day he made a judicial declaration before the Sheriff, saying that as he had not been within sight of Cecil when the accident happened he could give no explanation.

On 30th August Constable Donald Campbell searched Cecil's room at Ardlamont House. In the pocket of a jacket hanging there he found nineteen cartridges, eighteen for a 20-bore gun and only one for a 12-bore. All contained No. 6 shot. He also took samples of all the cartridges found in the house; the only amberite cartridges were for the 12-bore.

On 4th September Cecil's body was exhumed at Ventnor and examined by Dr Macmillan. He had the experienced collaboration of Dr (later Sir) Henry Littlejohn, police surgeon and lecturer on medical jurisprudence at Surgeon's Hall, Edinburgh, who was Professor Christison's successor as an indispensable witness in murder trials. Additional expert medical evidence was given for the Crown by Drs Macdonald Bell, Patrick Heron Watson and Joseph Bell.[1]

The defence too had distinguished assistance from Matthew Hay, professor of medical logic and jurisprudence at Aberdeen, and Dr W. G. W. Saunders, assistant to the professor of clinical medicine at Edinburgh. There was also expert ballistic evidence from James Macnaughton for the Crown, and Tom Speedy and George Andre (manager of the makers of amberite powder) for the defence. The expert evidence lasted in all over two days: this probably contributed to the confusion of the jury.

About the physical facts there was little dispute. The wound behind Cecil's right ear was triangular, with the base towards the front. It was $3\frac{1}{2}$ inches long and $2\frac{1}{2}$ inches broad at its maximum. Part of the right ear was missing. There was no blackening, such as comes from unburned carbon or powder, or scorching, from the flame of the explosive gases. There were no separate pellet marks round the wound.

When the scalp was removed, there was a hole 2 inches long and 1 inch broad from which the bone was missing; other pieces of bone round this hole were loosened. The brain was shattered in front of the wound but more or less intact behind it. Four irregularly shaped pieces of metal, identified as No. 5 shot pellets, were recovered from the brain.

These facts pointed clearly enough to a shot fired from the rear striking a glancing blow behind the right ear. A few pellets entered the head, but the main mass went on its way, possibly with some deflection. But at what range had the shot been fired? The two significant features were the absence of blackening and scorching, which indicated a rather longer range, and the absence of separate pellet marks, suggesting a closer range at which the pellets had not had time to spread.

[1] Dr Joseph Bell was Conan Doyle's model for Sherlock Holmes, whose death, as all Holmes scholars will remember, was prematurely reported from the Reichenbach Falls in this year of 1893. Unfortunately Dr Bell played only a minor role in the Monson case.

Both sides conducted experiments. For the Crown Macnaughton fired shots at sheeps' heads, cardboard, model skulls and even dead bodies from the Edinburgh mortuary. The Crown medical experts examined the results of these experiments and concluded, from the absence of blackening and scorching, that the shot had been fired from a distance of about nine feet; Dr Joseph Bell thought perhaps six feet or at the least four feet. If this theory was right, the shot must have been fired by some person other than the victim. But it minimised, if it did not overlook, the important fact that there was no sign of scattering on Cecil's head, although the same experiments showed scattering between three and six feet and very noticeable scattering at nine. In one case scattering was seen at two feet.

The defence experts, on the other hand, insisted on the importance of the absence of scattering and maintained that any blackening might have been washed off when the wound was dressed by Dr Macmillan. In any case, they said, amberite cartridges caused little flame or scorching. Tom Speedy demonstrated this by firing amberite cartridges at animal skins and hanks of human hair; finally he fired a shot at close range through his wife's hair.[1] From none of these experiments was there any scorching; there was not even a smell of singeing.

Other experimental shots at model skulls, wooden boards and horses' heads showed visible scattering at a range of two feet. The defence concluded that Cecil must have been shot at a range of two feet or less; this was quite consistent with accident.

The defence experts found further support for their theory in the bloodstained wad which Whyte had first found then lost. A wad does not fly far in the line of the shot; therefore if this wad had become bloodstained by hitting Cecil's head at the same time as the shot did, the shot must have been fired at very close range. Again the Crown disagreed. There was nothing impossible in a wad flying with the shot for at least nine feet. [The

[1] An even more dramatic, though unofficial, experiment was reported in the *Glasgow Herald* of 6th September 1893. A discussion was taking place in a public-house in the South of England about the Ardlamont mystery. Henry Card, a local gamekeeper, insisted that the wound could have been inflicted by Hambrough himself. To make his point, he held his gun behind his back with one hand and reached down with the other to pull the trigger. The gun was loaded and Card blew the top of his head off.

wad, of course might have become stained with blood by coming in contact with the pool of blood on the ground.]

The experts on both sides visited the scene of the death. Roughly south of where Cecil's head had lain on top of the wall and about nine feet away, there was a gap in the undergrowth. The Crown theory was that the shot had been fired from that gap. A line drawn from it through the position of the head passed through a rowan sapling and then through the branches of a lime and a beech tree further north. These three trees showed pellet marks in the leaves and twigs, and grooves, as if from pellets, on the bark. The height of the grooves, said the Crown, was such as would have been caused by a shot fired from the gap at shoulder level at a target about six feet above the top of the wall. The apparent age of the marks was consistent with their having been caused about 10th August. The defence argued that, if the shot, still travelling in a mass, had struck Cecil's head a glancing blow so that only a few pellets penetrated, the rest would have been deflected away from these trees. They thought the marks had been made before 10th August and pointed out that a great many trees in that part of the wood were scored with the marks of shot fired at wood pigeons.

The rowan sapling was uprooted and taken to Edinburgh for the trial. It is still in the basement of the High Court of Justiciary.

The defence stressed the rarity of homicide by shotgun and the great number of accidents reported every shooting season. Several witnesses said, more particularly, that Cecil Hambrough was careless with guns. He usually carried his gun by the barrel, muzzle pointing upwards, stock near the ground. In July he had been carrying it in this way when it went off; the charge passed very close to his head. Mrs Monson's brother, Philip Day, felt uncomfortable about his way of carrying a gun at full-cock even when he was going through fences. Edward Lang, a gunmaker in London, had shown Cecil a gun in his shop in April. Cecil put it to his shoulder after cocking it, pointed it at the foreman and snapped it. When he left, Lang remarked to his foreman "Did you ever see a fellow handle a gun in that way before? He will shoot himself or some of his friends." It is true that Cecil's carelessness in the shop was of a kind more dangerous to others than to himself but the two kinds of carelessness go together.

Near the end of the defence case George Henry Tillard, retired colonel of the Madras Staff Corps, told a spectacular story. In March 1871 he had been out shooting snipe, carrying a small double-barrelled gun at half cock. As he turned to call his servant, his foot slipped on some rocks and he fell backwards. He did not remember what happened next but when he recovered consciousness he found that both barrels of his gun had gone off. The shot had carried off part of his right ear and dug a trench behind it. Fortunately no part of the charge entered his skull. The direction of the shot was practically horizontal on the head. There was considerable blackening and scorching; the colonel had been using ordinary black powder and not amberite. He could not remember how he had been carrying his gun. The main difference between Colonel Tillard's accident and what happened to Cecil was that the colonel's wound was inflicted from the front, Cecil's from the rear. This may be significant. It is easy to picture a man throwing his hands, with the gun, forward to break a fall, or in a reaction even to a fall backwards. This seems to have been what happened to the colonel. It is less easy to imagine a shot from the rear. But it is not impossible. If a man was carrying a gun, as Cecil usually carried his, by the muzzle and jumped down from the top of a sunk fence, the stock and the trigger might possibly be caught in bushes behind the man: if the trigger was caught and the gun was cocked, it might well inflict a wound from the rear. Even without a jump down from one level to another it is not quite impossible to picture. The carrier of the gun would, of course, have to be very careless: but Cecil was.

The defence experts concluded from the position in which the body was found on top of the wall that Cecil could not have been shot from the gap as the Crown contended. If he first fell in the ditch (the official defence theory) his position on top of the wall, was, of course, quite irrelevant: but the defence had to be ready to cast doubt on the Crown argument even from the premises which the Crown assumed.

About a quarter to twelve on Thursday 21st December the Solicitor-General rose to address the jury. Before turning to the two charges in the indictment he described at some length the background—social and financial—to the case. He commented: "I think it must have struck you in watching the evidence that Mr Monson figures much more largely in this case as a financial agent than as an army tutor. Mr Monson has had full opportunity of placing any evidence his advisers though proper before you. We have had startlingly little information with regard to those phases of his life which it might be suggested were connected with the occupation of an army tutor. Testimonals were presented to Major Hambrough. Where are the gentlemen who gave the testimonials? Where are the pupils? Where are the names of the pupils? We have had glimpses of Monson's life, in certain spheres of social life, and in certain spheres of London life. These are, I should hope, rarely, if ever, closely associated with the profession of tutor to the young."

The comment about Monson's relationship to Cecil is fair enough; but in that passage, which came early in Asher's speech, there is a confession of the weakness of the Crown case. A strong prosecution case can dispense with criticism of the silence of the defence. And it was not the only time that Asher took this line.

He turned from the general financial background to the proposals for insuring Cecil's life. After several unsuccessful attempts to state an insurable interest, Monson had a new idea. "This impecunious occupant of Ardlamont has the boldness to go to McLean's office and say that he is about to purchase the estate of Ardlamont; that Mrs Monson, who has not two shillings in her pocket, was to pay £20,000 towards the price, and that the purchase was to be made in the interest of young Hambrough. . . . The proposal is entertained, an examination is made and the policies are completed. A premium has to be paid. There is no time to wait till the policy is got from New York, and the expedient is adopted of taking a temporary policy, subsisting in any event for sixty days, and upon the cheap terms of payment of a premium for half a year. A policy is effected, but the money has to be found. And I am bound to ask your close and careful attention to the circumstances under which that money was found. We are coming perilously close to the tragic event of 10th August. The acts of Monson, the motives of Monson, the objects he had in view, you must carefully scrutinise, watch and observe at and about the time which I have now reached. I have told you the misrepresentations under which this policy was obtained. I must now ask your attention to the flagrant misrepresentations under which the premiums were paid. The prisoner had reached a stage at which, apparently, even the bonds of that alliance which had subsisted between him and Tottenham, upon whom they were depending at the time for their daily bread, even these bonds were to be broken and treachery had to be employed towards the friend who had provided them with daily bread, for the purpose of obtaining the necessary money." There followed the story of Monson's appropriation of Tottenham's cheque for the mythical deposit of £250 for Ardlamont.

After his return from his meeting with Murray in Edinburgh, which on the Solicitor-General's interpretation had been deliberately unsuccessful, Monson persuaded Cecil to write the letter assigning the policies to Mrs Monson. Whatever might be the legal effect of such a document written by a minor, the mere fact of its being taken and handed to the insurance company showed that Monson believed it was effectual: and that was the question which the jury had to consider—not the legal effect but Monson's belief.

"Mr Monson manifestly thought he was armed with the necessary means of securing the total amount of both the policies in the event of anything afterwards happening to Cecil Hambrough. . . . He told the insurance company that the policies must be completed by the 8th of August. On the 11th of August several gentlemen were coming to Ardlamont. If the thing was to be done it must be before the 11th."

Nearly half his speech was over and the Solicitor-General was approaching the two crimes charged against the prisoner. He had shown—no very difficult task—that Monson was in very low water financially and that he was not the most scrupulous or truthful of men where money was concerned. He still had to prove murder.

As a preliminary, there was the attempt to drown Cecil on the night of 9th/10th August. "One would have thought that was sufficiently exciting and startling for one period of twenty-four hours; but you must take what followed along with you.

They returned home that night; they slept there during the night; they got up early in the morning, having returned home at one o'clock. It is startling to hear that at six o'clock in the morning of the next day, the same party were active and out for the purpose of undertaking a sporting expedition. It was not a morning which one would have thought calculated to invite those who had gone through the experiences of the night before, and with no further motive than amusement, to have entered upon a shooting expedition at seven o'clock in the morning.''

Hambrough died of a shot wound on the morning of 10th August. There were three persons there—Hambrough, Monson and "Scott". There were two guns, a 12-bore and a 20-bore, one carried by Monson and the other by Hambrough. There were only two alternatives: either Cecil Hambrough died as a result of a gunshot accident from his own gun or he was murdered by Monson. There was no suggestion of suicide or of accidental shooting by Monson.

Where was the body first found? Monson said several times immediately after Cecil's death that he found it in the ditch and lifted it to the wall: that was a deliberate statement made in the course of official enquiries. Was it true? And if it was not true, why did Monson make it? No witness saw any signs on the vegetation in the ditch of any person having fallen on it or having been removed from it. Then, though one of the largest veins in the head had been ruptured by the shot, so that Cecil bled to death, there was no sign of blood in the ditch: but large quantities were found on the bank where the body ultimately lay. If he had been carried from the ditch to the wall, there must have been blood between, there must also have been blood either on his own clothes or on the clothes of those who carried him: but there were no such traces. Even Dr Hay, the defence medical expert, had investigated on the hypothesis that the body was originally on the wall; it looked as though the defence did not believe that the body was ever in the ditch. This question was at the core of the case; "and if my learned friend is unable to displace from your minds the conviction that the body was upon the bank, and not in the ditch, then I am afraid he has the great task before him of giving some satisfactory explanation to you as to why the prisoner falsely, knowing the falsehood, made a representation with regard to the spot where he found the body, absolutely inconsistent with the facts of the case."

There was little doubt about the gun with which Cecil was shot. That was a 12-bore gun loaded with No. 5 shot.

If the jury could answer the next question, they would have a complete solution of the case. If they had conclusive evidence as to who carried the 12-bore, that would show whether it was an accident or murder. The facts were peculiar. There was no dispute that the 12-bore was Monson's usual gun and the 20-bore Cecil's. By an extraordinary coincidence, however, it was said that these guns had been exchanged on the morning of 10th August, the morning after Cecil Hambrough's narrow escape from drowning.

When was this exchange first suggested? The Solicitor-General drew attention to Monson's actions immediately after the death. He did not rush to the nearest point for help but passed the offices and went to the house. He took both guns with him, put them in the smoking-room and then removed the cartridges from both. It was only then that he told the servants that Cecil was dead. The jury would judge how far it was within the range of reasonable probability that the innocent friends would act in this way. "If he had exchanged guns with his friend . . . would it not have been the most natural thing for him to say, 'I wish to God I had kept my own gun this morning! Possibly if Cecil had been using his own this never would have occurred!' Not one word was said suggesting that any change of guns had taken place."

The doctor's reports showed that his first opinion, that death was due to accident, depended on the theory that Cecil was carrying the short 20-bore gun at the time; for this the doctor had accepted implicitly the statements of Monson and Scott. The first suggestion of a change of guns was when the Fiscal came from Inveraray after his suspicion had been wakened by the visit of the two insurance men.

The whole story of an exchange was an afterthought. It "was developed as an answer to what, on reflection, Monson must have known was standing as an indelible record against him. The pellets in the brain would be the pellets in the cartridges of the 12-bore gun, and by the removal of the guns and this theory of exchange, and the mixing up of the facts, this indelible record of evidence must in some way be displaced."

The next point was this: if Hambrough had the 12-bore he would have had cartridges to fit, and these cartridges would have been loaded with No. 5 shot. But in his jacket pocket there were found eighteen 20-bore cartridges loaded with No. 6 shot, and only one 12-bore cartridge—which was also loaded with No. 6 shot.

"You have to consider that, while I am treating these matters each one by one—the exigencies of argument compel me so to do—you will have to take them in the lump; you must take them not only separately but together. You will have to take the removal of the gun, not a word said about the fact that the man was shot by a 12-bore gun and a No. 5 cartridge and that that was the gun usually carried by Monson, not a suggestion made as to the exchange of guns till the police were on the spot, and in the pockets of the man cartridges found for the 20-bore gun, with the exception of one, and that with No. 6 shot.

"One would almost have said if I had stopped where I am, the chain was nearly, if not altogether, complete. But, gentlemen, I come now to facts about which there can be no doubt, facts the tendency and import of which it is for you to determine, but which I submit to you are eloquent only in one direction. I refer to the position of the body and the character and direction of the wound." All the medical witnesses agreed that Hambrough was shot from behind, by a shot passing nearly horizontally or a little upwards, which struck the head a little behind the right ear and carried away a portion of that ear.

Without repeating his previous arguments, Asher asked the jury to hold that Cecil had fallen on top of the wall where his body was seen by the witnesses whom Monson brought. In the immediate vicinity of that place there were trees with indisputable shot marks on them. It had been said that this was a wood in which there were shot marks on many branches: but no defence witness could point to any marks which could have been caused by the shot which killed Hambrough. "In determining how a man is shot, the next best evidence to the position of the body and the relative position of the weapon, which we have not here—for, if Monson's story is correct, both the body and the weapon were taken away—the next best evidence you can have is the ascertainment of the line in which the shot went that killed the man. Well, gentlemen, the body is found lying in an open space, between six and seven feet from a rowan tree. The head is towards the rowan tree; the feet away from it towards the south. If you put the body erect, and take a tape and draw a line which passes the head and, extended northwards, goes through that part of the rowan tree and the beech and the lime which, by general consent, show the marks of a shot—have you any doubt what that means? Can any person have any doubt that, on these facts, the man being shot there, and on minute and careful examination that continuous line between his head and the points of impact of the shot beyond being distinctly established—is there room for any doubt that the shot which caused the injury to the trees was the shot which caused the injury to the dead man's head?"

The defence suggested that the marks on the trees had been made before Hambrough's death. It was said that they looked about two months old when they were examined some five weeks after the accident. But minute accuracy in such a question was impossible.

If the shot through the trees was the one which killed Hambrough, it could not have been delivered by his own hand. Certainly accidents with guns could happen in an infinite variety of ways. But no rational explanation had been put forward to suit the conditions of a man being shot from behind by a shot fired horizontally at a height corresponding to the line of shot through the trees. The gun could not have been dropped. The angle of the line of discharge would have been quite different. But if the jury could discover any way in which a gun could be held with the muzzle opposite the point of entry, and at such an angle that the shot would pass horizontally past his head, they would give the prisoner the benefit of the discovery. "You will then have accomplished what all the men of skill who have been examined before you have conceded they could not find out."

The defence had produced some photographs to illustrate the experts' theories. But they all showed the gun being artificially supported behind the victim's head and were therefore of no value in this case.

The tracks found by Whyte led to a point from which a line could be drawn through the position of the head and the rowan, lime and beech trees. This gave some indication of the place from which the shot was fired.

From all these facts the Solicitor-General asked the jury to find that there was only one possible view of how the young man met his death.

Three men were involved, not two, in these happenings. What had become of the third man? According to the prisoner he came to examine the yacht. Why did he not do so? Why did he leave without making any attempt to do so? That was a secondary point. "Why has a person who was present on the scene absolutely disappeared from all human ken? . . . If the proceedings of the night of the ninth were purely accidental, and consequent on the folly of a youth cutting a hole with his knife in the bottom of the boat; if the death of the same youth next morning in the plantation was due to the accidental discharge of his own gun, why did one of the men who was there fly that same afternoon and conceal himself from that moment forward? You have got to consider and find an answer to that question, and I say again, listen to my learned friend when he explains to you that indisputable fact. If he can suggest to you a rational explanation of why a man should fly under circumstances like these, why, with reference to an alleged crime which has resounded throughout the world, that person should remain concealed up to the present hour, consistent with any other than this, that he was a participator in, or eye-witness of, a flagrant crime—if you can get any rational explanation which will displace that inference, by all means accept it and give the prisoner the benefit of it. But if you cannot then the result must be that this, like all the rest, like every incident from the beginning to the end, points conclusively in one direction. And you should place it in its proper class, and give it its proper weight in the deliberations which by and by it will be your duty to enter upon."

Then what was Monson's relation to the missing man? He had first described him as an engineer, well known in Greenock. Why was that statement made? It was manifestly false. The jury could have no doubt as to the true identity of "Scott". From the identical descriptions given of him and the London bookmaker Sweeney or Davis, and from the fact that the two men disappeared about the same time, only one inference could be drawn, that the two were not two but one.

Finally Asher reminded the jury of Monson's many misstatements about the insurances. Again he asked, what is the explanation?

"You must take the features of the case as they occur, and make up your minds, I repeat, severally and separately. But when you have done that, my wish is that you should place them side by side, look at them in their relationship to one another, and consider whether they do not establish the grave and serious chain to which I have referred—whether the circumstances do not infallibly and inevitably lead to one result, connecting the prisoner with the crimes with which he is charged. If you can find serious, intelligible and honest grounds that will influence you in coming to the conclusion that these facts are quite consistent with the innocence of the prisoner, by all means acquit him. But, gentlemen, if on the consideration of these facts you come to the conclusion that they are reasonably consistent with one, and only one, result, then your duty to the public, your duty to the oath which you have taken, is to find the prisoner guilty of the crimes with which he is charged."

The Solicitor-General had spoken until just before six o'clock and the Court adjourned. He had made the most of a case hampered by the failure of those on the spot to make enquiries at once; he had skilfully drawn together the suspicious features of the two incidents; but were they more than suspicious? Some difficulties he ignored: for example, the probable distance between the muzzle of the gun and the wound. And there were times when his logic seemed a little faulty. The main fault in his argument, however, was the excessive stress he placed on the prisoner's failure to do something which he was not bound to do, clear away the mystery of the death. In one passage of his speech he used the phrase "*if* [my italics] you begin by assuming the innocence of the prisoner in this case"; but that is what every jury ought to do—it is the meaning of the presumption of innocence which every prisoner enjoys. The phrase, as it was used by Asher, is like his calls for explanations from the defence, a confession of weakness.

Next morning Comrie Thomson rose in his turn about nine-thirty. He expressed confidence because of the inherent im-probabilities of the case and the difference of opinion on the main questions among the expert witnesses: "If these capable, intelligent, experienced, practical men honestly differ, is it for you to adopt an opinion which is adverse to the man charged with these crimes?" At the same time he felt anxiety because of the issue involved: "I remember more than five and thirty years ago sitting in one of these benches and hearing an advo-cate, who afterwards became a great judge, standing where I now stand, pleading for a woman who was sitting in that dock charged with the crime of murder. He opened his address with words which have become historical, but I repeat them to you now because of their great truth and their wonderful simplicity." The words, of course, were those with which John Inglis opened his defence of Madeleine Smith.

He warned the jury to disregard anything which they might have read in the newspapers, which had been full daily of news about the Ardlamont mystery, some of it highly prejudicial to the accused.

The Crown case could not be supported by direct evidence and was founded more upon so-called motive than any evidence, either direct or circumstantial. Two very important elements in the nature of indirect evidence were the direction of the fatal shot and the proximity of the gun to the deceased. The prosecu-tion had perilled their case on twelve pellet marks found in three trees. They had disregarded altogether the evidence about the distance between the gun and the dead man. That was con-clusively in favour of the defence.

Motive certainly had its place in considering the evidence but it was not enough. "You do not condemn a man because he had a motive to do a criminal act. Nay, if the evidence in regard to the act itself is scanty and insufficient you cannot add motive to eke out the otherwise imperfect evidence."

In any case the Crown position about motive was untenable. Admittedly Monson and his family were not well off, but Tot-tenham was able and willing to make advances to them to live and to maintain their boarder, Cecil Hambrough. By killing Cecil, Monson would have at once deprived himself of his only certain source of income, for Tottenham's bounty depended on Cecil's life.

There were the insurance polices and the unsuccessful attempts to insure. When the proposals were made there was a perfectly reasonable prospect that the contract with the Eagle Company would go to Monson. True, the company had agreed to sell to Major Hambrough and his friends by 1st August. But that contract was not completed and Monson was justified in assuming that, if it did not go through, the matter would once again be open. It was an essential part of the plan to purchase the life interests that the purchasers should have good life policies either on the major's life or on Cecil's. The major was not a good risk. Therefore it occurred to Monson to insure Cecil's.

But the success of the scheme depended on Cecil's taking steps to bar the entail when he came of age. Monson and Tottenham would then each take a large bonus. "The one thing that was essential to the carrying out of this arrangement was that the young man should live."

All Monson's insurance proposals, then, had been made in prudent anticipation of the time when the Eagle contract would again be open to him. It might have been suspicious if he had gone to some speculative and unknown office. But he approached well-known and thoroughly respectable companies. It was said that he told them untruths about his insurable interest. But it was quite true that certain advance had been made to Cecil and that was all the insurance companies really needed to know. Monson went on to say that the money was required "to cover certain liabilities incurred by Mrs Monson in connection with the Hambrough settled estates". That was an inaccuracy but a pardonable one, because, although the liabilities had not yet been incurred, they would be when Monson got his contract with the Eagle Company. In any case, it was an unnecessary piece of information which did not really concern the insurance companies.

The first proposals were made on the footing that Mrs Monson should insure Cecil's life and not Cecil himself. The reason was obvious: Monson was well aware that Cecil could not assign the policies. He must either have his father's consent or

he must adopt or homologate the assignation when he came of
age. Until that was done it was useless.

The policies with the New York Mutual Insurance Company
were taken in Cecil's name. It was part of the arrangement that
they should be properly assigned to Mrs Monson. The manager
had said in evidence: "Of course, we both knew that a minor
could not assign." So the position on the 10th August was that
there was no valid assignation to Monson or anybody else. No
doubt Cecil signed certain documents but these were not worth
the paper they were written on and Monson, in spite of what
the Solicitor-General had said, knew that. It might be that Cecil
thought, out of a sense of duty and common honesty, that he
should put his intention in writing: his father might make the
assignation good. But the case that Monson killed Cecil to get
the proceeds of the policies was completely without foundation.

Another pointer in the same direction was that it was one
of the conditions of the policy that the first premium should be
paid. It was not paid. It was true that Monson sent a cheque
on 8th August, but at that time there were no funds to meet
it. Tottenham's cheque for £250, which had been paid in on the
8th, represented nothing until 10th August, the date it bore.
"At the time the attempt to make payment was made there was
no money. It was waste paper, and certainly I am not responsible, my client is not responsible, for the good-natured but
somewhat loose actings of the agent of the bank at Tighnabruaich. It was the bank that made this policy a valid one and
therefore so far as the payment of the premium was concerned
it was not Monson. And notice, Monson knew that the cheque
which he had handed to the bank did not represent cash until
the 10th; and on the morning of the 10th, when this lad was
killed, he had no reason whatever to believe that the premium
had really been paid. . . . The whole Crown case based upon
motive crumbles into dust."

Monson's behaviour after the death was important. He made
no claim under the policies, but Tottenham did. "I do not want
to say hard words to you about a Crown witness, but I rather
think Tottenham produced the impression upon you of being
rather a queer fish. I do not think he is the kind of man that
you and I—quiet-going Scottish folk—are in the habit of meet-

ing, or even I do not know that any of us desire to make his more intimate acquaintance." He admitted that he was trying to bluff the insurance company. It was well known that such companies often paid up when they were not legally bound to do so and Tottenham was man of the world enough to know that.

It was said that Monson exercised influence over Cecil Hambrough. There was no harm in influence as such. The question was whether that influence was sinister and used for selfish and fraudulent purposes. From the whole correspondence in court it was clearly no treat for Cecil to go to see his father—knocked about from lodging to lodging, pursued by creditors and writs. The father's object in trying to make Cecil join him in London was not to enjoy his company, not to educate him, but to insure his life for his own scheme. Cecil's attitude was that he had to work for his exam and could not waste time in the middle of term, especially when Monson had engaged a tutor for himself and his other pupils—Rawstone and Jebb were mentioned. His letters were "the letters of a well-meaning, intelligent, dutiful son who has arrived at a time of life when he sees two things very plainly: in the first place, that he must not go on idling and fooling through the world, and, in the second place, that he must get himself educated and must try to get into the profession he had chosen."

"I have disposed of the motive" claimed Thomson. "I now come to consider the evidence as to the facts. Three persons almost certainly knew what happened and no other human being. They were the poor lad, who is dead; the prisoner at the bar, whose mouth is stopped; and the man called Scott, whom we cannot get.[1] Now, that being so, the first thing I purpose to to deal with is the position which Scott, and the evidence about him, occupy in the case."

First there was Donald's evidence that Monson said Scott came from the estate office. This might be the result of a genuine misunderstanding Monson probably said that he himself

[1] Even if Scott had been available in person, his mouth would have been stopped just as effectively as that of Monson. An accused person could not give evidence. And Scott was accused along with Monson on the same indictment.

F

had come from the estate office (i.e., Messrs J & F. Anderson in Edinburgh), as in fact he had.

Assuming that Scott was in fact an engineer, the fact that he did not go aboard the yacht was easily explained. The yacht was not to be delivered until the 10th and until that time he had no right to visit her. By the time the 10th came, the man who hired him was dead. There was no reason why he should stay. The doctor said in Scott's hearing, after examining the body, that he was satisfied that there would be no difficulty.

On the other hand, if Scott was the London bookmaker Davis, the evidence was that he was the gentlest and most amiable of men, who would not hurt a fly. Yet it was suggested that for some reason Monson invited this mild man down to be an eye-witness first to an attempt to murder and then an actual murder. Why? Monson needed no help either in the drowning or in the shooting. If he was guilty, Scott's presence would have been a danger: he could have given evidence against him. On the other hand, if Scott had been brought to be a witness that Cecil's death was due to accident, why was he allowed to go? "Gentlemen, it is probably the greatest calamity that could befall my client that Scott is not here. I do not pretend to know what he would have said, but according to my instructions—I go no further than that, but I am justified in going as far as that—I think it is the greatest calamity that ever befell mortal man that Scott has not been able to enter this witness-box.

"The result of this is, that without the three men, one being dead and the other with a closed mouth, and the third not to be got, the Crown has got to rely, as I said to you before, upon indirect or circumstantial evidence." That did not mean a lot of suspicious circumstances. Each circumstance founded on must be clearly proved by evidence in the usual way. Then they had to decide whether that body of proved facts was sufficient to exclude every theory except that of guilt. Before they could convict on circumstantial evidence they must be forced to that conclusion.

If the charge of attempted murder failed, it took the jury a long way towards finding that the second and more serious charge had not been established. Each charge was said to have been part of a design. If the Crown failed to prove the first at-

tempt to carry the design into execution, it made it far more difficult to prove the completed act involved in the second charge.

In most cases of crime the fact that a crime had been committed was easily demonstrated. "The peculiarity of this case
is that you have got to find evidence that a crime was committed, and you start with this, that the person alleged to have
committed it by shooting was entitled to have a loaded gun and
to discharge it; and that, on the other hand, the person who was
unfortunately shot had in his hand that with which his death
might be very easily brought about accidentally."

The probability was in favour of accident. Shot guns were
rarely used homicidally. Dr Littlejohn could remember only
two cases, one of which was in a poaching affray. But every
shooting season there were weekly reports of accidents to sportsmen, some fatal, all more or less injurious.

Shots were heard indicating that before entering the wood
the men had been firing nearer the sea. The three men came
round past the schoolhouse and went into the wood, according
to a witness, just as men would who were shooting a cover in
line. If they kept on walking in that order they would never meet.

The first point made by the Solicitor-General had been the
position of Hambrough's body when he was first struck down.
There was no doubt that the accused had conveyed to the mind
of more than one person that morning that when he found Hambrough his body was not lying on top of the wall; but he did not
say positively that he was in the ditch. He indicated points on
the far side of the ditch, on the sloping ground rising up from it.
There was no vegetation there which might have been expected
to break, only grass which would rise again as soon as any
weight was removed from it. It was said that there were no
traces of blood. But the blood was described as merely "oozing" from the wound and slight traces might have been washed
away by rain. It was also possible that the two pieces of bone
found near the body had originally been driven back into the
wound so as to plug it until after the body was removed. There
was therefore nothing to show that Monson's statement was
not perfectly true.

But assume that Cecil was shot at the place where his body
was found. He had been walking north, towards the rowan tree.

How did he get into his final position? If he fell forward, his head would be towards the north and he would be lying on his face. If he fell backward, he would be lying on his back with his feet towards the north. In fact, he lay on his back with his head to the north. Clearly, wherever he was shot, he had been moved before the witnesses came on the scene. And if that was so, the whole Crown case crumbled to pieces, because there were no longer any justified data for their calculations.

Admittedly Cecil had been shot with the 12-bore gun loaded with No. 5 shot. But who carried that gun? The only evidence was that of the underkeeper Lamont, who put the 20-bore gun into Monson's hands that morning. There was no evidence that it ever left him. Then long before there was any question of suspicion, Monson told the factor Steven and the pierkeeper McEwan that he had found Cecil experimenting with the 12-bore. It was a mistake to suggest that this was an afterthought.[1]

If the jury were satisfied of the truth of Monson's statement about the guns, there was an end of the case. But the defence did not need to go as far as that; it was enough if there was reasonable doubt.

The Solicitor-General had said how easy it would have been, if Monson was innocent, to have left the gun lying beside the body. "It did occur to me—it may be a very wicked suggestion —that if Monson had been guilty that is exactly the thing he would have done in order to make evidence for himself."

Another point was the finding of 20-bore cartridges in Cecil's jacket pocket. "It is essential to bear in mind that that discovery was made on 30th August. That jacket had been hanging, or at least had been within the power of Monson, ever since the time of the accident. If he were addressing you now, instead of me, he would tell you this, that he had been instructed to send to Inveraray the jacket and certain cartridges in the house, without any distinction, and that the day before it was taken away, or about that time, he had, in order to facilitate matters, put a certain quantity of cartridges into this jacket for facility

---

[1] The mistake was Comrie Thomson's. The evidence shows that Steven put this remark by Monson on a date when Monson was already under police surveillance. McEwan said nothing about the date and is therefore neutral on this point.

of carriage to Inveraray. That is not susceptible of proof. I am speaking as the mouthpiece of the accused in this matter. . . . That is the explanation that is given, one that is perfectly rational and natural; and even supposing there were no such explanation, what are you to assume from the fact that cartridges of that kind were found in this jacket which had been open to the whole house—open to the police constables, you will observe—because the police constables had been two or three nights in the house before this date? What are you to assume, after such an interval of time, and with the jacket hanging in this place, and cartridges of all denominations lying about in the smoking-room, from the circumstances that certain cartridges are found three weeks later in this jacket? It would have been a different story if, at the time when the jacket was removed, and when it was examined by the doctor, on the morning and afternoon of the 10th, it had been found heavy with cartridges that would not fit the 12-bore gun.''

The Crown case was said to depend on the pellets in the trees. But no one knew what kind of pellets these were. There were only twelve marks altogether found on the three trees. "We do not know whether they are No. 6 or No. 5. But we do know that a scientific man, who has paid great attention to such matters, depones upon oath that these pellet marks upon these trees were older by weeks and weeks than the date of the crime. Professor Hay and Dr Saunders concur in that statement and no one contradicts them. What significance are you to attach in a trial for murder to evidence such as that? We want to know if the pellets in these trees were fired at the time that the pellets were fired into this man's head. We know what the nature of the pellets in the head was. We can identify them. We have no identification of the pellets that passed through the trees. They were there till they got into the hands of the Procurator-fiscal. Where are they now? I am suggesting nothing improper; but I do suggest this, that for a blunder of that kind this man is not to suffer. There were pellets found in the bone. We have not these either. You can draw no safe deduction—and I do not require to put it higher—you can draw no conclusion, no safe deduction, from the evidence in regard to these pellets.''

The whole wood was riddled with pellets; it was a good cover, with winged game, wood pigeons and rabbits. Within seventeen yards of the body, Speedy had found branches broken and trees marked by pellets. There were between 200 and 300 pellets in each cartridge and the jury were being asked to convict because the marks of 12 unidentified pellets were found on three trees in the neighbourhood.

The Solicitor-General had passed over in a single sentence the question of the proximity of the gun to the head. This was important. The Crown witnesses had maintained that to the best of their judgments the distance between the muzzle and the wound was nine feet. The defence experts, however, had proved by demonstration that at nine feet there was a considerable scattering of pellets and it was clear and undisputed that there were no marks of stray pellets on any part of the person of the dead man.

There was no blackening. But amberite powder caused no scorching, merely some brownish discolouration which could easily have been washed off when the wound was sponged with soap and water. The absence of blackening was quite consistent with accident.

There was also direct evidence in favour of the theory of accident. Cecil Hambrough was careless with his gun. Then there was the evidence of Colonel Tillard. He had been shot from the front, but it was just as extraordinary that a man should have been shot from the front as from behind. Dr Macmillan was at first quite satisfied that the wound was just such as he would have expected from an accident. He changed his mind when he learned that there were no amberite cartridges for the 20-bore. And he ought to have returned to his original opinion when he learned that Cecil had been shot with the 12-bore, for which there were such cartridges.

Of the Crown medical witnesses, only one, Dr Littlejohn, was not open to entertaining any view but that of the guilt of the accused. The others admitted that their conclusions were in the region of conjecture and that there were infinite possibilities of accident. The defence medical experts were quite clear in their view that the shot had been accidental.

He concluded: " 'Moral impression, suspicion, feeling', to use my learned friend's expression repeatedly used yesterday, 'that everything has not been fully explained' will not do. All that falls very far short of what is necessary. Before you can return an adverse verdict you must have formed a perfectly clear opinion that you are forced by the evidence to find that these crimes, or one or other of them, have been committed; and I put it to you—not appealing to you for mercy, but asking you to give me simple justice—I put it to you, have I not demonstrated that there is ample room for entertaining serious doubt? Gentlemen, we are all liable to make mistakes. I pray you make no mistake in this terribly serious matter. The result of your verdict is final, irreparable. What would any of you think if some day, it may be soon, this mystery is entirely unravelled and it is demonstrated that that man was innocent, while your verdict has sent him to his death? He will not go unpunished if he is guilty. There is One in Whose hands he is, Who is Infallible and Omniscient. 'I will repay, vengeance is Mine, saith the Lord.' "

At 1.50 Comrie Thomson sat down and the Court adjourned for twenty minutes. Most of this time was spent by the Lord Justice-Clerk in prayer. He had, as he tells us in his autobiography, found it an anxious case, in which he had to take "scrupulous care lest the jury should be misled by feelings roused by the character of the accused". The result of this care was that, although the interventions from the bench during the trial seemed to be in favour of the prosecution, his directions to the jury were strongly in favour of an acquittal.

There were two charges, each involving the prisoner and another man. The Crown case was that both men were throughout acting in pursuance of a common scheme.

The background of the case showed a very dark side of social life. There was Major Hambrough, "reduced in the years 1891–1892 to the miserable position of living upon odd sums got from people who had their own schemes to serve by keeping him up. He was living in lodgings, occasionally unable to get his luggage removed through inability to pay the rent. He was an impecunious, broken-down gentleman, unable to find education for his son, except by arranging for a postponed payment, and it was this which brought him into contact with the prisoner. Mr Tottenham, who is a gentleman belonging to a particular class in London whose business it is to lend money, apparently at high

interest, and make his own income out of his loans, having come
to know Major Hambrough, and, knowing his circumstances,
and knowing that he had a son who was the next heir-of-entail
—as we would call it—of these large estates, introduces Major
Hambrough to the prisoner. It appears that the prisoner had
capacity as an army tutor, which capacity was shown by certi-
ficates from the parents of those whom he had educated for the
army, and Major Hambrough, being satisfied with the testimonials received, transferred his son to the care of Mr Monson."

The major and his son became estranged. The temptation to
the boy was very great. He was happy and there was something
of the nature of external affluence compared with his father's
squalid lodgings. Monson's unfortunate phrase, "I am not your
son's keeper", probably meant no more than that he had no
power to prevent Cecil from returning to his father if he wished
to do so. No doubt he felt perfectly confident that Cecil would
not want to return.

After a reference to Monson's bankruptcy and Mrs Monson's
judgment in absence against Cecil for £800 for board and lodging, the Lord Justice-Clerk came to the move to Ardlamont. It
was favourable to the prisoner that Tottenham was prepared to
advance money "on the general account of the show". So long
as Cecil was alive there was some financial backing. Tottenham
was also apparently prepared to get the purchase of Ardlamont
financed, though how he proposed to do so was not clear.

Monson's letter to Tottenham saying that he had fully discussed the purchase with the agents was "one of the most extraordinary episodes of this extraordinary case". No meeting
had taken place and the terms quoted bore no relation to the
facts. It was suggested that the purpose of the letter was to get
£250 from Tottenham. But Tottenham had undertaken to find
£450 for the rent which was due. The Crown made a lot of that
letter, but there was one suggestion in it which the jury should
bear in mind: Monson had suggested that Tottenham should
make the cheque payable to Messrs J. & F. Anderson. If this
had been done, there would have been no chance of using the
cheque for the insurance premium.

Up to this point there had been a long story of fraud and

lying. But it was a long step from dishonesty to murder.[1] The jury should consider these lying episodes only in so far as they were directly connected with the motive alleged by the prosecution.

By now Mr and Mrs Monson's affairs were practically desperate. The Crown said that the insurance policies were the motive for the murder. But there was evidence that Monson knew that Cecil's assignation was valueless. If the jury accepted this, it meant that Monson could do nothing worse for his own interests than kill young Hambrough, who "was, to use a vulgar expression, the decoy-duck by which money was to be got out of Tottenham". There was no positive evidence to show that Monson believed the assignation to be valid.

The law did not require a prosecutor to prove motive. If it was certain that a crime had been committed, proof of motive was not needed. But where the evidence was circumstantial, the question of motive became of vital importance.

On 8th August Scott arrived at Ardlamont. Here was the great mystery of the case, one which had not been cleared up. The Solicitor-General alleged that he was a party to the plot to murder. But why should he be there as a conspirator at all? "In regard to either of the crimes charged in this indictment, the drowning attempt or the successful shooting, I must say I have a difficulty in seeing what he was there for." He was not shown to have had any connection with young Hambrough. There was no evidence that he had any motive. The Crown theory must be that he was a hired assassin. But there was no basis for that view either.

His presence was mysterious, but it was for the Crown to solve the mystery. There was no evidence for saying that he had disappeared at the instance of the prisoner. If he had done so, that would make the case different. But it might be that his disappearance was unfortunate for the prisoner. The Judge's

---

[1] De Quincey would have disagreed. "If once a man indulges himself in murder, very soon he comes to think little of robbing; and from robbing he comes next to drinking and Sabbath-breaking and from that to incivility and procrastination. Once begin upon this downward path, you never know where you are to stop. Many a man has dated his ruin from some murder or other that perhaps he thought little of at the time." (*On Murder, Considered as One of the Fine Arts.*)

theory was that Monson had given this man "what we call a French invitation—'Oh, come and see us at Ardlamont and take a day's shooting'. It is meant for nothing; it is just the high talk of people who are wanting to show off that they have got a fine place." If Davis had found himself in the neighbourhood, he might have remembered and accepted this drinking-bar invitation. It would be natural for Monson, if this happened, to describe him as an engineer to prevent his wife and family from knowing that his companion was a bookmaker's clerk. Once he had told this story he had to stick to it.

After dealing with the charge of attempted drowning in a way that showed his own view that the evidence was not enough, he turned to the evidence about the second charge. Monson's actions after Cecil's death seemed quite natural: it was almost automatic, for example, for shooting men to unload a gun before taking it into a house. He then called for help and had Cecil's body carried to the house. A doctor was called. Dr Macmillan's first report was unfortunate, both for the Crown and for the prisoner. No suspicion was roused and so no proper enquiry was made at the time.

There was no definite evidence about where Cecil's body had first fallen. The expert witnesses for the Crown said that they would have expected to find blood on the ground where he fell and between there and the place where he was found if he had been carried from one place to the other. The defence witnesses said that that was not necessarily so. It was for the jury to decide between these views.

It was agreed that the fatal shot was fired from the 12-bore gun. There had been a sad want of care in such a serious case about looking to see what cartridges Cecil had in his pocket. It might have been expected that when the jacket was brushed and put away, all the cartridges would have been removed. Defence counsel had suggested an explanation for the mixture of cartridges that was found and the jury could consider that. The fact that one 12-bore cartridge was in his pocket might also show that Cecil did from time to time use the 12-bore.

In cases like this, the evidence of persons skilled in the use of guns and of doctors skilled in wounds was always of great importance, if it was recent after the event. That was not so here.

This might be a misfortune for the Crown, but it was no fault of the prisoner. If the case for the prosecution had been weakened because the investigation had been belated, the prosecution had to suffer.

The same observation could be made about the pellet marks found on the three trees which had bulked so largely in the Crown case. The expert witnesses on the two sides gave quite different estimates of the age of the marks. If the Crown did not prove that these marks were made by the shot that killed Hambrough, their whole theory fell to the ground.

The idea of the medical witnesses was that the shot struck a glancing blow *en balle*, before it had scattered. Some of it must then have been deflected after the impact, but they did not know at what angle. It was the Crown case that the shot had been fired at a range of some nine feet. The jury could look at the demonstration cards produced by the Crown and by the defence which showed the amount of scattering that took place at nine feet. They should try to consider what place in the spread of pellets the head would have occupied. There were no stray pellets in Hambrough's head or in his clothes. If that meant the range was under nine feet, it made murder less likely. The assailant would have had to come very close. And it also took the case outside the theory put forward by the Crown.

If the shot was fired from close range there was the possibility of accident and the prisoner was entitled to the benefit of the doubt. Colonel Tillard had told them of the most extraordinary accident that befell him in India. "I suppose if any doctor of experience had been asked before that accident happened to Colonel Tillard whether it was likely to happen in such a way, he would have had no hesitation in saying that such a thing could not possibly happen. But accidents do happen in very extraordinary ways."

They must also remember that Cecil had been proved to be very careless with guns.

"Now, gentlemen, you must consider how this case is to be disposed of. You have got a path to go on in this case in which you must see your way. You must neither walk through darkness at any point of it, nor leap over anything that you meet in it. It must be a straight path, and a path on which you have light. If you have light which takes you to the end of that path, so that you can give a verdict for the prosecution, then you must do it manfully, and you must not allow yourselves to be stopped, though Pity, with uplifted hands, stand pleading and entreating that you shall not go on. On the other hand, if there is any darkness or dimness on that path which you cannot clear away, you cannot go on to the end. If there is any obstruction on that path you have to stop there. The prisoner is entitled to that. And, lastly, if you yourselves do not see your way along that path without passing through darkness or dimness or other obstruction, you must not allow yourselves to be urged forward along that path blindly by any demon pushing you from behind, telling you that the prisoner is a bad man, a liar and a cheat, and that, therefore, you should send him to his doom. You must keep yourselves free from that. These things have a bearing on the case if you can go on, but you must not allow them to push you on. I am quite sure whatever verdict you arrive at will meet the justice of the case, so far as Providence has allowed its mysteries to be revealed. Do your duty. Think of nothing that people may say. Do your duty manfully, either in convicting the prisoner, if you must convict him, or in acquitting him, if you are not tied up to the conclusion on the evidence that you must convict. Gentlemen, that is all I have to say to you. You have listened attentively to this case, and know it in all its bearings. And now you have to do your duty by the Crown and by the prisoner."

At 3.53 the jury retired. Seventy-three minutes later they returned with a verdict of Not Proven on both charges. Monson was discharged. Comrie Thomson had opened his speech to the jury with an echo of John Inglis for Madeleine Smith: he now once more followed Inglis' example by not shaking hands with his client. Exhaustion may have been the reason in each case. Thomson is said to have remarked some time later "I don't know whether Monson killed Hambrough, but he nearly killed me."

The general impression was that the verdict was the only one to be expected in the circumstances. One strongly dissentient voice was heard, that of Monson himself in an interview with the *Westminster Gazette* the day after the verdict. Any English jury, he said, would have said Not Guilty. That, no doubt, is true: but would it have meant more than the verdict he got? He also complained of the conduct of the prosecution and blamed the whole thing on the Scottish system of "secret investigation". If there had been a coroner's inquest, as in England, the whole affair would have been done with in a day or two.

The *Glasgow Herald* pointed out in a leading article that the jury had not said emphatically that Monson did not commit the crimes with which he was charged but only that the Crown had not brought the charges home. "Shall we ever know the truth of what occurred in the wood on that tempestuous morning? . . . It is, in a sense, idle to dream or to conjecture. Yet it is almost impossible to refrain from doing both. The world generally is not able to say with Hamlet 'The rest is silence'. On one point, at all events, the public will follow the jury in giving the man who is no longer the prisoner at the bar the benefit of the doubt. Let us hope that he did not commit the crimes with which he was charged, for if he did commit them he was surely of all recent criminals the most despicable."

Though the verdict was approved, there were misgivings in the press. In a long correspondence in the *Scotsman*, many doctors and others called for an immediate examination, in all cases of sudden and unexplained death, by a doctor of some medico-legal experience instead of any general practitioner who was available. Cases were quoted where there had been no medical examination at all, or where a doctor had refused to certify the cause of death; in some of these cases the authorities had apparently been satisfied by an inspection of the corpse by the village policeman. The correspondence on this question branched out, as often happens with public correspondence, and the debate soon embraced the desirability of instituting coroners' inquests in Scotland. The general opinion was, and still is, against any such public investigation before trial. Although Monson said that it was generally recognised in Scotland that the native system was a bad one and that a bill was pending for its abolition, this had as little basis in fact as many of his other statements.

As a rule someone who has passed through the ordeal of being tried for murder is only too glad to avoid law courts in the future. Monson was an exception. He was acquitted on 22nd December 1893. His next appearance in court (a civil one this time) was in January 1894.

On 3rd January Tottenham called at Madame Tussaud's in London. He said he knew Monson well. He also said that a suit and a gun which he had with him were those which Monson had on 10th August. He offered them to Madame Tussaud's exhibition, and also offered a sitting by Monson to John Tussaud. For this he received a sum of £50 to account of the agreed price of £100; a day or two later he returned it, saying that Monson had changed his mind.

Shortly after that there appeared in the "Napoleon Room No. 2" of the waxworks exhibition the effigy of Monson wearing the suit and carrying the gun that had been supplied by Tottenham. Admission to this room was obtained by an extra payment of sixpence. Association with Napoleon may seem harmless, even flattering. But the Napoleon Room was the entrance to the Chamber of Horrors, which contained likenesses of many murderers and a representation of the scene of the Ardlamont mystery. In the Napoleon Room there was one recumbent figure of Napoleon. The other four figures formed a strange entourage: they were Mrs Maybrick, convicted of murdering her husband in 1889, Piggott the forger, who committed suicide to avoid arrest after the revelations of the Parnell Commission the same year, "Scott" and Monson.

Another member of the Tussaud family, Louis, had a similar exhibition in Birmingham. Monson's effigy appeared with royal and political celebrities just outside the Chamber of Horrors. They could be seen without the extra payment which was asked for admission to the Chamber. There was therefore less of a link between Monson and the gallery of murderers than there was in the London show. But the link was supplied by Louis Tussaud's advertisements: "See the Chamber of Horrors (extra room 3d) and the instruments of torture—See Vaillant, the Anarchist, and Monson of Ardlamont."

Monson sued the organisers of each exhibition for damages for libel. As a preliminary matter he applied for injunctions to

restrain them from showing his likeness until after the trials of
the actions. On 19th January Mr Justice Mathew and Mr Justice
Collins held, in the London case, that it would be clearly libellous to exhibit Monson's figure in the Chamber of Horrors; it
made no difference that it appeared in what was virtually its
anteroom. Irreparable mischief might be done if the figure was
allowed to remain until the date of trial and an injunction was
granted. An injunction was granted in the Birmingham case also.

The defendants appealed, armed now with affidavits setting
out Tottenham's part in the transaction. They also sought to
show that Monson was not averse to publicity by stating that he
was about to publish a pamphlet on the trial and that he had
advertised lectures on the subject. In reply, both Monson and
Tottenham swore that the idea had been Tottenham's and that
Monson, so far from authorising the approach, had indignantly
repudiated the agreement made in his name. As for the lectures,
he said he had changed his mind.

On 29th January the Court of Appeal allowed the appeals
and withdrew the injunctions. It was not that they thought there
had been no libel, but because of the question now raised
whether Monson had authorised the display in the first place.

The trial did not come on for another year. During that year
there were several public reminders of the Ardlamont case. First
there was Monson's pamphlet, to which I have already referred
more than once. It contained two portraits of Monson and a
photograph of a large Victorian building—not, as one might
have expected, Ardlamont, but "Riseley Hall (the Residence
of Mr A. J. Monson)". It threw no new light on the mystery and
received a thoroughly bad press—"catchpenny" was perhaps
the least unkind description. It consists mainly of complaints
about the Scottish legal system and praise of the English
coroner's inquest. Had the Scots adopted the English system he
would never have been tried. He tried, with little success, to
justify his financial manœuvrings. An interesting statement is
that he was inundated by applications from insurance companies anxious to have the business of insuring Cecil's life.

Appended to the pamphlet was a document described as
"Scott's Diary". It is quite obviously not a diary in the sense
of a daily record of events. It begins on 7th August.

"*Aug. 7 (Bank Holiday)*. As is pretty well known, I went to Glasgow on this date. I met Monson and Cecil Hambrough; I had to attend Paisley races, on the 10th and 11th; so thought I might as well look out for Hambrough, who, I knew, was somewhere in the neighbourhood, as I had some financial matters to settle with him; but our meeting was accidental.

"*Aug. 8*. I left Glasgow for Ardlamont; got there about eight o'clock at night. I had some talk with Hambrough on the matter of accounts, but nothing particular was settled.

"*Aug. 9*. I went out in the morning with Monson, and in the afternoon shooting with Hambrough. This was the day of the accident to the boat. I was not in the boat at the time, but heard all about it afterwards from Hambrough and Monson. We treated it as a joke.

"*Aug. 10*. Hambrough and Monson went out shooting. I had no gun, but went with them. I chaffed Hambrough about the way he carried his gun—everyone noticed this. Was present at time of accident. Dr McMillan asked me a lot of questions. I told him all I knew. He said that it was so evident that Hambrough's death was accidental, and that it was not necessary for me to remain. However, owing to the sad event, it was too late for me to go to the races that day, but I left for Glasgow. . . ."

The entry for 16th August begins with the words: "I met one of the Crown witnesses." As this was exactly one week before murder was suspected and a fortnight before Monson was arrested, the entry shows a considerable degree of prescience.

Most of the rest of the "diary" is taken up with long detailed stories of skirmishes with the police. I quote only the last two entries: "*Dec 12 to 22*. Have been present in court every day. Ready, if wanted, but never had any doubt about result.

"*Dec. 25*. A Merry Christmas."

The phrase "ready, if wanted" refers to an earlier entry, in which Scott claimed that he wanted to be at the trial in case his evidence was needed. But, as an accused person, he could not have given evidence.

It is difficult to see that this "diary" served any other purpose than to demonstrate, if demonstration were needed, that Monson was thoroughly unreliable and that the claims of accuracy and truth sat lightly on him.

In April 1894 there began a series of articles in the *Pall Mall Gazette*—"The Truth Out At Last, by Scott (The Missing Man)." These throw no light on what happened to Cecil Hambrough: Scott's memory on all material points was vague. But he said quite definitely that he had been invited to Ardlamont by Monson, who did not want him to be known as "Ted Davis, the London bookmaker" and devised the further *alias* of "Scott". He did not know Cecil Hambrough. He was not at the trial. He referred to Monson's version of his diary as "absurd and fictitious . . . not one word of truth".

In May of the same year he applied, under the name of Edward Sweeney, to the High Court of Justiciary in Edinburgh for recall of his sentence of outlawry. He stated that he had been out of Scotland at the date of the trial and that he now desired and was ready to meet the charges against him. The Crown made no appearance to oppose the application and it was granted. No proceedings, of course, were taken against him.

The next litigation involved Tottenham and his post-dated and stopped cheque for the £250 "deposit" for Ardlamont. The Royal Bank of Scotland, whose agent at Tighnabruaich had put it prematurely to Mrs Monson's credit, saw no hope of reimbursement from their customer and now sued Tottenham. On 4th July the Court of Appeal in London upheld Mr Justice Wills' decision in favour of the Bank for the full value of the cheque. Once it was credited to Mrs Monson's account, the Bank acquired a good title to it.

This was the first of two reverses for Tottenham. His old friend Monson turned on him. When the move to Ardlamont took place, Monson's furniture was stored in the name of John Kempton—Tottenham's *nom de guerre*. Tottenham removed some and sold it. Monson prosecuted him for theft. In spite of Tottenham's protests that Monson owed him considerable sums and that the furniture had been made over to him in security, he was convicted at Leeds Assizes on 13th December 1894 and sentenced to three months' imprisonment.

With all this litigation, Major Hambrough saw a chance to improve his position. As Cecil was a minor at his death he could not assign his life policies. The proceeds of any valid policies fell into his own estate and the major, as administrator, claimed

£20,000 from the Mutual Life Assurance Company of New York. The company repudiated liability, as they had done with Tottenham earlier. But the major sued them. The case was tried before the Lord Chief Justice (Lord Coleridge) and a jury, who found that the policies were bad because of false and fraudulent statements in the proposal forms. These statements, no doubt, had been made originally by Monson but they had been adopted by Cecil Hambrough. As they referred to his health, they were obviously material and had influenced the company to accept the risk. The major appealed. But the Court of Appeal dismissed his appeal on 25th January 1895, describing the statements as a "mass of impudent falsehoods".

While the major's case was going on, Mrs Monson tried in her turn to sue the company. After some preliminary procedure her case was dropped.

A few days after the major's unsuccessful appeal, Monson's libel action against Madame Tussaud's came for trial before the Lord Chief Justice and a special jury in London. Lord Coleridge, who had tried the major's case, was now dead. His place as Lord Chief Justice was taken by Lord Russell of Killowen. The new Lord Coleridge was Monson's senior counsel. The events of the past year had kept the public memory of Ardlamont alive, but in a way that was hardly propitious to Monson. His rash prosecution of his benefactor Tottenham was unpopular. Worse than that, it turned his only possible witness into a very hostile one.

After Monson had given his evidence, which included the admission that it was he who signed Jerningham's name to the Ardlamont lease, Tottenham entered the witness-box in the custody of a prison warder. He told how he and Monson went to Madame Tussaud's in a cab, stopping in Bond Street to buy a gun, which became "the gun used by Monson on the day of the tragedy". Monson did not go into the exhibition but arranged to meet Tottenham in a nearby hotel when the business was done. When Tottenham came out, Monson was not there. "It was not odd—for Monson." The witness thought that made it plain that the whole responsibility for the negotiations was to be put on his shoulders. Monson then repudiated the bargain, only because he thought the price too low. He complained bitterly of the way in which Monson defrauded him over the celebrated £250 cheque. Counsel asked him why he had not prosecuted. "I am going to prosecute him as soon as I have done my turn, for perjury and theft. He stole letters from my office of the correspondence about which he prosecuted me at Leeds and about other matters. There was a lot of hard swearing, and counsel told the jury that I was a moneylender and that put an end to the case. I shall prosecute Mr and Mrs Monson as soon as I get out."

In charging the jury, Lord Russell said he had no doubt that the exhibition was libellous. If the jury agreed they had to consider damages. Here different considerations applied. He dealt with the Jerningham forgery, described Monson as being "quite ready to perpetrate a sordid and vulgar fraud upon Cecil Hambrough" and remarked that the whole story "reeked of fraud". The jury duly found for the plaintiff and awarded one farthing damages. They also gave him one shilling for the detention of his suit of clothes. Each side had to bear its own costs and the exhibitors undertook to withdraw the figures from the show.

In a leading article on 31st January 1895 the *Scotsman* observed: "There is a Portuguese coin called a maraveda, a shovelful of which are said to go to make up a penny. A maraveda would have been a more accurate estimate of the solatium due in this case; but a farthing is near enough for practical purposes.... Mr Monson may count himself fortunate that he has got off in the meantime with his farthing and his shilling of compensation for the detention of his clothes, and still more fortunate if the law takes no further trouble with him in return for all the trouble he has given the law."

In April 1895 the scene returned to Edinburgh. Charles Morritt, "the well-known hypnotist", was advertised to appear at the Operetta House there. On 25th April, the *Edinburgh Evening Dispatch* printed a letter from Monson, in which he challenged Morritt to practise on him in order to clear up the Ardlamont mystery. On 29th April Morritt publicly accepted the challenge and undertook to obtain from Monson under hypnosis his whole knowledge of the affair.

On the same Monday morning, the late William Roughead, that indefatigable collector of crime, recognised Monson in

Lothian Road, Edinburgh, with another man. The two turned
into a public-house. That evening Roughead was in the Operetta
House and recognised in Morritt the stranger he had seen with
Monson. Morritt announced that if Monson was in the building he would accept the challenge. Monson rose and said he
was willing to undergo the test. The time of nine o'clock next
evening was fixed.

At that hour the theatre was crowded. Morritt induced an
apparent trance and invited members of the audience to ask
questions. The *Scotsman* reported that they were answered to
the apparent satisfaction of the audience. One dissatisfied
spectator was Roughead, who quotes two questions with their
answers: "Did you murder Mr Hambrough? No!" and "How
was Cecil Hambrough killed? I don't know." Another dis-
believer called out "Stick a pin in him" and the supposedly unconscious Monson smiled.

Roughead's scepticism of Morritt's *bona fides* was justified.
The day before Morritt's first appearance in Edinburgh, a traveller from London shared a railway compartment with two men
who were on friendly social terms. When the train approached
Waverley Station, the younger of the two left the compartment
and did not return. Next night the traveller recognised in the
Operetta House, in the person of Morritt, the companion who
remained. His first feat was to resuscitate a man whom he had
brought unconscious from London in a box. This man was the
younger companion from the railway compartment.

The name Monson was not much in the news for the rest of
1895.

In December, Alfred John Wyvill, who lived near Douglas,
Isle of Man, was so unfortunate as to have his house burned
down—a misfortune which had befallen Monson in 1886, just
after he had insured against such an event. Wyvill claimed £500
for jewellery destroyed in the fire. The insurance company refused to pay. Wyvill instructed a solicitor to sue. The solicitor
had been an interested spectator at the Tussaud trial and recognised in Wyvill the well-known Alfred John Monson. He refused to act.

Monson was now arrested to stand his trial for perjury in his
prosecution of Tottenham. The charge was that he had falsely

sworn that a letter produced by Tottenham in his defence was in part a forgery. After evidence from Tottenham and a hand-writing expert, the stipendiary magistrate at Leeds agreed with a defence submission that there was no case to answer and Monson walked out of the dock once more a free man.

In 1898, Monson was carrying on business as an insurance and financial agent in London. The words in his case meant that he was a moneylenders' tout. His functions were to steer towards his associates young men with little or nothing in the present, but with large reversionary interests which could be sold or pledged—other Cecil Hambroughs.

One of his more unsavoury associates was Victor Honour, whose many aliases included John Milton and William Shake-speare. On 29th and 30th July 1898 Monson found himself in the dock at the Central Criminal Court, London, before Mr Justice Lawrance and a jury. Beside him were Victor Honour and a younger man, Robert Ives Metcalf. The charge was con-spiracy to defraud the Norwich Union Life Insurance Society. C. W. Mathews and Horace Avory prosecuted. Honour was de-fended by Marshall Hall, who had recently taken silk, Monson by Rawlinson, Q.C., and Metcalf by H. C. Richards, Q.C.

This was the story as told by the witnesses for the prosecu-tion. In 1894 Honour met Percival Edwards Norgate, a young man who needed money. Honour lent him £40. Later Norgate needed more money and applied again to Honour. This time Honour asked Norgate, before money passed, to sign his mother's name to ten promissory notes for £25 or £30 each. Norgate did so and Honour lent him a small sum for his im-mediate needs. In 1895 he sued Mrs Norgate and she, to avoid exposure of her son, settled the claim.

Norgate, however, still needed money and still went to Honour for it. When he next asked for a loan, he had to sign his mother's name to a note for £120 and promised to repay this sum in in-stalments. He found this difficult. Honour helpfully suggested that he should insure his life and assign the policy. In that case nothing would be heard of the forged note. Honour suggested a policy for £2,000. Norgate protested, as was the truth, that he was in such poor health that he would never be accepted. Honour told him that the company would issue a policy for

£200 without examination and Norgate agreed to take out such a policy.

Monson now came on the scene, using his Isle of Man name of Wyvill. He introduced Norgate to Metcalf, the third man in the dock. Metcalf undertook to arrange the insurance. His method was unorthodox. He got his partner, Stanley Hobson, to fill up and sign the proposal form in the name of Norgate and then to present himself, still as Norgate, for the medical examination necessary for the £2,000 policy. This he did successfully. Norgate was surprised at the size of the premium asked but was satisfied with Honour's explanation that this was because the policy had been issued without medical examination. According to Norgate, the first time he realised that he had been impersonated was when he had to sign some documents relating to the insurance. Honour asked him to sign his own name as like as possible to another signature which was laid before him as a model. This was presumably Hobson's version.

Honour now had the insurance policy. He also still had the £120 promissory note signed by Norgate with his mother's name. He did not propose to lose this and in spite of his promise to Norgate, took proceedings against Mrs Norgate. In July 1897 Monson called on the young man's father, the Reverend Mr Norgate. He called himself "Hobson" and explained that his young brother Stanley and the parson's son had got into some little difficulty over insurance. He could, however, smooth things over if Mr Norgate paid £350. In February 1898 Mr and Mrs Norgate paid Honour £210 to recover the forged note.

There was no explanation from the accused of this unsavoury story. They themselves could not yet give evidence (the Criminal Evidence Act of 1898, which allowed accused persons to testify, did not come into force until October). They led no evidence of any kind. The only argument advanced by Marshall Hall was that Honour had been imposed upon by young Norgate; he also made an impassioned plea that the jury should not allow themselves to be prejudiced by his client's profession and his race.

Monson's defence was that he had no connection with the fraud at all. "It was common notoriety that Monson had been charged before this but it was also common notoriety that he had never been convicted. He had struggled hard against prejudice to lead an honest life and there was no evidence that he knew of this fraud or that he had anything to do with it, except trying to stop its effect by settling the matter on behalf of the parties concerned."

For Metcalf, it was contended that the prosecution case was tainted by depending an the evidence of informers.

The jury took only fifteen minutes to convict all three accused, with a recommendation to mercy for Metcalfe. Mathews informed the Court that, so far as Honour and Monson were concerned, this was not an isolated case. Mr Justice Lawrance sentenced the two principal villains to five years' penal servitude each and Metcalfe to eighteen months' hard labour. He said he had no doubt whatever that Victor Honour had treated other persons who had got into his hands, or been put there by Monson, in the same way as he had treated Norgate.

Commenting on the case on 1st August, the *Scotsman* quoted a saying attributed to Lord Braxfield: "You're a clever chiel, but you'll be nane the waur o' a good hangin'." The London correspondent of the *Scottish Law Review* noted with pardonable pride that English law had done something which Scots law had failed to do, keep Monson out of harm's way for some time. It is not recorded whether Monson's preference for English law survived this blow. He issued no more pamphlets.

The crowded five years after his acquittal in Edinburgh show pretty clearly that Monson was a menace to young men with expectations. Other cases, according to what Mathews told the Judge, were known to the authorities. It is also clear that he had a taste for insurance. Does this history throw any light on what happened at Ardlamont? Its only effect is to emphasise that Monson was a financial trickster and an insurance expert. And this in its turn underlines the probability that he knew well enough that Cecil Hambrough could not assign his life policies until he was twenty-one. He therefore had no motive for murder and that is a serious gap in a circumstantial case.

But from one piece of information we can make a guess at the real purpose of "Scott's" visit to Ardlamont on 8th August

1893. During her husband's imprisonment awaiting trial and afterwards, Mrs Monson, a shadowy figure in the background, had been a loyal wife. She took every chance she could of maintaining his innocence in press interviews. When he was acquitted, she seems to have stayed with him for some years. But they parted at last. In 1898 she gave other interviews to a weekly publication, in which she described her home life as "unbearable". Monson was a hard drinker, whose head remained unaffected by any quantity of drink. He used this immunity to the disadvantage of those less favoured. It will be remembered that a house-party was expected at Ardlamont for the 12th. This consisted mainly of young brother-officers of Cecil. Put young officers under the influence of drink, have a bookmaker handy, and there are the makings of a nice plot. Can there be any real doubt that that is why Scott came on the scene? It may be thought that Monson could have easily fleeced his friends by himself; but, as a gentleman, he may have thought it unworthy of his lineage to soil his hands with the mechanics of the swindle. Or he may have thought it safer for the future to be able to put the blame on another. At any rate, it seems to me a much more likely reason for the presence of a London bookmaker than that put forward by the Crown.

In 1898 it was stated that Monson was taking divorce proceedings against his wife for her adultery with an unknown man and also with the late Cecil Hambrough. This does not, however, help with motive. Mrs Monson bore her husband two children after Cecil Hambrough's death and the presumption must be that at the relevant times he did not know of the fact of her adultery, if fact it was. I have been unable to find whether the divorce case proceeded, and if so, with what result. In fact, nothing seems to be known of Monson after his conviction in 1898.

Year after year, on 10th August, the anniversary of Cecil's death, there appeared in the press an *In Memoriam* notice: "In loving memory of our dear son, Windsor Dudley Cecil Hambrough, found shot dead in a wood at Ardlamont, Argyllshire,

August 10th, 1893. 'Vengeance is Mine. I will repay, saith the Lord.' "

On 10th August 1898, five years after the event, and a few days after his old client's conviction for fraud, Comrie Thomson, who had used that text in his peroration, slipped and fell. He received injuries from which he never recovered and from which he died on 23rd August of the same year.

In his last illness he was attended by one of the Crown witnesses against Monson—Dr Joseph Bell.

(IV)

JOHN DONALD MERRETT

Well within the capacity of the poor old police.
No experts need apply.
Case-Book of Sherlock Holmes: The Three Gables

SOONER or later most visitors to Edinburgh find their way to Queensferry to see the Forth Bridge stride gauntly across the mile-wide river. If they leave the city centre by Queensferry Street they have to cross an older bridge, Telford's Dean Bridge, carrying its hundred and fifty yards of roadway a hundred feet above the village of Dean. Once across this bridge the street takes a broad sweep to the left between two garden strips whose trees hide the Victorian buildings on the parallel roads behind. That on the left is Buckingham Terrace. The first-floor flat at No 31 was the scene of the next mishap which we have to consider.

Mrs Bertha Merrett was a Lancastrian by birth who married, in New Zealand, John Alfred Merrett, an electrical engineer. John Donald, the only child of the marriage, was born in New Zealand on 17th August 1908. From New Zealand the Merretts went to Russia but the climate of St Petersburg did not suit the child's health. When war broke out in 1914 he and his mother were in Switzerland. During the war Mrs Merrett nursed wounded British prisoners released from enemy camps; later she worked for the Ministry of Food in London. After the war she returned to New Zealand and Donald went to school there until he was sixteen. By this time Mrs Merrett believed that her husband had been killed in the Russian Revolution. Apparently, however, he had deserted her and was in fact alive and in India.

In 1924 Mrs Merrett took up house near Reading and Donald went to Malvern College which he left in December 1925 with a good record for work. His conduct was less satisfactory. Instead of sending him to Oxford as she had planned, Mrs Merrett decided that he should continue his studies for the diplomatic service at Edinburgh University. She would live in Edinburgh and Donald would live with her and under her watchful eye.

Mother and son arrived in Edinburgh in January 1926 and Donald entered the Faculty of Arts. They seemed happy and devoted. After living at two other addresses they came to 31 Buckingham Terrace, of which they had a four-months lease, on Wednesday 10th March. Every morning Donald left home with his books, returning later in the day to study in the seclusion of his bedroom, until his mother anxiously urged him not to work too hard. She was a good parent, who wanted him to get on and make a name for himself, but not by ruining his health by overwork.

Her fears were misplaced. Whatever caused Donald's tiredness, it was not overwork. After the first two or three weeks of term, though he still left in the morning with his books, he did not go near the University. And at night, when he was in theory studying or sleeping in his locked bedroom, he was often at the Dunedin Palais de Danse in Picardy Place, where he became friendly with two dancing instructors, Betty Christie and George Scott. To get out from Buckingham Terrace he used a rope which was ostentatiously tied across his bedroom window by day. He explained that he walked in his sleep and that the rope was for his protection.

As in Monson's case, we must understand something of the financial background. Mrs Merrett had an income of £700 a year, out of which she paid all the living expenses and Donald's fees. Donald had nothing, though at the age of twenty-one he would come into a substantial sum under his grandfather's will. Mrs Merrett gave him 10s. a week as pocket money. She was careful in money matters—she had to be—and she insisted that Donald should follow her example of keeping strict accounts of how he spent his money. Each week he had to submit his account book, which showed his expenditure on such things as sweets, cigarettes and church collections. But there were some items which his book did not show—"booking out" Betty Christie by paying her estimated earnings at 6d a dance (15s. for an afternoon session and £1 or 30s. for an evening); the price of two rings he gave her; £2 5s. for an automatic pistol and cartridges on 13th February; and £28 for an AJS motor bicycle on 6th March. Possibly he thought it would be inappropriate to show these sums in an accounting for 10s. a week. They certainly did not come out of that allowance.

Mrs Merrett had two bank accounts. Her income was paid into one with the Midland Bank, Boscombe, Bournemouth. She had another with the Clydesdale Bank, George Street, Edinburgh, which she kept in funds by cheques drawn on the Boscombe account. It was her habit to note the balance on each account on the counterfoils of her cheque books so that she could tell at a glance when her Edinburgh account had to be replenished and how her expenditure was marching in step with her income. With the same object she had her bank books brought up to date at intervals by the two banks, checking her figures against theirs.

In spite of these precautions the Clydesdale Bank account was twice overdrawn in March 1926 and the bank wrote to her on 13th and 16th March. Each time a cheque on the Midland Bank was paid into the Clydesdale account, putting it again in credit. The bank's figures, as we shall see, did not agree with Mrs Merrett's. But it is uncertain whether she knew this. It was Donald who took in any letters delivered at Buckingham Terrace, and it was he who collected mail sent to their previous address, a boarding-house in Palmerston Place.

About 9 o'clock on the morning of Wednesday 17th March Mrs Merrett's daily maid, Mrs Henrietta Sutherland, arrived as usual and was admitted by Mrs Merrett. She took off her hat and coat and went into the sitting-room to clear away the breakfast dishes. Mrs Merrett and Donald were both there. Mrs Merrett was putting some things from the table (salt cellars, sugar bowl and so on) into a drawer in her bureau, which stood against the right hand wall as one looked from the door toward the front bow window. Mrs Sutherland took the dirty dishes and washed them in the kitchen at the back of the flat. She then went back to the sitting-room to clean the fireplace. Mrs Merrett was sitting writing at the large table on which breakfast had been served, her chair being between it and the bureau, which was behind her and a little to her left. Donald was sitting in a chair reading. Mrs Sutherland did not disturb them but went back to work in the kitchen.

Soon there was a shot in the sitting-room and a scream from Mrs Merrett. She had received a pistol wound through her right ear. Mrs Sutherland went to the telephone and called for the police. They arrived in a few minutes and sent Mrs Merrett by ambulance to the Royal Infirmary. She died there a fortnight later on 1st April.

The first police officers on the scene were two uniformed constables, Middlemiss and Izatt. Merrett told them that his mother had shot herself. Middlemiss asked him why she should have done such a thing and Merrett said "money matters". Middlemiss asked "Too much or too little?" to which Merrett answered "No, just money matters". Izatt gave a different account: Middlemiss asked if there were any financial worries and Merrett replied that his mother was well off.

Mrs Sutherland told the constables that she had been working in the kitchen when she heard a shot. Merrett then came in and told her his mother had shot herself.

At about 10 o'clock Inspector Fleming and Sergeant Henderson arrived. By that time Mrs Sutherland was alone in the flat. She told them that, on hearing the shot, she went into the lobby and through the open sitting-room door saw Mrs Merrett falling off the chair on to the floor and a pistol falling out of her hand.[1] On Sunday 21st March other officers were sent to ask her about the discrepancy in her two statements to the police. She went back to the first one, that she had been in the kitchen when Merrett came in and told her that his mother had shot herself.

After interviewing Mrs Sutherland the inspector and the sergeant looked round the flat. On the table there was an unfinished letter to a friend in Stirling saying that she had found a flat at last and that after some trouble she had engaged a daily maid. There was no blurring or dragging of the pen as though the writer had been violently interrupted. The two letters from

[1] That evening she had occasion to consult her doctor, Dr Rosa. She gave him the impression that she heard the shot just as she was leaving the room, turned round and saw Mrs Merrett falling. She added the picturesque detail that Mrs Merrett had removed her false teeth.

the Clydesdale Bank which told her that her account was overdrawn were lying open on the bureau behind her. The pistol
had already been removed by the constables.

Before Fleming went to the flat he was told that the case was
one of suicide and his cursory investigations did not suggest
otherwise. He went back to the police station and detailed plain-
clothes officers to make inquiries with a view to charging Mrs
Merrett with attempted suicide. The authorities at the Royal
Infirmary, where Mrs Merrett lay in the ward reserved for attempted suicides, were asked to notify the police when she was
about to be discharged.

Donald Merrett had left the flat with his mother in the ambulance. He called again at the Infirmary between 12 and 1 o'clock
and told Sister Grant that his mother had been worried about
money matters. He asked the sister not to tell her, if she got
better, what had happened. His story was that he had been
sitting reading and his mother had been writing at the table.

About 2 p.m. he met Betty Christie outside the Palais de
Danse, booked her out for the afternoon and took her to
Queensferry on the pillion of his motor bicycle. He was looking very white and said that his mother had had an operation.
A few minutes later he said she had shot herself: it might have
been an accident. He said he had been sitting in the room and
that the maid was in the kitchen.

When they got back from Queensferry they went to the flat,
where they were joined by George Scott, the other dance in-
structor. Merrett went to the Infirmary by taxi with Betty
Christie. She waited in the corridor while he went in to see his
mother. He also visited the Infirmary with her later that evening. Sister Grant asked whether, if anything happened during
the night, she should send the police to Buckingham Terrace,
but he said no, that he was staying with friends at the County
Hotel, Lothian Road. She asked for his telephone number and
he gave that of the Dunedin Palais, and asked her to telephone
there at any time up to 1 a.m. and ask for Mr Scott.

In fact he spent the evening with Betty Christie at the Caley
Cinema, next door to the County Hotel. The next afternoon and
evening he spent with her again.

On Thursday Dr Holcombe, in whose charge she was, asked

G

Mrs Merrett what had happened. She said she had been writing.
"Donald was standing beside me and I said 'Go away, Donald,
and don't annoy me'." Then she heard a "kind of explosion"
and remembered no more. The doctor reported this statement
through his chief to the police.

Next day the doctor saw Merrett and put the same question
to him. Merrett said that his mother had been writing and said
"Go away, Donald, and don't annoy me". He went over to the
corner of the room. He heard a shot, looked round and saw his
mother falling to the floor and a pistol falling from her hand.

The two accounts are remarkable for their agreement.

The doctor told him that his mother was seriously ill but that
she had a fighting chance. Merrett commented "So it is still on
the cards that she will recover". Sister Grant suggested that the
relatives should be sent for and Merrett eventually agreed,
though he said that they were not on friendly terms.

He had already summoned from Brighton a New Zealand
friend, Mrs Hill, who arrived that morning. On learning that
Mrs Merrett's illness had been caused by a bullet, she asked if
anyone else could have got into the flat. Merrett turned down
this suggestion and told her much the same story as he had told
the doctor. Mrs Hill asked why his mother should have done
such a thing. He said that she was in money difficulties, having
had a letter that her bank account was some £20 overdrawn.
[This was the amount mentioned in the first of the two letters
from the Bank.]

When Mrs Hill saw her old friend Mrs Merrett, it was the
patient who asked what had happened. Mrs. Hill said tactfully
that she had had a fall, but Mrs Merrett denied this. She had
been writing a letter "and a pistol went off under my ear". Her
further remarks, however, showed some confusion and Mrs
Hill, not wanting to excite her, left.

Before she went back to Brighton, Mrs Hill wrote to Mrs
Merrett's sister Mrs Penn, who was then with her husband on
the Riviera. Mr and Mrs Penn, who had heard nothing from
their dutiful nephew, left at once. On their way they met Mrs
Hill in London and got a full account of what she knew. They
arrived in Edinburgh between 6 and 7 o'clock in the morning
of Wednesday 24th March, a week after the shooting, and went

straight to the Infirmary. Mrs Merrett was asleep but they called again between 10 and 11 o'clock.

Mrs Merrett was delighted to see her sister and talked to her apparently very sensibly. She asked her to find a present for Sister Grant, who had been very kind, and to go to the flat and look after Donald: Edinburgh was "a particularly wicked city".

She also asked Mrs Penn to get an ear specialist for her. She had been told that she had had a fall but she doubted this official story. Her recollection was that she had been sitting at the table writing "when a sudden explosion went off in my head as if Donald had shot me".

Mrs Penn said that would be impossible and the subject was dropped.

Later that day Mr and Mrs Penn, Donald Merrett and a Mr Jenks, Mrs Merrett's business agent in London, discussed the mystery in a room at the Infirmary and afterwards at 31 Buckingham Terrace. Merrett, in answer to Mrs Penn, said that he did not shoot his mother and suggested suicide, a theory which his aunt indignantly rejected. Someone suggested accident: the pistol might have been among papers in the bureau and have been accidentally discharged when the papers were taken out.

Next day Mrs Merrett was able, when Mrs Penn visited her in the morning, to sign a cheque. Later that night she became delirious; she continued incoherent on Friday 26th March and lost consciousness on Saturday 27th. She died very early in the morning of Thursday 1st April, still in the suicidal ward of the Royal Infirmary. Her death was recorded in the *Scotsman* of 2nd April: "MERRETT. At Edinburgh, on the 1st inst., Bertha Merrett, third daughter of the late W. H. Milner, of Manchester. (By accident.)"

A post-mortem examination was carried out by Professor Harvey Littlejohn, son of Sir Henry of the Monson trial. He found a perforated wound of the inner ridge of the right ear. A small-calibre nickel-plated bullet was embedded in the bone of the base of the skull, the direction of the wound being horizontal and slightly forward. Professor Littlejohn's report concluded: "There was nothing to indicate the distance at which the discharge of the weapon took place, whether from a few inches or a greater distance. So far as the position of the wound is concerned the case is consistent with suicide. There is some difficulty in attributing it to accident, although such a view cannot be wholly excluded."

Mrs Merrett was buried in Piershill Cemetery on Saturday 3rd April, the ceremony being in the shortened form considered appropriate for suicides. Mr and Mrs Penn took over the occupancy of the flat until the lease expired in June and their nephew stayed with them. He continued his nominal studies and his more enthusiastic visits to the Dunedin Palais de Danse and to Betty Christie. He had tea with her on the afternoon of his mother's funeral.

His behaviour indeed did not alter, except to become more extravagant, during his mother's illness. He had bought an AJS motor bicycle on 6th March for £28; on 22nd March he ordered an HRD racing motor bicycle with sidecar at a price of £139. He was allowed £30 for his old machine and had to find £109. From 23rd to 27th March he made four cash payments amounting to £70. Then the payments stopped. As the sellers insisted on payment in full he never received delivery.

On 30th March—and this explains why the payments stopped when they did—Inspector Fleming called at 31 Buckingham Terrace. He had learned from Mr Penn that an empty cartridge case had been found in the sitting-room, where it had apparently lain, undisturbed either by Mrs Sutherland's cleaning or the police investigations, for nearly a fortnight. It was near the window, some six or eight feet in front of the place where Mrs Merrett had been sitting when the shot was fired.

During this visit Fleming took the opportunity to interview Merrett. He had not done so before.

After being cautioned, Merrett explained that he had bought the pistol in February as they thought of going to France at Easter. At Buckingham Terrace relations between his mother and himself were good, but at their previous address she "got on to me for spending too much money. She also got on to me for going out too much and neglecting my lessons". Some letters had arrived that morning. One from the Clydesdale Bank said that she had overdrawn her account. After breakfast he went into his room and when he came back Mrs Merrett was sitting at the table writing. He pointed out that she had wrongly addressed the envelope for the letter she was writing. She told him to go away, as he worried her. He went to the other end of the room to get his books, heard a report, turned and saw his mother falling. He rushed over, saw Mrs Sutherland in the hall and told her that his mother had hurt herself. He then telephoned for the police.

He further explained that he had loaded his pistol on the Saturday before, as he meant to go to the Braid Hills to shoot rabbits on Sunday morning, but his mother took the pistol and put it into one of the drawers of the bureau. He did not see it again until he lifted it off the floor after his mother had fallen.

This statement agrees with what Mrs Sutherland told Fleming, that she had come out of the kitchen when she heard the shot and had seen Mrs Merrett falling. But Mrs Sutherland had told different stories and so had Merrett. His statement to the constables who arrived first was that he had gone into the kitchen to tell Mrs Sutherland what had happened. It should also be noted that this statement explains why the pistol was on the bureau (if in fact it was there) when these officers called. But the evidence on this important matter is contradictory.

On the same day, 30th March, Inspector Fleming carried out a search and took possession of a number of articles. First there was a Midland Bank cheque-book in a drawer in Merrett's room. The first five cheques and their counterfoils were missing. In the same drawer there was an envelope addressed to Mrs Merrett containing her Midland Bank pass-book and a letter dated 5th March. A note-book headed "J. D. Merrett—Accounts" was also found.

In the bureau the inspector found Mrs Merrett's account book and another mutilated cheque-book with counterfoils missing. He asked Merrett for the Clydesdale Bank pass-book but Merrett professed ignorance. Fleming also asked for the unfinished letter which he had seen on the table on 17th March, to be told that it had been destroyed as it was stained by blood. The inspector could not remember seeing blood on it.

A few days later the inspector returned and Merrett handed him two of the five missing Midland Bank cheques, which he said he had found in a drawer in his mother's room. He did not

know where the other three were. He told the inspector that he
had bought the pistol at Hardy Brothers in Princes Street and
that he did not think his mother knew he had it. It is difficult
to reconcile this statement with his account on 30th March of
how she had confiscated it.

Later still the inspector called again, this time with the remaining Midland Bank cheques, which he had obtained from
the bank. They were dated 24th, 26th and 27th March and
made out to J. D. Merrett for £30, £30 and £28 9s 6d respectively. All bore the signature "Bertha Merrett". Merrett now
explained that his mother used to sign cheques in blank for him
to fill in as required, either to replenish the Edinburgh account
or for cash. He had used the proceeds of these three cheques
to make payments to account of the price of his new motor
bicycle. [This statement, at least, seems to be true.]

On Tuesday 13th April Merrett followed one of the conventions of detective fiction and went to London to consult a
famous detective: he did not mention any names. Rather ex-
travagantly for such a serious business trip he took with him a
friendly taxi-driver and two young ladies. One of them came
back very soon at the bidding of the police, who had discovered
that she was under sixteen. The other three members of the party
arrived back about a week later. They said they had walked
from London as they had no funds left.

When he came back Merrett stayed at Buckingham Terrace
with Mr and Mrs Penn. When the lease ran out in June, he
went to Ramsay Lodge, a University hostel, until the end of
the summer term.

On 3rd June he was invited to call at the Central Police
Office and write the name "Bertha Merrett" six times on
a piece of paper, four times in his own writing and twice in imi-
tation of one of the Midland Bank signatures. Apparently even
the credulity of the Edinburgh police was being strained by
some of their discoveries. But still no action was taken. When
term ended, Merrett was free to go on a yachting holiday on
the Clyde, based at Tighnabruaich. We do not know whether
he visited, or even consciously noticed, the house at Ardlamont.

Meanwhile the Edinburgh University authorities were dissatisfied, as well they might be, with Merrett's academic dili-

gence and told him that he would not be allowed to continue his studies after the summer vacation. Other arrangements had to be made for his education. The Public Trustee, who was executor and the young man's guardian under Mrs Merrett's will, was advised that his ward should prepare for academic life at Oxford in healthy open-air surroundings in the country. In August Merrett began this new and probably distasteful life at the vicarage of Hughenden, near High Wycombe in Buckinghamshire.

There for the moment we may leave him and return to the wicked city of Edinburgh, where the authorities were still slowly puzzling over Mrs Merrett's financial affairs and the manner of her death. On 6th August Professor Littlejohn obtained cartridges of the same make as Merrett's and fired a series of experimental shots at cardboard targets with Merrett's pistol. Generally speaking these showed that at a range of three inches or less there was a clearly visible area of smoke blackening and tattooing caused by particles of powder which had become embedded in the cardboard. Above that range there was little to be seen except the entrance hole of the bullet. Similar results were obtained from experiments carried out with Professor John Glaister of Glasgow University in December.

On 4th November, Gerald Francis Gurrin, a London handwriting expert, made a report about a number of cheques which had been recovered from the Midland and Clydesdale Banks. On 29th November a warrant was granted by the Sheriff of the Lothians and Peebles for Merrett's arrest on two charges: first, that he murdered his mother, and second, that he "uttered as genuine"[1] twenty-nine cheques each bearing her signature, such signatures being forged. He was arrested at Hughenden and handed over to two Edinburgh police officers who brought him back to Edinburgh.

The pattern of the case so far is not unlike that of the Ardlamont shooting. In each case three persons were at or near the scene—the victim, the alleged killer and one other—instead of the two whom any prudent murderer would have thought enough; the weapon must have been in the hand either of the accused or of the victim; if it was in the accused's hand, the

[1] I.e., presented for payment.

shot was deliberate and the death was murder; the authorities were satisfied by the first statements of the accused and the third party that the victim was responsible and accordingly made only casual investigations; discovery of the financial background made them think again; the doctors, too, changed their minds; and in each case the result of all this was that the charge was first made when the evidence was already stale—much more so in Merrett's case than in Monson's.

It is true that Mrs Sutherland, the third party, did not disappear like "Scott". But the variations in her statements must have made the Crown wish that she had done so after her first one.

The trial began in the High Court of Justiciary on Tuesday 1st February 1927, ten months to the day after Mrs Merrett's death. The presiding Judge was the Lord Justice-Clerk, Lord Alness, who held that office from 1922 until his resignation in 1933. He reached the bench not from the office of Lord Advocate (which he held from 1913 to 1916) but, more unusually, from that of Secretary for Scotland (1916 to 1922). The prosecution was conducted by the Lord Advocate, the Right Honourable William Watson, KC, assisted by Lord Kinross as advocate-depute. The defence was in the hands of Mr Craigie Aitchison, KC, Mr R. Macgregor Mitchell, KC, and Mr J. L. M. Clyde, advocate, instructed by Messrs Norman Macpherson & Dunlop, SSC.[1]

It was a strong bar. In 1929 the Lord Advocate, with the title of Lord Thankerton, took his seat in the House of Lords where his father had sat before him as Baron Watson. Mr Aitchison was Lord Advocate from 1929 to 1933 and then Lord Justice-Clerk until his death in 1941. Mr Macgregor Mitchell was Chairman of the Scottish Land Court from 1934 to 1938. Mr Clyde was Lord Advocate from 1941 to 1955, when

---

[1] Next year the same team, with the substitution of J. C. Watson for Macgregor Mitchell, conducted Oscar Slater's successful appeal against his conviction nineteen years earlier on the charge of murdering Miss Gilchrist.

he was appointed to the offices of Lord Justice-General of Scotland and Lord President of the Court of Session, offices held by his father before him from 1920 to 1935.

First Mrs Sutherland told how she had been employed by Mrs Merrett. She then said she had been bending down to clean the kitchen grate when she heard a shot, a scream and the sound of a body falling. She stood still for a few seconds. She then heard a noise like books falling in the lobby and the accused came in, very upset. He said "Rita, my mother shot herself" and made to put his head on her shoulder. Mrs Sutherland remarked that his mother had seemed all right when she arrived. Merrett said that he had been wasting her money and that his mother had quarrelled with him about that. He thought she was worried.

She and Merrett then went into the sitting-room. Mrs Merrett was lying with her head toward the door; that is, as if she had fallen to the floor to her left. There was a lot of blood. She saw a pistol on top of the bureau at the corner nearer the door, which was not within Mrs Merrett's reach from where she had been writing.

Mrs Sutherland went to the telephone and called the police. Merrett had to take over, as she was not sure how to spell the name, whether a single or double "t". [One feels that this detail could have been left till later.] Merrett asked her to help him put his mother on the sofa but she said they should leave her where she was. He then said "I cannot bear to look at it any longer", and both went downstairs to meet the police, who arrived just as they got to the foot of the stairs. She asked one of the constables to take the pistol away.

Later two detective officers came to the flat to interview her. One was Inspector Fleming. She did not know what she told them. She was mixed up at the time. She did not remember saying that she had seen the pistol falling from Mrs Merrett's hand. She did not in fact see that.

On Saturday 13th March Mrs Merrett asked her if she had seen a cheque-book which was missing. Next day she heard her ask the accused to write and ask for another one to be sent on.

In cross-examination she agreed she did not know Mrs Merrett intimately. She had been in her service for only a week. On

Monday Mrs Merrett told her that she had had a hard life and that she had lost her husband in the Russian Revolution. Mother and son seemed affectionate and happy.

When she last saw Mrs Merrett, she was sitting at the table. To reach the bureau she would have had to turn, stretch out her arm and probably tilt her chair on one or two legs. When she went out, she left the sitting-room door open. She did not hear it being closed at any time. It was open when she came back after the shooting.

She insisted that she stood still in the kitchen after hearing the shot and did not go out until after the accused came in. She agreed, however, that she might have said she ran out at once. The accused was very upset and agitated when he came in. She tried to comfort him.

When Inspector Fleming came, she told him that Mrs Merrett had shot herself. "Did you say anything more?" asked Aitchison.

"I said other things that I cannot rightly remember . . . I think I said I saw the lady falling, but I did not. I had got mixed up with other things."

Further cross-examination led her to say "I must have said I saw her falling instead of saying I heard her falling." She still denied having in fact seen the fall.

That evening she consulted her doctor, Dr Rosa, and told him that she felt unwell, that the lady for whom she worked had shot herself and that she was sorry for the boy because he was so young. That was all she said about the case. It was "a downright lie" to suggest that she told him anything about Mrs Merrett's false teeth—although she thought that, when she left the room, Mrs Merrett had them in her left hand.

At times Mrs Penn, Mrs Merrett's sister, showed hostility to the accused but not about this case. She did not discuss the matter very often with Mrs Penn.

After a surveyor had formally identified plans which he had made of the flat, the Lord Advocate brought his police witnesses, beginning with Thomas Middlemiss. He had left the police to become a piper with the KOSB and now planned to emigrate to Australia. As one of the officers who came in answer to the first summons, he was an important witness. It was all the more unfortunate for the Crown that he was very vague about the position of the pistol: he could not remember whether he picked it from the floor or from the bureau. He was, however, sure that there was blood on it. He interviewed the accused, who gave "money matters" as a reason for his mother's action, and Mrs Sutherland, who said that she was in the kitchen when the accused came and told her that his mother had shot herself. The witness reported the case as one of attempted suicide.

Cross-examined, he said that there was a lot of blood about. He made enquiries and found that Mrs Merrett had shot herself. He did not agree that the accused gave his information freely and willingly: "but, you know, he is a fellow that I could not really tell you what he is. You know you could not read him very well. You could not sum him up. If he had been a pal . . ."

"If he had been a pal you would have known him better?" —"Yes."

He took a statement from Mrs Sutherland and made a report. "It was my duty."

"And I suppose it was your duty to keep your eyes open?" —"It was, but in cases like this, when you are a policeman in uniform, you have to get your skates on quick; but it was reported to the CID. I did my best. I could not do anything more in my duty."

"There was nothing in the circumstances to arouse your suspicion?"—"Well, not at the time, but after . . ."

"At the time there was nothing whatsoever in the circumstances as you found them to arouse your suspicion?"—(No answer).

"Do you follow the question?"—"I follow it."

"Am I right?"—"I was telling you at the time when you get a job like that you have to do it in quickness and try to save life."

"I am not blaming you in the least, because I think you were right in your conclusion; but was your conclusion at the time that it was a case of attempted suicide?"—"Well, after I reported the matter, I was beginning to think different things, just the same as the public."

"But at the time when you were there officially, was it your view that it was a case of attempted suicide?"—"I reported the case as that."

"And may I take it that that was the view you formed at the time after your interview with the accused?"—"Yes."

"And with Mrs Sutherland?"—"Yes, with the statements I got I could not do anything else."

[The witness obviously felt on the defensive, uneasily conscious of less than total efficiency. He took Aitchison's question about keeping his eyes open as a sneer that he did not do so. He reacted by trying to create suspicion in order to show that he himself had not been as credulous as might appear. The point, of course, was to suggest that Middlemiss had in fact done his duty and kept his eyes open and that his observations at the time had pointed to or confirmed the idea of a self-inflicted wound.]

Constable Izatt corroborated in his fashion. He was sure that Middlemiss picked up the pistol from the floor and not from the bureau. He then rolled it in a piece of paper and put it in his pocket. The accused told Middlemiss that it was not money matters that caused his mother to attempt her life: "my mother's well off."

Constables Watt and Gibson told of their visit to Mrs Sutherland on 21st March to find out just what she had seen or not seen. In his cross-examination Watt said that on Friday 19th March Dr Holcombe told him at the Infirmary of a statement made by Mrs Merrett. He reported this to the CID and asked if he should interview her. The CID, however said that a detective officer would do so that afternoon.

The last police witness called for the Crown was Inspector Fleming. He went to the flat with Sergeant Henderson about 10 a.m. on the 17th after the ambulance had left. Mrs Sutherland told them she had seen Mrs Merrett falling and the pistol falling from her hand. Mrs Merrett's unfinished letter was lying on the table and the inspector read it—"not exactly out loud, but I think Sergeant Henderson would probably hear it and the maid too." If Mrs Merrett had been sitting at the table writing that letter, the blood stains on the floor were consistent with a fall to the left. He saw the two open letters from the Clydesdale Bank about the overdrawn account.

As a result of his observations he concluded that the shooting had been suicidal.

On Friday 19th March he went to the Infirmary. Dr Holcombe was not there but the inspector saw him next day and was told what Mrs Merrett had said. As a result he sent Watt and Gibson to see Mrs Sutherland.

After that he was not concerned with the case till 30th March, when the empty cartridge case was belatedly found in the flat. He went there and took a statement from the accused. He also took possession of cheque-books and other articles.[1]

In cross-examination he said that on their first visit they did not at once make enquiries. "What did you go there for?" asked Aitchison. "We were informed it was a case of suicide by shooting and we simply went down there to see what had happened. We were told what had happened and in consequence we left the matter for divisional plain-clothes officers to make inquiries."

After that visit a charge of attempted suicide was formulated against Mrs Merrett. Mrs Sutherland and the accused were both noted as witnesses. When Mrs Sutherland said she saw Mrs Merrett fall she was quite clear and seemed to know what she was saying—not "mixed", though a little excited. As an experienced officer, he saw no reason to doubt her accuracy. The accused's statement on 30th March, that he saw the maid in the hall as he rushed over to his mother, was quite consistent with what Mrs Sutherland told him.

When the accused visited the Central Police Office by invitation on 3rd June, he signed the name "Bertha Merrett" willingly and without hesitation. The fifth and sixth signatures were intended to be copies of a signature on one of the Midland Bank cheques. The inspector could not say which cheque was used as a model.

From 3rd June the questioning returned to Fleming's curiously desultory dealings with Dr Holcombe on 19th and 20th March. The inspector did not think what the doctor told him was important, although it was about statements by Mrs Merrett which might have some bearing on the events of 17th March. He knew Mrs Merrett had had a severe head injury which had

---

[1] See above, p. 197.

made her unconscious for some time. He did not, however, discuss with the doctor the taking of a dying deposition[1] "because I did not consider at that time that the woman was so dangerously ill as she appears to have been. I asked Dr Holcombe if her life was in danger and he said it was." Later he hedged about the doctor's opinion; but he seems to have treated the medical advice he was given in a surprisingly cavalier fashion. The importance of the evidence for the defence was once more to emphasise the complete lack of suspicion in the minds of the police at the time. The inspector agreed that it would have been wise to have had a deposition taken if the circumstances had been suspicious.

Dr Richard Bell brought the day's evidence to a close. He was the surgeon on duty in the out-patient department of the Infirmary when Mrs Merrett was brought in. He examined the wound and saw no blackening or tattooing. He did not remove any of the blood round it. After his preliminary examination he sent the patient to the surgical theatre.

The defence had had a good day. The Crown witnesses had unanimously at the time attributed the shooting to suicide, with all the evidence lying before them. True, the accused seemed to have changed his story a little; but so, and more spectacularly, had the principal witness for the Crown.

On the second day Dr Holcombe told how he dressed Mrs Merrett's wound when she was admitted. He washed her ear, using a swab to get the blood out. Then he examined the wound but found no blackening or tattooing. In cross-examination he agreed he had to use a certain amount of force to rub away the coagulated blood. In searching for blackening he used the naked eye only, unassisted by microscope or hand lens.

In his examination in chief he told of the account Mrs Merrett gave him of the "accident". This evidence was admitted only after lively objection from Aitchison, who argued that statements by deceased witnesses could be admitted only if they were (1) part of the *res gestae* (circumstances immediately con-

---

[1] This is a statement taken on oath before the Sheriff from a witness in imminent danger of death. If he dies it is competent evidence; if he recovers it is not. The witness must be of sound mind at the time but he need not know his critical condition.

nected with the crime, like the muttered "They got me" of a cliché-ridden film) or (2) made in the presence of the accused or (3) made formally as a dying deposition. Mrs Merrett's statements to Dr Holcombe did not fall in any of these categories. The Lord Justice-Clerk, however, was not prepared to exclude the evidence and so the jury heard Mrs Merrett's story from the doctor, and also the very similar one given by the accused next day, each with its use of the words "Go away, Donald, and don't annoy me."

Once the evidence was admitted Aitchison had to try to minimise its effect. Mrs Merrett recovered consciousness before 12.30 p.m. on 17th March. She was fully conscious until delirium set in on 25th March. There was a full week when a deposition could have been taken. The doctor saw no sign of mental disturbance before the onset of the delirium, which he took to be the first sign of inflammation in the brain and co-incident with it. The defence theory was that the inflammatory process must have been going on for some time before delirium set in, but the doctor did not feel able to deal with this.

When she was first asked how the accident happened, Mrs Merrett was quite willing to answer. She did not repudiate the use of the word "accident". Later she became annoyed and impatient when he asked to whom she had been writing. It was quite common in the doctor's experience that a patient's mind was blank as to the events immediately before a head injury, even when the injury was self-inflicted.

Aitchison's cross-examination ended with a hint of an attack he was to make on Mrs Penn, the dead woman's sister.

"Was not she rather inclined to make suggestions as to how the thing had occurred?"—"She was."

"And suggestions against the accused as to how it had occurred?"—"She never actually made it against the accused to me."

"Not in terms?"—"No."

"Not in terms; but can you say that Mrs Penn was not pointing the finger at the accused and insinuating that he had something to do with it?"—"I cannot say she was actually insinuating against him."

"Was she coming pretty near to insinuating that the accused

had something to do with it?"—"You could take it that way."

Sister Grant and Nurse Innes, who attended Mrs Merrett in the Infirmary, gave evidence of statements made to them by their patient. She said she had been sitting writing at a table "when suddenly a bang went off in her head like a pistol". Sister Grant asked "Was there not a pistol there?" and Mrs Merrett replied in surprise "No, was there?" Neither saw any sign of confusion in Mrs Merrett when she spoke of the accident.

It is more important perhaps that the next witness, Mrs Bertha Hill, failed to see any confusion. An old friend was less likely to accept unusual behaviour as normal than were strangers like the nurses and the doctor. But Mrs Hill said she seemed quite clear. At one stage Mrs Merrett said "You know my little purse; there is £6 in it; take what you want to go on with." This seems clear enough but its accuracy was not checked. The purse was at the flat and Mrs Hill did not go there. In any case, £6 was not likely to have remained untouched for long while Donald Merrett was about.

Mrs Hill described Mrs Merrett as "highly strung, emotional, a keen grip on life and everything it contained, but never a suggestion of doing away with herself. . . . Very clever in everything." Neither her conversation nor her conduct suggested that she was likely to attempt her own life. She was not nervous, though perhaps more easily upset than other people by little things that went wrong.

Mrs Eliza Penn, sister of Mrs Merrett and aunt of the accused, corresponded regularly with her sister and was on very affectionate terms with her. Mrs Merrett never complained about money difficulties. "She was an extremely careful person about money matters and an excellent business woman."

In view of the attack which Aitchison was going to make on her it is interesting to see that her evidence of what Mrs Merrett said to her in the Infirmary on 24th March reads more like that of a reluctant witness than a hostile one. Mrs Merrett said she had been writing when a sudden explosion went off in her head. "Did she add anything further to what you have told us?" asked the Lord Advocate.—"May I be excused, my Lord?"

The Lord Justice-Clerk: "Answer the questions which the Lord Advocate puts to you."

The Lord Advocate: "You have told us she said 'I was writing when a sudden explosion went off in my head'. What I want to know is if she added anything further to these words and, if so, what?"—"Yes, 'as if Donald had shot me'."

"Did you say anything to that, or what further passed between you? I just want to know the whole truth, nothing more and nothing less?"—"I replied that would be impossible."

Later that day there was a meeting at which Mrs Penn asked the accused if he could explain matters. He said he had not shot his mother but did not then suggest that she had done it herself. He had done so earlier but Mrs Penn had refused to consider that explanation. There was some suggestion of an accident, that the pistol might have been in a drawer in the bureau and that it might have been taken out by mistake with some papers and gone off accidentally.

Aitchison's cross-examination made no concessions to subtlety. From the start he treated Mrs Penn as a hostile witness. "Did you refuse a precognition[1] to the accused's advisers in this case?"—"I did not."

On one occasion, said Mrs Penn, when the accused's solicitors approached her and her husband for a statement, her husband wrote and said that they did not want to be bothered about the matter then: she was ill at that time. It was untrue to say that they had to be ordered by the Procurator-fiscal to give such a statement. They went willingly and eagerly to the solicitors' office, but were insulted and left before they were asked a single question. The insult was a remark that Mr Penn was "too good to live". It was untrue to suggest that at the interview Mr and Mrs Penn showed such temper that they were asked to leave. On 7th January they had been staying at Rumbling Bridge, in Perthshire, and had refused to be interviewed there. They were coming to Edinburgh and thought the matter could wait [three weeks before the trial began]. Once Mrs Merrett had visited the witness at Bosham. She stayed in the village, not in Mrs Penn's house. It suited both of them. It was not the case that the sisters had had a row and that Mrs Penn had turned Mrs Merrett out.

After these preliminary questions, Aitchison turned to the facts of the case. Mrs Merrett was very bright when the witness

---

[1] I.e., a statement of the evidence which the witness can give.

first saw her and not at all confused. She did not taken any
written note of the conversation at the time but "her words are
burnt into my mind". She had always told the same story. It
was her own recollection, not something suggested to her by
anyone else.

Her reaction to the phrase "as if Donald had shot me" was
to say "that was impossible".

"Did you think it impossible?"—"Yes, I did, then."

"Have you changed your mind?"—"I do not know."

"You expressed that opinion then. I would like it if you
would express an opinion now?"—"I have nothing to say."

". . . I put it to you that it was you who suggested to her that
Donald had shot her and that it was his mother who warmly
repudiated the suggestion as being impossible?"—"That is
quite untrue."

"I think your nephew Donald is heir to his grandfather, is he
not?"—"Yes."

"And, failing Donald, who is the heir?"—"My own son."

"Have you never at any time expressed yourself strongly that
Donald should not succeed to the estate?"—"No, never at any
time."

The witness had always resented any suggestion that her sister
had committed suicide. There was nothing in the family history
to suggest such a thing. One brother was in a lunatic asylum in
Manchester but "there is nothing inherited in my family whatsoever. He brought it entirely on himself."

A careful examination by the Lord Justice-Clerk next day
left matters very much as they were.

The next witness, Walter Penn, her husband, was deaf and
irritable. He seemed to find it quite unnecessary that he should
have to give evidence at all: the police had his statements and
should have notes of when things happened. This may have
been a display of the artistic temperament (his own description
of himself was "a poor devil artist"): whatever it was, it brought
him into frequent conflict with counsel and the Court. His most
dramatic evidence was about the meeting at the Infirmary. Mrs
Penn, he said, "looked across at Donald, who was on one of
the settees, and she said 'Donald, didn't you do it?' and Donald
said 'No, auntie, I did not do it, but if you like I will confess'."

After a few questions in cross-examination about this meeting, Aitchison asked whether the witness had been using his earphone at the time. He said he had not. Aitchison invited him to remove it in the witness-box so that they could have an idea of what his normal hearing was like. The witness did so.

"At the moment" asked Aitchison "is your hearing normal or abnormal?"—"No, I cannot hear that. I cannot even hear that you are saying anything."

Counsel stepped back to the dock. "I will confess if you like."—"I can hear you talking; I can almost hear your articulation."

He came nearer. "I will confess if you like."—"It seems to me you are not trying to raise your voice at all."

Nearer still, up to the witness-box. "I will confess if you like."—"You said 'I will confess if you like'."

"Was Donald's head as near your head as mine is to yours at the time?"—"That I cannot be quite sure of."

The danger had passed. To make matters sure Aitchison brought out that the words must have been heard by Mrs Penn and by Jenks, Mrs Merrett's business adviser. Finally the witness said he thought the remark was just a childish way of brushing it on one side. It is not surprising that the Lord Advocate did not rely on this evidence in his speech.

Nurse Grant was present at the conversation between Mrs Merrett and Mrs Penn. Mrs Merrett asked what had happened. Mrs Penn said "You had a nasty fall". Mrs Merrett denied this and said "There was a sound like a pistol or gun shot in my head". She added "Did Donald not do it? He is such a naughty boy." She did not remember Mrs Penn saying "That would be impossible". According to her Mrs Penn was so upset that she left the room without saying anything. Mrs Merrett seemed quite serious. She was suffering a lot of pain and having morphine injected to deaden the pain.

This is not exact corroboration of Mrs Penn; it may come close to it.

Then Betty Christie told of Merrett's visits to the Dunedin Palais de Danse (about four nights a week and once or twice a week in the afternoons) and of the visit to Queensferry on the afternoon of the shooting. In cross-examination she said that she suggested the visit, to try to take his mind off things. He was very upset. Before 17th March he danced quite a lot at the Dunedin, but she could not remember his doing so while his mother lay ill.

Finally Aitchison asked "Did you just regard him as a big romping boy?"—"Yes."

The way was now cleared for the expert evidence. First, Charles Nichol Stott, an assistant with Hardy Brothers, described the pistol he had sold Merrett on 13th February for £1 17s 6d. It was a .25 automatic made in Spain, cheap in comparison with the English makes but not necessarily inferior. It had quite an effective safety catch. When it was fired the spent cartridge case was ejected, usually to the right, but one could never be absolutely certain.

Another gunmaker, Alan Macnaughton (son of James Macnaughton who gave evidence at the Monson trial), agreed with Stott's description. He added that the gun had a fairly heavy pull for such a small weapon (5 lbs 9 oz) and was therefore unlikely to go off accidentally. He had made no experiments about the distance at which blackening was caused, but he thought that with so-called smokeless powder there would be blackening only at a very short distance. He would expect hair to be singed at a range of one inch. Again experiments would be needed to be quite sure. Pistols like this were of little use for rabbit shooting or target practice. The short barrel made it difficult to take a steady aim. They were useful mainly for self-defence.

In cross-examination he said that some people bought pistols without having any clear idea why they wanted them. Firearms sometimes went off accidentally for no accountable reason. The explosive used was a modified type of cordite known as smokeless powder. It would not cause the real blackening which gunpowder would.

These two witnesses were followed by Professor Harvey Littlejohn, professor of forensic medicine at Edinburgh University. He was in poor health and died in August of the same year. In his first report he had expressed the view that the case was consistent with suicide and that accident, though difficult, could not be excluded. In his second report he described the results of his experiments with the pistol and cartridges. He concluded: "In considering the question of a possible accidental discharge of the pistol by the deceased, I am of opinion that this is not easily conceivable when one considers (1) the position in which the pistol must have been held, viz., behind the ear and not less than 4 inches from it; (2) the angle at which it must have been held, with the muzzle pointing forwards, and (3) the considerable force required to discharge it.

"Intentional self-infliction is in my opinion equally inconceivable.

"The suicide, as a rule, leaves nothing to chance. He holds the weapon close to his head in a natural position and fires at the temple or side of the head in front of the ear. The wound always shows the characters of a 'near' discharge.

"In the present case the discharge was not a near one. The wound was in a very unusual position, while the direction, considered along with the distance of the discharge, indicates that the hand and arm must have been in a strained position—a most unlikely circumstance in a would-be suicide. With the weapon held in such a position, the person could have had very little knowledge of what part of the head he would hit, also a very strong point against self-infliction.

"From these considerations I am of opinion that suicide was in the highest degree improbable.

"The direction of the bullet wound, the position of the wound, the distance at which the discharge took place, all point to the weapon having been fired by another party."

The professor had compared the results of his experiments with those obtained for the defence by Robert Churchill and Sir Bernard Spilsbury. The first experiments by these experts were made in London and showed different results, owing to a difference in the powder used. Their later experiments in Edinburgh, using the same gun with cartridges from the same box as those used by the Crown experts, gave similar results.

Cases of suicide by shooting by women were rare but they did happen occasionally. The witness demonstrated, however, that the position to be taken up by Mrs Merrett was an awkward one. It involved holding the pistol three inches or more from the ear and behind it, with the arm in a strained position. Accident was also extremely unlikely. Mrs Merrett would have had to take the pistol out of the drawer with the butt in her hand and then turn her hand so that the muzzle pointed towards herself. Then she would have to have her thumb or finger on the trigger and give it a pull of at least 5 lbs. If the safety catch was on, it could not have been released accidentally.

Washing with a sponge got rid of some of the blackening on cardboard and also on skin, but it left the darkest part next the wound unaffected. The smoke blackening went, but the deep black, caused by unconsumed particles driven into the surface, could not.

In cross-examination by Aitchison, the witness agreed that all the data should be known before an opinion was formed. His opinion was stronger than a probability: he thought that both suicide and accident were inconceivable. He had no doubt that the discharge had been at a greater range than three inches; but if he was wrong about this suicide and accident were both possible. In order to get over the difficulty of the direction of the wound, Aitchison suggested that the pistol might have been held at right angles to the longitudinal line of the head and that at the very moment of discharge Mrs Merrett might have instinctively averted her head so that the angle between it and the pistol was increased. The witness with some reluctance agreed that this was possible. He also agreed that women often have a considerable range of movement in the shoulder joint.

He did not agree that the skin experiments showed less blackening than those on cardboard. Passages from a number of textbooks were put to him to emphasise the danger of drawing inferences about range of discharge from the mere absence of blackening. These included the works of Professor (now Sir Sydney) Smith—to which Littlejohn had written a eulogistic introduction—and Littlejohn himself. The witness was unshaken. Pure cordite might cause no blackening, but the so-called "smokeless powder" of automatic ammunition was not pure cordite and did cause blackening.

He was closely examined about the possibility of blackening being washed away when the wound was cleaned. He maintained his opinion that only the smoke blackening would have been affected: powder tattooing would have been obvious, even without a hand lens, if there had been a near discharge, i.e., one closer than three inches.

The site of the wound was "very, very rare" for suicide, though not impossible.

After Aitchison put different theories of accident to him he admitted that accident was just possible.

He was reluctant to express a view about the reliability of statements made by Mrs Merrett before she became delirious. If she seemed normal to the persons who heard the statements, he would have been inclined to rely on them.

Professor Glaister's report summarised the information which had been made available to him from the Infirmary and from Professor Littlejohn's post-mortem report. Like his colleague he thought that the wound could have been self-inflicted only if the hand and arm were in a very strained and unnatural position. He found the site of the wound unusual. In his experience, suicides usually chose the easiest and most certain position to secure their object—the temple, the forehead or the roof of the mouth. From the absence of blackening he concluded that the muzzle was at least four inches and probably more than six inches from the head at the moment of discharge. He concluded "while I am unable to exclude absolutely the possibility of the production of such a wound as in this case by self-infliction the improbabilities so outweigh in my mind the possibility that I have come to the conclusion that the head injury which caused the death of Mrs Merrett was not self-inflicted."

For the rest he agreed substantially with Professor Littlejohn. Perhaps most important, he would not be shaken from his view that blackening would not have been washed away with the coagulated blood round the wound.

Next day the Lord Advocate turned to the charge of uttering the forged cheques. First of all, the London expert Gerald Francis Gurrin told how he had examined a number of undisputed signatures by Mrs Merrett to make himself familiar with their characteristics. They bore signs of having been written quickly and without hesitation and blotted while the ink was still wet, so that only a thin film was left on the paper. He then examined fifty-six cheques the signatures on which were disputed, twenty-three on the Clydesdale Bank and thirty-three on the Midland Bank. They were so arranged that only the signatures were visible. He picked out twenty-nine as being heavier in appearance than the genuine signatures. When he looked closer, he found under the ink of these signatures a deep violet outline, either carbon paper or very soft pencil. The presence of such an outline was quite inconsistent with genuineness. The inking over had been done slowly and hesitantly.

Another suspicious circumstance struck him on his preliminary examination. A number of the disputed signatures were far more similar to one another than is usual with genuine signatures. He made a tracing of one of these recurring signatures and superimposed it on the other disputed examples. It corresponded exactly to sixteen of them, so that seventeen signatures were identical. By the same method he found another signature to appear eleven times. These twenty-eight recurrent signatures were all within the group of twenty-nine on which carbon lines had been found.

All twenty-nine cheques were made out to J. D. Merrett. In none of them was the body written out by Mrs Merrett, although she had written the body of all the others.

Cross-examination by Macgregor Mitchell did not have much success. It was hardly to be expected. Detailed questioning about the sizes of letters and so on could not disguise the hard fact that the signatures on twenty-nine cheques had been inked over carbon or pencil outlines—and people just do not sign their names in that way.

When an Edinburgh expert, William Morrison Smith, gave evidence that he had independently picked out the same twenty-nine cheques for the same reasons, there can have been nobody in court who had any doubt that the signatures were forged. The evidence of bank officials, who said that they had honoured the cheques without question, did not affect that issue.

Some less important witnesses described, among other things, Merrett's behaviour before and after his mother's death and his transactions with the motor bicycles. The most interesting point was the discovery of the missing Clydesdale Bank pass-book, which was found in the boiler-room of the Dunedin Palais de Danse.

Finally John Michael Geoghegan, CA, reported on an examination of Mrs Merrett's private accounts and the books of the two banks. These showed discrepancies but they could be made to agree by taking into account in Mrs Merrett's accounts the twenty-nine cheques in favour of her son which had already roused the suspicions of the two handwriting experts. There was no cross-examination.

The Crown case had taken a week—Tuesday to Saturday. The defence evidence began on Monday 7th February. First there came witnesses to tell of the original official theory of attempted suicide and the steps taken toward bringing such a charge. Then Dr Rosa, Mrs Sutherland's doctor, told of his patient's visit to him and the story she told on the evening of 17th March. When he read of Merrett's arrest in December, he did not know what to do and consulted his solicitors. They in their turn took counsel's opinion. As a result of the advice he got, he reported his information both to the Crown and to the defence solicitors. His recollection was quite clear and he was unshaken by cross-examination.

After evidence that Mrs Merrett and the accused seemed devoted to one another, the defence concluded with the big guns of their experts.

First there was Professor G. M. Robertson, President of the Royal College of Surgeons and Professor of Mental Diseases at Edinburgh University, and the holder of a number of other important posts. He knew Mrs Merrett's medical history through reading newspaper reports and studying the Infirmary records. During her first three or four days in the Infirmary, her temperature was subnormal, indicating a degree of physical shock to the whole body. On the fifth day her temperature rose suddenly to 101 and this lasted for two days. This indicated some infection of the wound. The temperature went down but never again reached normal. It rose once more and she died with a temperature of 103. This showed that an infective process was producing a state of inflammation which ultimately caused her death. There was a discharge from her ear, indicating that the brain covering was damaged, liberating the surrounding cerebral spinal fluid. She was paralysed on one side of her body; she must have suffered very serious damage to the brain or the nervous system. During her whole time at the Infirmary she was in a very grave condition. She was receiving morphia in large doses.

The injuries she received were such as to produce very serious mental changes, including altered consciousness or disassociation. Her severe head injury, physical shock, pain and probably disturbed emotional state were the commonest conditions for producing altered consciousness. This state might not be noticeable even to a trained observer who had not previously known the patient. The patient, though apparently quite normal, might look at things in a different way; his prevailing mood might be slightly different. The test was when he came to himself and had absolutely no recollection of what had happened. He remembered one patient who tried to hang himself with the cord of his dressing-gown. He was cut down and saved by his wife. The witness had been very anxious to find out exactly what had passed through his mind but the patient, a medical man, could not remember the attempt. Such a patient might remember incidents almost bordering upon such an act and the impulses leading up to it.

In another case two motor cyclists collided. One was knocked unconscious. A doctor was sent for and arrived while the victim was still unconscious. When he went home the cyclist told his parents that the accident had been caused by the doctor. He was not confused, but perfectly clear that the doctor had been responsible.

People who had had head injuries were very suggestible. The intelligence and the efficiency of the brain were both affected.

Although Mrs Merrett might have been outwardly normal, it would be unsafe to exclude a state of altered consciousness, especially as her case developed into one of delirium. There had been no real examination of her mental condition: she had a very serious physical injury and the doctors' whole attention had naturally and properly been directed to that.

Having regard to the whole circumstances, he thought that any statements she made about what happened on 17th March should be received with the greatest hesitation. Her inflammatory brain condition must have been developing for some time before the delirium was obvious to anyone. A state of delirium did not come on suddenly. He would not say that no reliance should be placed on what she said, but it would be hazardous to accept her statements as being strictly accurate.

Cross-examination was short and directed mainly to possible differences between Mrs Merrett's case and the examples quoted by Professor Robertson. The doctor who tried to hang himself, for example, had been suffering from a mild degree of melancholia: he was not in good mental health. The Lord Advocate concluded: "You would agree, I suppose, that if corroboration is found to a material extent of what Mrs Merrett had said, it is of value as evidence?"—"That is so."

"As I understand you—and, if I may say so, I agree with you—what you are doing is throwing out a note of warning that there should be careful consideration of the circumstances in which she made the statement, and the true circumstances as otherwise known, and then to test what she has said?"—"That is my position."

In re-examination he said that, in uttering his warning against accepting her statements, he had in mind that the nurses and even Mrs Merrett's friends saw no abnormality. These people paid little attention to mental symptoms.

Finally Lord Alness summed up: "Does your evidence therefore really come to this, that it is necessary to proceed with caution in accepting statements made by Mrs Merrett at such time in respect that they may be accurate or may be inaccurate?"—"That is so."

Robert Churchill, gunmaker, London, and an experienced expert witness in England, said he had made experiments in London with Sir Bernard Spilsbury. They fired a number of shots with a similar pistol to Merrett's at different ranges and at different substances, particularly cardboard and skin. Cardboard showed more blackening than skin. Later experiments by Sir Bernard in Edinburgh showed the same relative sensitivity. The blackening was easily removed. The defence produced a piece of skin at which a shot had been fired at a range of one inch. It now showed blackening on one side of the wound only. Originally there had been blackening on both sides but Spilsbury had cleaned the other by wiping it lightly with a piece of damp cloth. That experiment was made in London but a similar result was obtained in Edinburgh. If a wet swab had been used to remove coagulated blood, it would also have removed any blackening about the wound. No inference therefore could be drawn about the range from the mere absence of blackening.

The direction of the wound was quite consistent with both suicide and accident. An instinctive turn of the head would cause the wound to be forward from a point behind the ear. He taught shooting and found that women tended instinctively to turn their heads away from the discharge.

The witness then demonstrated ways in which an accidental wound might have been inflicted.

The position of the wound in suicide by shooting varied with the weapon. If a shotgun was used, the wound was often in the mouth; a long-barrelled revolver was placed at the temple or in the mouth; a short-barrelled weapon, like the one here, was often aimed at the side of the head.

In cross-examination he admitted that it was uncommon for women to commit suicide by shooting. He had known some cases. One did so in the presence of her husband, who was asleep in a chair beside her.

If the shooting was accidental, he agreed that Mrs Merrett must have had her thumb or finger inside the trigger guard. She must have known that the pistol was there.

The experiments in London and Edinburgh were carried out with different, though similar, pistols. The cartridges were similar. The London cartridges produced more tattooing and more of a flame colour than the Edinburgh ones.

There was a brief re-examination and then Sir Bernard Spilsbury entered the witness-box to bring his great reputation and experience to wind up the evidence for the defence. It was one of two cases where he crossed the Border in that unaccustomed role.[1] In England he invariably appeared for the prosecution.

After the great man had given his qualifications, Aitchison opened his examination with the growled and almost inaudible jest "Now, St Bernard". The witness said he had studied the history of the case and the medical records and had applied his mind to the question whether the wound was homicidal, suicidal

---

[1] The other case in which Spilsbury appeared in Scotland was that of Peter Queen, found Guilty of murder in January 1932. Lord Alness presided at that trial also. Craigie Aitchison was now Lord Advocate. As the case was tried on circuit in Glasgow, he did not appear personally. But as defence counsel was Macgregor Mitchell, Spilsbury must have felt quite at home.

or accidental. Its site was not inconsistent with either suicide or accident. He had a case where a man shot himself, the bullet entering half an inch behind the right ear and emerging above the left ear. The weapon was found grasped in his hand and death must have been instantaneous. Nor was the direction of the wound in any way inconsistent with suicide with a light, short-barrelled pistol. Accordingly he agreed with Professor Littlejohn's first report.

It would not be safe to draw any inferences about the range at which the shot was fired. Any indications of near discharge might easily have been removed when the blood was washed away. He had carried out experiments both in London and in Edinburgh. These showed that there was less blackening when the muzzle was in contact with the target than when it was one or two inches away. Where there was blackening on cardboard, a good deal could be removed by washing. There was less blackening on skin and that, even from a range of one inch, could be wiped away so as to be invisible to the naked eye; a trace could be made out with a hand lens. He had used a piece of cotton wool wrung out in water and tried to use about the same force as he would have done to remove coagulated blood round a wound. When the target was smooth skin, like the skin round the ear, it was easier to remove blackening. The wound must have bled freely; and that might have removed some blackening.

His Edinburgh experiments confirmed the results of his London ones.

From Mrs Merrett's injuries and the treatment she was receiving, he thought her statements should be accepted only with the greatest caution.

In cross-examination, he agreed that the side of the head was not one of the more usual points at which a suicide directed the weapon. It was also true that a suicide would tend to place the weapon against the head or very near it. But he might not keep the weapon so close if he averted his head as the trigger was pulled.

It was important to experiment with the actual weapon and as near the actual cartridges as possible. He would therefore prefer the Edinburgh experiments, both his own and Professor Littlejohn's, to the London ones. But he did not accept Littlejohn's unsuccessful attempt to rub away blackening. He knew that there had been little destruction of the tissues round the wound. The muzzle therefore could not have been in contact with the skin when the shot was fired; it was a question of a near discharge or one further away.

His theory of accident depended on the victim having the weapon in her hand in a position to shoot and then falling and perhaps striking some object with her elbow.

In answer to the Lord Justice-Clerk he said that if there had been no blackening originally the muzzle must have been at least three inches from the head.

The evidence was over and the Lord Advocate addressed the jury. There were two quite separate charges but the second one (uttering forged cheques) had a very important bearing on the first. On the second charge the Crown did not have to prove that the accused himself wrote the forged signatures; it was enough if they proved that he knew they were forged.

He reminded the jury of Mrs Merrett's methodical business habits. The accused had ten shillings a week pocket money. On 8th March he paid £28 for a motor bicycle. There was no trace of this sum in his accounts or his mother's. His account book showed one entry of 5s. for the Palais de Danse; no trace of the 15s or 30s for booking out Miss Christie. The girl Christie said he always seemed to have plenty of money. The Crown case was that from 2nd February the accused was operating on his mother's bank accounts by forged cheques. There were twenty-nine cheques, twenty-three used before 17th March and six after that date. There was no doubt that the body of these twenty-nine cheques was written by the accused; there was no doubt that he endorsed them; there was equally no doubt that the signatures were not written by Mrs Merrett.

The two handwriting experts had found double signatures on all these twenty-nine cheques. That was enough to show they were forged: nobody ever wrote his own signature twice over in two different colours. Then the signatures on these cheques were halting instead of being fluent and free. There could be no doubt that the accused either did the tracing himself or got somebody else to do it in collaboration with him. "Why do I say that? He was the party . . . who presented the cheques and got cash or credit to himself and who endorsed each one of them."

That was enough to establish the crime of uttering.

There were some other facts of intense interest. They had between 120 and 130 cheques with Mrs Merrett's signature on them. The only ones on which the accused's name appeared as payee were these twenty-nine. Then, although Mrs Merrett used her cheques strictly in rotation, the forged cheques were taken out of order until she was in the Infirmary.

The accused told Inspector Fleming that Mrs Merrett gave him blank cheques. That was not impossible. But it was no reason for the counterfoils being torn out of the cheque-books, nor did it explain the number of cheques involved. The Lord Advocate analysed the transactions with the suspected cheques up to 17th March: in six weeks the accused secured a sum of £205 3s out of his mother's fixed income of £700.

There were disturbing factors which suggested possible trouble to the accused before 17th March. If the pass-books were made up and Mrs Merrett examined them, she would see the entries relating to these cheques. If they were her own she would not mind. But if they were not, undoubtedly there would be trouble. The Clydesdale book was made up to 13th March. At that date it would have shown a very considerable number of forged cheques. The Bank did not have it after that date. Who did? That was the book found in the boiler-room at the Dunedin Palais de Danse, which the accused frequented.

The Midland Bank pass-book was left at Boscombe and Mrs Merrett wrote for it to be sent on. It was sent to her on 23rd January. On 21st February she sent it back and asked the bank to keep it meantime. On 4th March she wrote and asked for it, saying that she had drawn "one or two, for me, rather large cheques lately". There were several more she did not know about. The book was sent off on 3rd March. Did Mrs Merrett ever see it again? On 12th March she wrote for a new cheque-book and said she had not yet received her bank-book. There was a postscript to that letter in the accused's handwriting to say that the book had just arrived from the old address: "it is quite in order".

That was a most significant letter, written on the Friday

before 17th March. Fleming found the book in a drawer in the accused's bedroom. If Mrs Merrett had seen it, it would have shown a balance at her credit of £286 instead of her own figure of £374. The difference of £88 was the amount of the forged cheques on the Midland Bank up to 6th March. That would undoubtedly have alarmed her: £88 was a big slice out of £700. An inquiry would have been very awkward for the accused.

The next question was the overdraft on the Clydesdale Bank. On 13th March the bank wrote to tell Mrs Merrett that her account was overdrawn by £21 11s. A few days later the accused presented a cheque on the Midland Bank for £30, £25 of which was paid into the account and £5 taken in cash. The second letter from the Clydesdale Bank on 16th March intimated an overdraft of £6 10s. It arrived by post on the morning of the 17th.

On the evidence, Mrs Merrett was in no way alarmed financially or otherwise up to this stage. What happened that morning? There was the evidence of Mrs Sutherland, the evidence of what Mrs Merrett said in the Infirmary, and the evidence of statements made by the accused.

First, Mrs Sutherland. The Lord Advocate read her evidence —how she was in the kitchen when she heard a shot and then a thud, like a body falling, and after a few seconds the sound of books falling in the lobby: and then the accused came in. Now, if the accused had been reading and gone straight to the kitchen, one could understand how he came to have books. But if there was a delay—and his own statement was that he went across to the body and picked up the pistol—how did he come to have books when he went to tell Mrs Sutherland what had happened?

Mrs Sutherland's accuracy was attacked on the ground of her admittedly faulty statement to Inspector Fleming and her statement to Dr Rosa. Whether she would have had time to go across to the hall, as she told Fleming she did, when she heard the shot, and to see Mrs Merrett falling, was for the jury to judge. The story she told Dr Rosa was different, that as she was leaving the room she heard a shot and turned round. But the first statement she made and the one she gave to Watt and Gibson on 21st March were the same as the one she told in the witness-box. That story was confirmed by what the accused said to

Betty Christie and George Scott. Mrs Sutherland was probably upset. But while the accused and the policemen were there and they were all helping Mrs Merrett, she might have kept her wits about her. Then she was left alone in the flat until Inspector Fleming came. That was just when you would expect a reaction, when she might be somewhat mixed.

He agreed that anything Mrs Merrett said had to be taken with caution and they had to consider whether there was any corroboration. All the evidence of those who saw her was that she was clear and normal. Against that there was the expert opinion, especially that of Professor Robertson. The illustrations he gave were mostly of cases where a bit had been cut out of a person's memory by an accident. But if Mrs Merrett's statements were not correct she must have been imagining something which did not happen at all. He asked the jury to accept these statements. She made five which were all consistent, four being almost identical. They were vital to the case, because one of the most important things was whether Mrs Merrett knew about the pistol at all. Her statements were quite inconsistent with such knowledge. If that was so, then her death was due neither to suicide nor to accident; the pistol was never in the bureau. If it was homicide, if the shot was fired by the accused while his mother sat writing peacefully at the table, the position and direction of the wound were exactly as one would expect to find them.

Then there was the accused's story. He gave various versions to different people. On the day he suggested to Constable Middlemiss that his mother was worried about money matters. He suggested to Betty Christie and to Scott that it might have been an accident. But it was not until Fleming interviewed him on 30th March that he suggested to anyone that the pistol was in the bureau, something which was necessary to support any theory of accident.

Lastly, there was the expert evidence. There was no doubt about the position and direction of the wound—through the right ear, forward and slightly upward. "There is a question as to whether a person could easily shoot himself suicidally in that way. Nothing is impossible in this world—doctors' evidence always shows that; but what you have got to judge of are all the

H

circumstances, not only the medical possibilities or physical possibilities; and it is perfectly clear on the evidence that if a person did shoot himself in that way it is not a usual form of shooting. This lady was in the room with her only child, and, even if she had any motive for committing suicide, is it likely that she would do so in these circumstances—sitting writing quietly a letter to her friend that had nothing to do with money matters, when it is alleged she suddenly leant over to the bureau, took out the pistol and shot herself in the presence of her only child? It is possible; all things are possible. But the purpose of having juries is to deal with such matters on reasonable grounds; and the question is whether that is a reasonable possibility."

On the question of the range of discharge, the experts agreed among themselves except on one point. With a near discharge, within three or four inches from the head, there would be a substantial amount of blackening. The issue was whether that blackening might have been washed away before the wound was properly inspected by the doctors at the Infirmary. The defence suggested that the whole surface of the wound might have been covered with blood. Against that there was the evidence of Dr Bell, who saw her first. He did not wash the wound, but he looked at it carefully for signs of blackening or tattooing and smelled for explosive. He was fully alive to the question. Sir Bernard Spilsbury said he would expect to find most of the blackening on the upper part of the ear. That was just where Dr Bell looked in vain. There had been no washing at that time and it could be ignored. After washing, Dr Holcombe and the nurse who dressed the wound in the evening found it free from blackening.

The experiments made by Sir Bernard Spilsbury and Mr Churchill were made in London with different powder and could not be set against those made by Professors Littlejohn and Glaister: in the latter a considerable portion of the blackening remained after washing. It must have been visible to Dr Holcombe and the nurses.

Although practically no position was impossible for an accident, the jury had to consider whether, in the circumstances of this case, accident was a reasonably possible alternative to murder.

Before concluding, he returned to the second charge. Mrs Merrett was taken unconscious to the Infirmary on 17th March. By his operations with forged cheques after that date the accused obtained in cash £165 9s 6d. Add that to the £265 he got before 17th March. "It comes to £361 9s 6d that he got in a period of under eight weeks out of the moneys of a lady who had only £700 a year of income to keep them both. £361 in under two months!"

The jury could come to only one conclusion, that the accused was guilty on both charges. What motive could Mrs Merrett have for committing suicide? They knew what her character was, what her habits were. She probably saw the letter from the Clydesdale Bank intimating an overdraft of £6 10s. She might have been a little worried about it. But would she commit suicide because of that? The important account for her was the Midland Bank account.

The accused was getting ever nearer the risk of discovery. He had staved off some alarms already—the Midland Bank passbook which was found in his bedroom and the first overdraft letter from the Clydesdale Bank. He had a motive; his mother had none. She was sitting quietly writing a letter. If there had been any quarrel it was over. Donald was leaning over her and she told him to go away; both agreed about that. The next thing she knew was a noise like the explosion of a pistol in her ear. "I submit it is clear that that is how it happened. She says 'Don't worry me, go away'. Donald is standing there with a pistol in his hand, and, whether the fear of detection and the impulse is too much for him or not, he is in exactly the position to inflict the wound which was in fact found in Mrs Merrett's head. . . .

"Is it conceivable that Mrs Merrett would suddenly commit suicide on an impulse, and nothing said; and after the shot a scream, and after the scream a thud, and then some delay until the accused appears in the kitchen? What is happening during that delay? On his own statement, he picks up the pistol and puts it on the corner of the bureau. Did he do that, or did it go from his hand on to the corner of the bureau, which is the natural thing to happen? Observe, if he is standing behind his mother and shoots her, the corner of the bureau on which the pistol is seen after the event by Mrs Sutherland is exactly on his right hand. And an important point in this connection is his coming down the passage. Is he running excitedly because his mother has shot herself? No. He had been over to the body, on his own admission. He has been handling the body. He comes down the passage with books in his hand which must have been picked up from the table in the recess and he drops them on the way. What is that for? Is that consistent? I suggest that the whole of this was an attempt—a hurried attempt—to try to stage a scene.

"Ladies and gentlemen, my submission to you on this first charge is that, when you look at all the evidence, and when you look at the facts, it is beyond all reasonable doubt clear that the accused was guilty of the first, as well as the second charge, and I ask your verdict accordingly."

The Lord Advocate resumed his seat. Once again the High Court had heard from the public prosecutor a calm, logical and dispassionate argument. The fireworks were left to the defence.

Before he turned to the evidence, Craigie Aitchison had some preliminary comments to make. "I hold a very strong view indeed that when a man is on trial for his life he ought to be on trial for his life, that no prisoner should ever be put in the position of having to fight a charge of murder with his right hand and a charge of uttering with his left. Yet that is the situation in which the accused is now placed. I do not dispute that it was competent for the Crown to place two charges in the one indictment, but there are bigger things than competency, and there are bigger things than legality; there is fair play."

It was for the Crown to prove their case. "The presumption of innocence is not now, and it never has been, a fiction in the law of Scotland; the presumption of innocence is the cardinal principle of the criminal jurisprudence of Scotland. . . . There is one other thing of a preliminary nature I would like to say to you. There is a great tradition in the criminal courts of Scotland, a tradition of which we who are engaged in the administration of the criminal law in any capacity are justly proud. It is a tradition which has grown up with the growth and development of our criminal law, a tradition that has come to a rich maturity, and the tradition is this: wherever you are dealing with a question affecting the life or the liberty of a fellow-man, the angle from which you approach that question is not the angle of trying how many points you can get against the prisoner, but rather the angle of trying how many points you can get in his favour. That is the spirit of our justice. It is a great tradition, a splendid tradition of the criminal courts in Scotland, and you members of the jury, I am sure, will worthily maintain that tradition today.

"There is perhaps one further observation I ought to make. This is a stale prosecution. The trial is taking place some ten months after the occurrence of the events which are being investigated, at a time when every circumstance that might have exonerated the accused has been obliterated. I do not hesitate to tell you that we, who have been responsible during these anxious days for the conduct of the defence, have felt ourselves very gravely handicapped by the absence of proper investigation made at the time by the police who were charged with the duty of inquiry. It is all very well for the Lord Advocate to come before you and suggest that if the police had made fuller inquiry at the time they might have discovered something that would have been conclusive against the accused. I can tell you that our view for the defence is a very clear and a very definite view, that if there had been proper investigation at the time these charges would never have been brought and the accused would never have been put on trial. And when you are dealing, as you are dealing here, with a stale prosecution, there is an imperative duty upon you which I am certain you will not forget—a very imperative duty indeed—to see that the utmost fair play is shown to the accused."

The question for the jury on the first charge was not to decide whether Mrs Merrett died from a homicidal wound or a suicidal wound or an accidental wound. They might be unable to do so. The question for them was: have the Crown, by the evidence, proved that the accused murdered his mother? Unless the Crown had excluded accident and suicide as reasonable hypotheses, the accused was entitled to a verdict as a matter of legal right.

He was not going to examine the evidence in great detail.

The jury had to judge on broad considerations and a broad view of the facts. If they took the evidence and analysed it fairly, they would find that the Crown asked for a verdict simply because the accused was in the room when his mother received the wound of which she died. Their case began and ended there.

First they had the evidence of Mrs Sutherland. They had two versions from her. That was one of the strange features of the case. They would find two versions in Professor Littlejohn's evidence also. It did not matter very much which version of Mrs Sutherland's evidence the jury accepted. Both were favourable to the accused. The revised version[1] was that she saw Mrs Merrett at the table writing and the accused at the other side of the room reading. She went out leaving the door open. She heard no quarrel. Then a shot rang out and the accused came through in very great distress. "Is that not far more consistent with innocence than with guilt? I would like to know what the Crown theory about it is. Does the Lord Advocate suggest that the accused on the morning of 17th March deliberately shot his mother at a time when there was a maid in the house, at a time when the dining-room door was open, in a room into which the maid could see, and into which at any moment she might enter? That won't do. It won't fit the facts. But you might say 'Well, it may not have been a deliberate act of murder; it may have been an impulsive act of murder,' That, I think, must be the Crown view of it. But it is a very dangerous theory for the Crown to say that the accused in a moment of impulse might take the life of his mother; is it not equally probable that his mother in a moment of impulse might take her own life? Impulse is a dangerous theory for the Crown in this case. The accused is bone of her bone and flesh of her flesh. If he could impulsively take her life, could not she impulsively take her own life?"

He also claimed in his favour the sound of falling books as corroboration that the accused was reading on the other side

---

[1] Aitchison treated the statements to Inspector Fleming and to Dr Rosa as the original version and [that given in the witness-box as the revised version. He overlooked the fact that Mrs Sutherland's first statement, to Constables Middlemiss and Izatt, was the same as her evidence.

of the room when the shot was fired. The delay between the scream and his appearance in the kitchen was unimportant. A second might well seem like a minute to Mrs Sutherland at a time like that.

Fortunately for the ends of justice there was another version, that given by Mrs Sutherland at the time to Inspector Fleming and Sergeant Henderson at the flat and to Dr Rosa in the evening. If she made these statements, was the Lord Advocate really asking for a verdict of murder against the accused? If there was even a doubt it was fatal to the Crown case. "I have never heard a more extravagant or a more monstrous proposition than to ask a jury to find a verdict of guilty of murder in a case where the only witness said at the time 'I was an eyewitness, and I saw the weapon falling from the hand of the woman after the shot rang out'."

There was another point about the events in the flat that morning. Constable Izatt said he saw Middlemiss pick the pistol up from the floor, roll it up in a piece of paper and put it in his pocket. How did they get round that? It would not do for the Crown to say that Mrs Sutherland or anyone else saw the pistol on the bureau. Izatt, a Crown witness, said he saw Middlemiss pick it up from the floor. That was remarkable corroboration of Mrs Sutherland's statement that she saw it falling from Mrs Merrett's hand.

When the Crown tendered evidence of what Mrs Merrett said in the Infirmary, he felt bound to object to its admission. That objection was overruled and he accepted that. But he was in no way precluded from commenting on the value of that evidence. It depended on the memory of witnesses ten and a half months after the event. It was dangerous to rely on that. Then there was Mrs Merrett's condition when she made the statements. The medical facts were not in dispute. But the Crown doctors said they could take these statements as if they were made by a perfectly normal woman. "I do not care in the least what the Crown doctors say in these matters. In these matters a layman is as good as any doctor. Do you think it right, in a case of this gravity, involving an issue of life and death, to place any reliance whatsoever upon the statements made by Mrs Merrett in the physical and mental condition in which she was?" The use of these statements showed the bankruptcy of the Crown case.

There was good ground for thinking that behind some of Mrs Merrett's statements there was the active and suspicious mind of Mrs Penn. He had not been impressed by her apparent reluctance to answer questions. "I do not want to make any harsh comment, but it struck me as playacting, and bad playacting at that." On the evidence, Mrs Penn was at least coming near to insinuating that the accused was responsible. She certainly rejected any thought of suicide, Mrs Merrett at the time was in a very suggestible state. Could the jury exclude the view that what Mrs Merrett said might have been suggested to her when she could not resist?

There had been innuendo against the conduct of the accused. If the suggestion was that it was callous, why did the Lord Advocate not say so openly? It was easy to jump to conclusions. The accused was a stranger to Edinburgh, with few friends. Why should he not go to the Dunedin Palais de Danse where he had a friend in Miss Christie? What was more natural? The evidence was all against the accused being callous. Was his expression that it was "still on the cards" that his mother would recover any more casual than the doctor's remark that she had a "fighting chance"? "Do not forget that a boy at the age the accused was—and he was only seventeen and a half—is very apt to be ashamed of anything that looks like emotion, and if there is anything in his conduct at all to suggest that he was casual or callous, you will bear that in mind."

The accused had made a number of statements. Minor discrepancies were not important, especially when they depended on the memory of witnesses. But from first to last the accused told substantially the same story, with one variation, and that a variation that was strongly in favour of innocence. When Mrs Hill suggested that someone might have got into the flat and shot Mrs Merrett, the accused would not hear of it. Would not a man with a guilty conscience have welcomed any suggestion that took suspicion away from himself? Later, though he had first suggested suicide, he said accident. It seemed a tremendously strong point in his favour that he would not have the idea of any third party causing his mother's death and, when he learned that she was going to be charged with attempted suicide, although that would have exonerated him, he said it was not attempted suicide, it was accident.

Two or three days before 17th March Mrs Merrett said she had had a hard life and that her husband had died in the Russian Revolution. Then Mrs Penn said Mr Merrett was not dead in Russia but alive in India! What was the family history? What did Mrs Merrett mean by her hard life? What were her worries over money matters? Was there anyone concerned with those money matters they had not heard? They had not seen Mr Jenks, who might have enlightened them.

The second charge was the charge of uttering. It had not been fully explained to the jury. First of all, the accused was not charged with having forged his mother's signature. Second, he was not charged with having misappropriated a single penny belonging to her. Uttering just meant passing. It was essential that the accused knew that the cheques were forged. The Lord Advocate had said "There can be no doubt that the accused either did it [sc., the forging] himself or got somebody else to do it in collaboration with him." He was not entitled to make such an observation. The Crown had not charged the accused with forging the signatures; they could not prove such a thing. If they were going to bring home guilty knowledge to the accused they had to find that knowledge in something other than the mere fact of forgery.

Was there forgery at all? The Crown case stood on the evidence of experts. It was a commonplace that there was hardly any evidence as unreliable as that of handwriting experts. It should be received with the utmost caution. It made no difference that they were dealing with what was said to be a peculiar type of forgery; the imagination of handwriting experts could be as active in alleged forgery by tracing as in any other. Gurrin had founded on certain "coincidences". When fifteen or twenty dissimilarities were pointed out to him, he said they did not matter; they still had the coincidences. Against Gurrin, they had the evidence of the banker. One honest banker was worth half a dozen experts. True, he said he had no experience of forged cheques. That was why his evidence was important.

People who lived in an atmosphere of forged cheques were very apt to find them where they did not exist.

Nobody ever knew a handwriting expert who had any doubt about anything. In a celebrated case, Adolf Beck had been sent away for a long term of penal servitude not merely on wrong evidence of identification but on wrong evidence by handwriting experts, who said they were "perfectly satisfied". "Perfectly satisfied! Members of the jury, I find it difficult in this case to get out of my mind this fact, that the name of the handwriting expert who led to the conviction of Adolf Beck was Gurrin—not the present Mr Gurrin. Out of respect to the present Mr Gurrin we refrained from asking what relationship he bore to the expert who gave evidence in the case of Adolf Beck."[1]

They had heard evidence of the so-called double signatures, but the Crown had not thought it worth while to make any chemical analysis of the ink of the signatures to see how far the solid matter might have separated from the fluid matter so as to give the appearance of a double signature.

If the signatures were not forged, that was an end of it. But if they were forged, that would not entitle the Crown to a verdict. What facts were relied on as showing guilty knowledge? First, there were cheques drawn in favour of the accused. What about it? The Crown did not allege any misappropriation. All they had been able to discover was £2 10s for a ring. That did not suggest extravagance. Then there was the fact of cheques being taken out of sequence and the bank-book found in the boiler-room of the Dunedin Palais de Danse. If it was to be evidence of crime that cheques were not drawn properly in sequence, all of us would be more or less suspect. The finding of the bank-book was in the accused's favour. If he wanted to get rid of it, why did he not burn it? It was found only a step or two down from the passage leading to the cloakroom. The natural conclusion was that it had fallen from the accused's pocket and been kicked into the boiler-room. He was paying money into the bank for his mother: what inference could they draw from his possession of the bank-book?

The evidence about the motor bicycle was unconvincing. In order to draw any adverse inference they had to exclude a great

[1] He was a son.

many possibilities which the Crown had not done. Mrs Merrett
might have arranged for her son to get a new bicycle for the old
one. There was no evidence to the contrary.

A good deal had been said about Mrs Merrett's businesslike
habits. But there was evidence that she had sent off at least one
cheque unsigned: was that businesslike? She wrote for her Midland Bank pass-book as she had drawn one or two large cheques
and wanted to know how her account stood. Why did she not
know if she kept the careful books which the Crown said she
did?

That was the case on the second charge. It was not proved. If
it failed, then not only were the jury bound to acquit on it but
they could not take it into account as bearing on the question
of motive for the first charge. But even if they convicted, it was
a long way from uttering to murder. It would be extremely
hazardous to say that, because the accused uttered, therefore he
committed murder. That was why he had protested against the
two charges on the one indictment.

On the medico-legal evidence, the direction and the position
of the wound were consistent with suicide and with accident.
The medical theory for the Crown was based on the absence of
blackening, which was consistent in their view only with a shot
fired at more than three inches distance and not with a shot
from a greater distance. The jury would not leave out of account
the evidence that the wound had to be thoroughly washed, that
pressure had to be applied to remove the coagulated blood and
that the wound might have been subjected to friction in the
ambulance. Professor Littlejohn had said in his own book
"With a sponge the blackening of the smoke and any blood
would be wiped off". How could the jury draw any adverse conclusion against the accused from so slight a circumstance as that
upon which the Crown founded?

In this case they had had the great assistance of Sir
Bernard Spilsbury. Professor Littlejohn and Professor Glaister
were both men of eminence "but I do not hesitate to say that
there is no name in Britain, there is no name in Europe, on
medico-legal questions on the same plane as the name of Sir
Bernard Spilsbury. And I am certain that you cannot fail to
have been impressed by the moderation and restraint and fair-

ness and by the complete absence of partisanship displayed by him in the evidence which he gave in the witness-box yesterday. Standing the evidence as it does, I claim that on this, the medical aspect of the case, it is emphatically in my favour."

He was not going to develop the theory of accident. It was a platitude that accidents could occur in the most unexpected ways. They might think suicide was unlikely. Was homicide less unlikely?

"You may say to me in conclusion that there are many things you would have liked explained in this case. So be it. I would only say this to you: there are greater things in life than loyalty to one's own life, and there is no greater loyalty in life than loyalty to the memory of one's mother. And why do I say that? I say that because I want you to be on your guard in this case when you come to consider your verdict—I want you to be on your guard against saying 'Why not this, and why not that? We would have liked light on this, we would have liked light on that.' Members of the jury, do not forget that there are people —and thank God there are people—who would rather go to their death with their lips sealed than that they should speak a single word that would reflect upon the name of a mother—a name which is incomparably the greatest name in all the vocabulary of our human life. I leave the case there. Judge with truth and judge with insight. And I beseech you, if you have not got all the explanations you would have liked, do not jump to conclusions. There may be reasons which you do not know, and of which you can know nothing. I need not remind you, members of the jury, of what your verdict means to the accused, who has undergone the ordeal of these trying days. Do not forget that he is without the guidance of a father, who should have been his guardian and his mentor as he was passing from boyhood into manhood. You have seen some of his relatives—and his mother is in her grave. But you have got to send him out into life; and I say to you, with the utmost respect, that if you send that lad out into life with a verdict of Not Proven, with a verdict that implies a stigma on him, upon the evidence that has been led in this case, then I say to you that you take a tremendous responsibility upon your shoulders. Members of the jury, I claim from you with a clear conscience a verdict of Not Guilty upon both these charges. Give him by your verdict a reputation up to which he will have to live for the rest of his life; and I will only say this to you, as one who has been much and intimately in contact with him during these last few days—and it is my final word—send him out from this courtroom this afternoon a free man with a clean bill, and, so far as I can judge, he will never dishonour your verdict."

Craigie Aitchison had done a magnificent job for his client. Although his argument limped a little in dealing with the minor charge of uttering, as was inevitable in view of the very strong evidence brought by the Crown, there was a fine sweep to it as he boldly seized the very points taken by the Lord Advocate as pointing to guilt and claimed them for his own. His peroration has a curiously old-fashioned air to it but, vigorously delivered, it had a passionate effectiveness. It was marred at the very end by his statement of his personal opinion of his client—a statement that should not be made by any advocate: but there was no judicial rebuke. Some of his predecessors had not escaped. In Madeleine Smith's case, both the Lord Advocate and the Dean of Faculty were reprimanded for stating their belief in the rightness of their respective causes.

So far from administering a rebuke, indeed, was the Lord Justice-Clerk that he began his charge to the jury with tributes to both counsel for the way in which they had conducted themselves.

The case, he went on, was an extraordinary one. There were two charges of diverse nature against the accused. For murder the law knew only one punishment, death. There was the relationship of mother and son between the alleged victim and the accused; cases of matricide were fortunately rare in the annals of Scottish crime. There was the comparative youth of the accused. The cumulative effect of these facts was to show that the case was a quite exceptional one in its character and its gravity and the responsibility of the jury was correspondingly increased.

"On the threshold of the case, one fact strikes my mind, unchallengeable and significant, and that is that the charge of murder brought against the accused is an afterthought on the part of the Crown. Do not misunderstand me. That consideration is by no means conclusive one way or the other. Though the charge is an afterthought it may none the less be a correct afterthought. But that it is an afterthought appears to me on the evidence to be manifest. At the time of the occurrence which we are investigating, the Crown, after inquiry through its officials, were satisfied that they were dealing with a case of attempted suicide, not a case of homicide."

Certain obvious consequences followed. Precision regarding the surrounding circumstances and the statements of the alleged victim was now unattainable. In a case treated as murder from the outset, an exact record of all matters relating to the issue and in particular to the state of affairs at the scene of the alleged crime was always preserved. Here they did not even know whether the pistol was found on the bureau or on the floor by the victim's side. Mrs Merrett's alleged statements were made to a number of people in different circumstances and no notes were taken at the time. Precision was entirely lacking.

There were four possible theories: suicide, accident and homicide, either by the accused or by another person. The last could be disregarded. Unless the Crown excluded accident and suicide as reasonable hypotheses—not merely possible explanations, but reasonable explanations—the accused was entitled to a verdict in his favour.

The onus was on the Crown to prove guilt, not on the accused to prove innocence. The evidence by which the Crown sought to discharge the onus came from four sources: first what happened at the flat; second what happened at the Infirmary; third what happened at the University—the experiments by the experts; and fourth the statements and conduct of the accused.

There were three persons at the flat that morning. One had since died. They were Mrs Sutherland, Mrs Merrett and the accused. They had to ask whether Mrs Sutherland's evidence as given in the witness-box advanced or retarded the Crown case or was neutral. They had also to remember that she had not always told the same story. The story she told Inspector Fleming was detailed and circumstantial. It contained three statements of fact: that she went into the lobby, that she saw Mrs Merrett fall and that she saw the pistol fall from her hand. Was any temporary confusion adequate to explain that triple misstatement, as she now called it? Could they rely on Mrs Sutherland? Then there was the evidence of Dr Rosa. If they thought he was completely mistaken, they would disregard it. But having regard to what he did when he read of the arrest of the accused, they might find it difficult to do so. It was difficult to believe that he invented or imagined the passage about the false teeth. If these statements were made, the jury had to consider whether they were not destructive of the case of murder.

He felt bound at this stage to add that the police evidence about what they saw and did at the flat was loose and hazy in the extreme.

Second, there were Mrs Merrett's alleged statements. "I ruled that these statements were admissible in evidence, but that does not abate my regret that you have not before you a sworn, authentic and complete statement made by Mrs Merrett to a responsible officer by way of deposition." He analysed the statements said to have been made. Mrs Penn said Mrs Merrett used the phrase "as if Donald had shot me" to which she replied "that would be impossible". Nurse Grant was there at the time. She said Mrs Merrett did not say "as if Donald had shot me" nor did Mrs Penn say "That would be impossible". On the other hand, she said that Mrs Merrett said "Did Donald not do it? He is such a naughty boy". That was a fair illustration of the hazard of relying implicitly on witnesses' memories after so many months. "It would appear that, on one important matter, Nurse Grant does not confirm Mrs Penn and that, on another important matter, Mrs Penn does not confirm Nurse Grant. You will consider whether the difference between them does not go a little further than that, and whether, so far from confirming one another, they go the length of contradicting one another."

The Crown said these statements were inconsistent with the theory of suicide. They also said that Mrs Merrett's character was such as to preclude any motive for suicide. But he thought the jury would be disposed to regard the statements with caution. Professor Robertson doubted if any of them could be relied on. Dr Holcombe demurred to his competence to deal with this. Professor Littlejohn was disposed to rely on the evidence of the doctors and nurses about Mrs Merrett's mental state.

"The questions which I invite you to put to yourselves, before you leave the Infirmary branch of the case, are these: First, were the statements imputed to Mrs Merrett made by her at all? Second, can you be sure of their complete accuracy as reproduced more than ten months after the event? Third, if made and accurately reported, can they be implicitly relied upon, having regard to her mental condition as conceived by Professor Robertson? And, lastly, accepting them as accurate and accepting the view that her mental state was such as to render the statements intelligible and reliable, how far do they advance the Crown case, which is one of murder?"

No motive for suicide had been disclosed in evidence; none of any weight had been suggested in argument. But the jury would consider whether as a rule motive for suicide was either suspected or disclosed. It was said with some force that the time and place were unlikely for suicide. But were they not equally unlikely for homicide?

"My comment, for what it is worth, upon these statements alleged to have been made in the Infirmary, before leaving them, would be this: so far as I know, but you are the judges, no one who heard these statements made at the time thought that they attributed or involved the guilt of the accused. The Crown certainly did not, otherwise he would have been arrested. If those statements are of so unequivocal a character as the Lord Advocate attributed to them, is it not a fair question: why, if they involved one inference and one only, did the Crown stay its hand? Ask yourself this, are you being invited to draw an inference of guilt from these statements which no one at the time drew? Consider, further, whether the statements may accurately be described as ambiguous, inconsistent, inconclusive, not upon oath, not noted at the time, not testified to at the time. All these vices would have been avoided by a sworn deposition."

Lord Alness, however, did not share counsel's view of the duty of the police in this matter. There was no suspicion of crime on the part of anyone except Mrs Merrett herself. And it was only where there was suspicion that a deposition was taken. "I should have thought that the view of counsel for the defence would have been not so much to blame the police for not taking a deposition as to affirm that the absence of a deposition was the best proof of the innocence of his client as regarded by the police at that particular juncture. But these, ladies and gentlemen, are matters for you, and I do not for a moment—I have no right to—dogmatise regarding them. I merely submit to you, for your final consideration and adjudication, the observations which I have made."

On the third branch of the case, the expert evidence, they had on one side Professors Littlejohn and Glaister, both men of great eminence and fairness. But in approaching their evidence they must ask: was not the reconstruction of a crime notoriously difficult and was there not a danger that the original conditions might not be accurately reproduced? They had to consider the evidence very carefully. Professor Littlejohn wrote two reports. In the first, he declined to rule out suicide or accident; in the second he virtually ruled out both. His reasoning was: no blackening, therefore no near wound, therefore neither accident nor suicide. After Professor Littlejohn's evidence they must take it that the Crown case depended on the absence of blackening and that alone. Two questions arose: was there blackening originally, and if so, had it been rubbed off? There was a direct conflict of skilled opinion between Professor Littlejohn and Sir Bernard Spilsbury. The jury should consider the experiments made in Edinburgh, and they were in favour of the Crown view on the first question. The experts also differed about the possibility of blackening being rubbed off. Professor Littlejohn said it might be partly rubbed off but not completely: Sir Bernard Spilsbury, "to whose evidence I should imagine you would be disposed to attach the very greatest weight", said that it could be substantially removed by washing. It was indubitable that there had been washing and rubbing.

Professor Glaister was unable to exclude the possibility of self-infliction and said that you could never exclude questions of suicide or accident so long as you did not know the facts and circumstances. Did the jury in this case know the facts and circumstances?

They had to say whether they accepted the evidence of one set of experts and rejected that of another. The evidence did not seem reconcilable on these vital matters.

The last compartment of evidence on the murder charge consisted of the statements and the conduct of the accused. His impression was that there was no substantial variation in what the accused said to different people. He agreed with the Lord Advocate that it was important to know whether Mrs Merrett knew of the existence of the pistol. The evidence did not seem to disclose that the accused concealed the fact. Was there anything which would justify them in asuming that Mrs Merrett was in ignorance of a fact which several other people knew?

He did not think counsel was justified in saying that the Lord Advocate had insinuated that the conduct of the accused was callous. No such statement had been made nor could it safely be inferred. They might think that his obligations to his mother should have overborne his obligations to his "pal" at a critical time. But they were not a court of morals nor had they to approve or disapprove of conduct except as it had a bearing on the commission of the crime they were considering.

Certain pieces of evidence pointed in a different direction. His mother was attached to him and he to her. The shot was fired when Mrs Sutherland was in the flat; it could have been fired quite easily in her absence had anyone so desired. It was in evidence that the accused was very upset and Mrs Sutherland thought he was going to cry. Was that all acting? He left the pistol lying about, admitted ownership and that the pistol did the deed. He said that it was impossible for a third party to have done it. He visited the Infirmary. He kissed his mother. Was that the kiss of Judas? Did Mrs Penn harbour for two months her sister's assassin? Was the conduct of the accused more consistent with guilt than with innocence? Was there anything in his statements or his conduct which advanced to any material extent the Crown case?

At this stage he invited the jury to ask whether the Crown was claiming at their hands a verdict of murder upon evidence which at the time they had deemed insufficient even for arrest. The Crown had evidence before them in April. They knew the results of Professor Littlejohn's experiments in August. But there was no arrest until Gurrin's report. Was this the new factor which induced the Crown to arrest the accused? Did they conclude that they now had a motive? Before he passed to the second charge, he warned them that proof of motive, though

often supremely important, would not atone for the absence
of sufficient evidence to prove the commission of a crime. They
also had to ask whether the motive was at all commensurate
with the crime charged. That was a matter of common sense
and experience. It was one of the many questions for them.

The jury must bear in mind exactly what the second charge
was. There was a lot of evidence about cheque-books, cheques,
pay-in slips, bank-books and bank accounts, and it was all en-
veloped in an atmosphere of suspicion. The accused was
charged with uttering, not forgery. Uttering was using a forged
document knowing it to be forged. Three questions arose and
three only. Had the Crown proved that the cheques were
forged? Had the Crown proved that the accused presented them
for payment? Had the Crown proved that, if he did and if the
cheques were forged, the accused knew that at the time? If the
Crown failed to prove the first point, that was an end of the
case.

It would not do just to jeer at the evidence of hand-writing
experts. It was true that their evidence, like that of all experts
(and the defence had called at least two), had to be carefully
examined. They had to go into the matter fully. First, both
experts claimed to have detected a double signature in the same
twenty-nine cheques. Were they both suffering from hallucina-
tions? Then there was the marked similarity in the mechanical
formation of the same signatures. There was the contrast between the stilted and halting formation of the letters and Mrs
Merrett's usual free and flowing hand. For these reasons the two
experts agreed that the cheques were forged. There had been no
counter skilled evidence. He himself was not disposed to attach
so much importance to the second and third features as he was
to the double signature. But it was for the jury to judge.

Did the accused present the cheques? They were all payable
to him; they were all endorsed by him; and they had all been
honoured. Had the jury any reasonable doubt? He did not think
the defence raised any question on this.

Did the accused know they were forged? Direct evidence of
the state of a man's mind was generally, if not always, un-
obtainable. It was a matter of inference from the facts. The
accused had an allowance of 10s a week. On 6th March he

bought a motor bicycle for £28. There was no trace of that in his or his mother's accounts. There was no trace of the cost of booking out Miss Christie, no trace of the rings he gave her. Where did the money come from? The twenty-nine cheques were the only ones in which the accused was payee. They were not drawn in sequence as Mrs Merrett's usually were. The counterfoils were missing. There was the mystery attaching to the two bank-books. These were some of the facts relied on by the Crown. Did they or did they not, taken in cumulation, prove that the accused knew all about it? They had to judge whether any explanation worthy of the name had been put forward for these devious and suggestive dealings.

If they thought the cheques were forged, that they were presented by the accused and that he knew they were forged, it was their duty to convict him upon the second charge.

That was the whole case. The jury had not to consider whether they believed the accused was guilty of one or other or both of the charges. "The only question—I end as I began—the only question is: has the Crown satisfied you beyond all reasonable doubt that the accused committed either or both of these crimes? Mathematical precision in such matters is unattainable; it is a question of common sense. But if any reasonable doubt exists in your minds with regard to either charge, the accused, in accordance with our traditions, is entitled to the benefit of that doubt. If you are not satisfied that the Crown has made out its case, then, according to the view you take of the evidence, you will find the accused not guilty of either or of both charges, or find either or both charges not proven. If, however, you are satisfied that the Crown has proved its case with regard to either or both charges, then, unpleasant though your task may be, I doubt not that, bearing in mind the oath which you have taken, you will faithfully and fearlessly perform it."

The jury retired at twenty-five minutes to five and returned at half-past. On the first charge their verdict was Not Proven by a majority; on the second charge their unanimous verdict was Guilty. The Lord Justice-Clerk, with a certificate from the Prison Commissioners before him that the accused was unsuitable for Borstal training, sentenced him to twelve months' imprisonment.

He then discharged the jury, with a word of thanks for their attention to a long and anxious case. Practical expression to his thanks came in the form of a promise that they would be exempted from jury service for five years.

"An unsatisfactory ending to an unsatisfactory case" said the *Scotsman*. But was it not inevitable on the evidence? The police investigation at the outset was of the most cursory nature. Even in stock detective fiction the official investigators rarely show up so badly. Roughead comments that the two constables who first appeared might have filled places in the chorus of *The Pirates of Penzance* and the same comment might be made of their superiors as well.

It is a remarkable thing that throughout the whole case no reference was made to fingerprints. The art or science of identification by such means was known by the time of Merrett's trial: the first instructions to the Scottish police about it were issued in 1904. When Constable Middlemiss picked up the pistol and wrapped it in paper, it might have been thought that his object was to preserve any possible prints. Apparently, however, it was to save himself or his uniform from being contaminated by bloodstains.

So the death of Mrs Merrett was allowed to remain clouded by obscurity, like those of John Gilmour, Pierre Emile L'Angelier and Cecil Hambrough. As in Madeleine Smith's case, we can hardly refrain from asking: how was the accused going to extricate himself from the position into which he had brought himself?

In nearly every trial there is at least one witness whom one would have liked to see and hear for oneself: the printed word is so hopelessly inadequate. In Christina Gilmour's case, that witness was John Anderson; Madeleine Smith's trial is perhaps an exception; Beresford Loftus Tottenham and Major Hambrough share the role in Monson's case, and in Merrett's, there are Mrs Sutherland and, even more so, Mrs Penn.

Mrs Sutherland's contradiction and re-contradiction of her own statement may well have made the Crown case almost hopeless. The Lord Advocate suggested that she became confused by some kind of reaction while she was left alone in the flat waiting for the arrival of Inspector Fleming and the sergeant. But the inspector saw no sign of confusion. Craigie Aitchison ignored Mrs Sutherland's first statement to Middlemiss and Izatt and took the statement to Fleming as the original version and therefore deserving of credit. But is not the explanation probably this, that she told the first two constables the truth; that, as she waited, the drama of the situation impressed itself on her and she improved it by making herself almost an eye-witness; when she saw her doctor, her story had improved still further, bringing her to the very threshold of the room where Mrs Merrett was shot; and then, when she realised how serious the matter was, with a trial of one kind or another in the future, she reverted to the original truth?

The phrase which Mrs Penn attributed to Mrs Merrett "as if Donald had shot me", was a striking one, full of sinister implication for the accused. It was emphasised by the way it had to be drawn out of the witness after her request to be excused. That emphasis may have been intentional or not. Was Mrs Penn really friendly to the accused and a reluctant witness against him? Or was she in truth hostile to her nephew and prepared to have him convicted of murder? If her reluctance was real, why did Aitchison assail her so violently? I am told that, as one would expect from the very detailed cross-examination, she had in fact refused to give a precognition to the defence solicitors until pressure was brought to bear on her. On this view, of course, her reluctance to say the words "as if Donald had shot me" was feigned, and feigned in the pretty certain knowledge that she would be compelled to speak out. She would then have it both ways—win the reputation of being a kindly aunt who did her best for her nephew in his peril, and yet be quite sure that the evidence would be forced from her willing lips. In his speech to the jury Aitchison described her behaviour as "playacting and bad playacting at that".

There is some support in the evidence for the view that she was hostile to the accused. Very soon after she had seen her sister in the Infirmary, she challenged him with having done it; Mrs Sutherland said she showed hostility to him at times, though not in connection with the case; Dr Holcombe was compelled to admit that she sometimes came very near to insinuating that Donald was guilty; and there is in the evidence of her husband, Walter Penn, a hint that the Penns and Mrs Merrett had been on bad terms. According to him, Mrs Merrett said to him "Walter, you have been awfully good, and I have been most unkind at times. You will forgive me, won't you?" A state of affairs which calls for an olive branch like this between relatives is rarely the fault of one side alone.

On the other hand, there is the testimony of William Roughead, who attended the trial and who lived very near Buckingham Terrace, so that he had a good working knowledge of local gossip: indeed the case was reported to him as one of murder on the day of the shooting, a fortnight before Mrs Merrett died, when he was dining with friends in Buckingham Terrace itself—not No 31. In his introduction to his edition of the trial[1] he says that Mrs Penn "displayed in the box no animus whatsoever against the accused, and, indeed, as one happens to know, refrained from stating matters to his prejudice within her knowledge."

The Lord Justice-Clerk expressed the view, in his charge to the jury, that Aitchison's observations on Mrs Penn's hostility "seem to me to be a little less than just".

We, who were not at the trial and who cannot revive the transient, unrecorded features of the evidence, are left to wonder in frustration: but it is likely that Mrs Penn was hostile to her nephew, and with good reason.

In his peroration Craigie Aitchison vaunted his belief in the future good behaviour of the accused. His faith was soon betrayed, though it is fair to remember that it was conditional on his client's full acquittal.

On his release from Saughton Prison the accused travelled south in a sleeping compartment which had been reserved for him. The next compartment was occupied by the Lord Advocate who had prosecuted him. They did not meet.

[1] *Trial of John Donald Merrett*, (Hodge, Notable British Trials Series, 1929).

Merrett went to stay at Hastings with an old friend of his mother, Mrs Mary Bonnar. She had a daughter Vera, aged seventeen, who was a ward in chancery. In March 1928, Merrett and Vera eloped and were married in Glasgow. With a second-hand car and a tent they went on a camping honeymoon.

Merrett was being allowed £2 a week by the Public Trustee. Part of his mother's income had stopped with her death and part of her funds had been expended on the defence of her son. He was not yet twenty-one so that he could not put his hands on his grandfather's money. Two pounds a week was hardly enough for a married man who had no intention of getting a job. But Merrett had a cheque-book and an imposing manner and presence for one so young. He was able to buy goods in the shops in different parts of the country, paying for them by cheque. He and Vera always struck camp and left town well before the banks opened. The shopkeepers lost their money and could not trace their unprofitable customer.

In June the wanderers left Scotland and returned to England. In Newcastle-on-Tyne, Merrett (now known as John Donald Milner—his mother's maiden name) opened a new bank account with twenty-five shillings and was given a cheque-book. At last he bought Vera an engagement ring, but this was pawned almost at once: a bracelet had the same fate. Then he became greedier and tried to obtain goods worth £90 in another shop. The manager was suspicious and informed the police. The honeymooners, who had not struck camp, were arrested and charged with obtaining goods on false pretences. Merrett was sentenced to six months' and three months' imprisonment on two charges, the sentences to run concurrently. Vera was discharged.

The Public Trustee paid the costs and also made good the losses incurred by the shopkeepers. The funds in his hands were dwindling.

Merrett was released on 28th January 1929 and went to live with Vera. About this time he assumed the name of Ronald John Chesney; Vera still called him "Don". They had a three-roomed flat in Hastings, where they were soon joined by Vera's mother. She had married again. Her husband claimed a baronetcy, without justification, and Mrs Bonnar now became

"Lady Menzies". She left her husband but retained that fictitious title.

When Chesney (as he had better now be known) came into
his grandfather's money, Vera persuaded him to buy a bigger
house. He was never unwilling to spend money, whether he had
it or not. He also bought a Bentley open tourer and spent
lavishly on other women. Some months after he succeeded to
his money he made a marriage settlement of £8,400 on his wife,
at the suggestion of the Public Trustee. She would enjoy the
income for her life and if she died before him the capital would
revert to him.

In 1930 the Chesneys and Lady Menzies moved to Ports-
mouth, where Vera had persuaded her husband to buy a small
grocer's business. The business failed. Chesney was not made
for application to legitimate business and there were counter-
attractions in some of his younger customers and also in the
society of naval officers. In 1931 they moved to live a life of ease
in a twenty-roomed house in Weybridge with Lady Menzies and
the two children they had adopted. They gave lavish parties and
subscribed generously to local charities. Officially Ronald John
Chesney was a merchant. In fact he had taken to smuggling,
an appropriate choice of profession for one of his appearance.
Big in every dimension, he had grown a large black beard and
wore a gold ring in his left ear. About 1935 he began to work
on a large scale. He had bought an aeroplane and had his pilot's
licence; he had a pilot cutter for sea work; and he had cars both
in Britain and on the Continent. Land, sea and air were provided for.

His family used to accompany him on his cruises in the
cutter, innocent partners in smuggling rifles to Spain and gold
and diamonds everywhere. Vera took to drink, encouraged by
her husband. It meant that he needed to take even less trouble
to hide his numerous affairs with other women.

In the winter of 1938–1939 he owned a luxurious motor
yacht, which he managed as a gambling ship. He sold her in the
summer of 1939 and returned to his cutter, the *Gladys May*. But
by September 1939, when war broke out, he had lost her by
gambling with an Egyptian merchant in Algiers, where he
planned to settle.

He had to return to England. Vera had found a house at 2 St Mary's Road, Ealing, which she turned into a guest house for old people. Her mother acted as housekeeper. In January 1940 Chesney, who cannot have found the atmosphere of an old people's home congenial, joined the R.N.V.R. and was commissioned. No investigation was made into his history. Boastful and colourful he impressed many of his fellow-recruits—and their women. Senior officers were less appreciative but he survived.

In 1942 he was in command of a smuggler-like craft sailing to and from the beleaguered garrison at Tobruk. In June of that year he was captured when his ship was almost (but not quite) sunk under him. He was the last to leave her. In the library of one prison camp he found a copy of his own trial, edited by William Roughead. The photographs, or according to one version the book itself, soon disappeared. Ronald John Chesney was taking no chances.

In March 1943 he was repatriated in exchange for a sick Italian sailor and resumed his naval service. Vera followed him round his different postings and just before the war ended she was with him, quite irregularly, in Kirkwall. She left him there and returned to London, where she restarted her old people's home, this time in Montpelier Road, Ealing.

Chesney was posted to Wilhelmshaven in Germany. The state of occupied Germany gave ample scope to his talents for smuggling and the black market. Theft came inevitably into it: his most spectacular exploit in this line was to steal a luxurious car which had belonged to Admiral Doenitz. For this he was sentenced by court martial on 7th November 1946 to four months' imprisonment. He served his sentence in England.

When he was released he returned to Germany and his German mistress Gerda Schaller. He resumed his old life. I do not propose to trace this in detail and it is enough to say that he came up against the law in many European countries. Fines and imprisonment followed and he was banned from a number. This did not interfere too drastically with business: the post-war years were good years for the Chesneys of the world.

From time to time he visited Vera at her old people's home, not out of love or affection but to plead for a divorce. She was a nuisance to him, always insisting on maintenance and still keeping the marriage settlement. As a faithful Roman Catholic she refused. Chesney himself was a member of that church, which he had joined after his marriage: the only practical effect it had on his conduct was that he devoted to St Anthony ten per cent of the profits on every successful smuggling deal.

In 1952 he was sentenced at Lewes Assizes to twelve months' imprisonment for trying to export coffee and currency notes. In prison he met a number of experienced criminals and discussed business with them. Smuggling, of course: but that was not the most important thing now. Vera's marriage settlement was becoming more and more tempting. With the improvement in normal supplies and the increasing alertness of the police in so many countries smuggling was becoming less profitable. He offered good money to any man who was prepared to stage a motor accident that would be fatal to his wife. When she died the capital of the settlement would revert to him.

None of his prison friends would help him.

Soon after his release he returned to Germany, this time to a new mistress, Sonia Winnicke. It would, he thought, be easier for him to kill Vera in Germany, so he wrote in seeming affection inviting her to resume married life there. Vera ignored his invitations: she too thought she would be in danger.

In June 1953 he visited London and stayed with Vera for a short time. Quarrels became unbearable and he left. Sonia Winnicke joined him in London.

He saw one day in a public-house a man whose face had some resemblance to his own—a photographer named Chown. Chesney found out his full name. Then he obtained a copy of his birth certificate from Somerset House and applied for a passport in the name of Leslie Bernard Chown. All that he needed to do to use that passport was to shave off his beard.

Once he had obtained this passport he went back to Germany. Again he tried to persuade Vera to join him; again she refused. In December he spent some time with her in London, outwardly affectionate once more. They parted with a kiss and a promise from him that he would soon come and see her again.

On Thursday 11th February 1954 a maid in the old people's home was looking for Mrs Chesney or Lady Menzies. A new guest had just arrived. The maid could find neither lady. This was unusual and she reported the matter to the police. They arrived and found Mrs Chesney dead in a bath with her night-dress on and a cardigan round her shoulders. A post-mortem examination was later to discover that she had been drunk when she died. The search continued and Lady Menzies' body was found, her head battered and a stocking tied tightly round her neck. Scrapings from under her fingernails showed traces of blood and skin.

There were few clues. But it was obvious that the older woman at least had been murdered. Vera might have died by accident because of her drunken condition, but murder was at least possible in her case also. Whoever had murdered Lady Menzies had taken care to wipe clean every surface that might have held a fingerprint. The police found many letters signed "Don" and learned that "Don" was Vera's husband, Ronald John Chesney. They also found that he had been staying with his wife a few weeks previously.

There were two dogs at the old people's home. Neither barked during the night.

This curious incident of the two dogs in the night-time made the police think that the crime or crimes had been committed by a man who knew the house and the dogs well. Two men seemed to fit that description. One was Ronald John Chesney. But so far as the police could trace he was in Germany at the time.

He was not yet cleared from suspicion. That suspicion grew when the Criminal Record Office reported that Ronald John Chesney had a long criminal career and that he had been charged, as John Donald Merrett, with the murder of his mother in Edinburgh twenty-seven years earlier. It grew further as Superintendent Daws studied the letters from "Don", outwardly affectionate, but with references to Gerda Schaller, Sonia Winnicke—and the marriage settlement. The police theory was that Chesney somehow got into Britain from Germany without using his passport, visited Ealing and made Vera drunk. He then carried her to the bathroom and drowned her. As he left, he may have bumped into Lady Menzies and, to avoid discovery, struggled with and killed her. The old lady had, from the appearance of the room where she was found, put up a good fight for her life, only to succumb in the end to a battering of blows with a heavy coffee-pot on her head.

Investigation at the ports showed that Chesney came over from Germany to Harwich on 3rd February and returned next day. There was no evidence of his landing at any other port after that.

Scotland Yard asked for the co-operation of Interpol. On 16th February a message reached them from Cologne that a man believed to be Chesney had been found dead. Superintendent Daws went to Cologne. The dead man was Chesney. He had been found shot through the mouth with a Colt revolver which lay by his side—according to the experts at his trial in Edinburgh one of the more usual places for a suicidal wound. He had in his pocket an English newspaper which carried the story of the double murder at Ealing.

The police continued their investigations. They found evidence that Chesney had travelled to England on 10th February with the false "Chown" passport. A number of witnesses remembered him. His arms were scratched; the skin torn from them corresponded with the traces found under Lady Menzies' fingernails. Under his own fingernails were fibres like those of the wool of his wife's cardigan. His clothing was stained with his own blood and also another type. Fibres and hairs found on his clothes matched fibres and hairs from the house. The case was complete and a coroner's jury had little difficulty in deciding that Chesney committed both murders.

In his recent autobiography, *Mostly Murder*,[1] Sir Sydney Smith, who succeeded Professor Littlejohn in the chair of Forensic Medicine at Edinburgh in the year of Merrett's trial, blames the police and Sir Bernard Spilsbury for Merrett's acquittal and therefore for the deaths of the other two victims in 1953. It is undoubtedly true, as the most cursory glance at the trial shows, that the police mishandled the case from the start, just when careful observation and recording is most important. But he seems to put the greater share of blame on Spilsbury,

[1] Harrap, 1959.

whom he accuses of coming to an opinion too hastily and sticking to it too stubbornly. Sir Sydney is a very experienced and very distinguished expert in his own right and his opinion is entitled to the greatest respect. But if the police had investigated more thoroughly—if they had taken the precaution of finger-printing the pistol—it is hard to imagine that there would have been much material for Spilsbury and Churchill to work on: or perhaps there would have been too much. There may well be differences of opinion about the amount of blackening at differ-ent ranges and the ease with which it can be washed off. Wash-ing and rubbing by human force involve a certain subjective element: it is not easy to measure accurately the degree of force employed. Two cartridges, even from the same box, may not be exactly the same in their composition, though the difference is likely to be minute.

One strong criticism of Spilsbury and Churchill, which Sir Sydney makes, is that they experimented in London with a different pistol and cartridges of a different make. This vitiates the London experiments. But he seems to overlook the fact that the experiments were repeated in Edinburgh with the same gun and cartridges from the same box as those used by the Crown experts. The London experiments played only a small part in the evidence. Spilsbury admitted that the Edinburgh experiments were more valid and the Lord Justice-Clerk almost directed the jury to ignore the London experiments altogether.

The really fatal mistake was not to fingerprint the pistol. It must have shown prints; there was little time to clean it before it was taken away. But if it did not show prints, then it must have been cleaned or it must have been fired by someone hold-ing it in a handkerchief or something like a handkerchief. Who could that person have been but John Donald Merrett?

In an interview in the *Sunday Pictorial* of 28th February 1954 Gerda Schaller said that Chesney confessed to her that he had killed his mother. He claimed that she found the pistol and asked him how he got it. He tried to take it from her, there was a struggle and it went off. If that story is true (and there is no reason to believe it), it could also have been established by fingerprinting.

In *Portrait of a Bad Man*,[1] Thomas Tullett vividly describes another confession to Gerda Schaller. This does not involve a struggle but a cold deliberate murder. There can be little doubt that this is the more accurate confession. Mrs Sutherland, that changeable witness, never heard any sounds of quarrelling or struggling in any of the versions she gave of what happened at 31 Buckingham Terrace on that March morning of 1926.

[1] Evans Brothers, 1956.